Visual QuickStart Guide

Pro Tools 8

For Mac OS X and
Windows

Tom Dambly

 Peachpit Press

Visual QuickStart Guide
Pro Tools 8 for Mac OS X and Windows
Tom Dambly

Peachpit Press
1249 Eighth Street
Berkeley, CA 94710
510/524-2178
510/524-2221 (fax)

Find us on the Web at: www.peachpit.com
To report errors, please send a note to: errata@peachpit.com
Peachpit Press is a division of Pearson Education.
Copyright © 2010 by Thomas E. Dambly

Editor: Rebecca Gulick
Development and Copy Editor: Kim Saccio-Kent
Contributing Writer: Mark Wilcox
Proofreader: Liz Welch
Production Coordinator: Becky Winter
Compositor: Danielle Foster
Indexer: James Minkin
Technical Reviewer: Dave Darlington
Cover Design: Peachpit Press

ISBN 13: 978-0-321-64685-9
ISBN 10:   0-321-64685-1

9 8 7 6 5 4 3 2 1
Printed and bound in the United States of America

Dedication

To my lovely wife Debra, whose kindness, creativity, beauty, and grace are an inspiration to me.

Acknowledgments

I'd like to thank Kim Saccio-Kent for her patience, skill, and kind guidance through the process of creating this book. Thanks also to Rebecca Gulick, for her encouragement and flexibility as this project took shape. I am very grateful to master engineer Dave Darlington for his assistance as technical editor. Thanks to Mark Wilcox for his authorship of the chapters on plug-ins, mixdown, and video.

My appreciation goes out to the wonderful people at Peachpit Press: Publisher Nancy Ruenzel, editor Karyn Johnson, proofreader Liz Welch, production coordinator Becky Winter, compositor Danielle Foster, and indexer James Minkin.

Finally, thanks to everyone at Digidesign, whose passion and boundless energy have changed the audio industry and made Pro Tools what it is today.

—Tom Dambly

CONTENTS AT A GLANCE

TABLE OF CONTENTS

Chapter 8   Importing Audio and MIDI   155

Chapter 9   Working with Selections   171

Chapter 11   **Editing Audio**   **231**

TABLE OF CONTENTS

INTRODUCTION

Pro Tools is a digital audio production system that brings together hard disk recording, non-linear editing, digital signal processing, MIDI sequencing, and digital mixing in a program that runs on the Mac OS and Windows.

Used in recording studios, post-production houses, broadcast facilities, and sound design companies worldwide, Pro Tools has become the professional standard for working with audio. It has also been widely adopted by independent artists, educational institutions, and home enthusiasts.

Pro Tools owes its popularity to its ease of use, its compatibility with a wide range of third-party software and hardware, and the availability of entry-level versions that have many of the same features as professional systems.

With Pro Tools 8, Digidesign has redesigned the software interface and added many enhancements for music creation, including new windows for editing MIDI, multiple track lanes for viewing automation and comping takes, and the ability to edit and print musical notation.

Pro Tools Systems

There are three types of Pro Tools systems, which integrate hardware and software:

Pro Tools HD is a professional-level system that uses dedicated cards for audio processing tasks. Pro Tools HD systems feature expandable input and output capability; and they offer increased track counts, higher sample rates, and more plug-in and mixer processing capacity than other Pro Tools systems.

Pro Tools LE is designed for home studios, portable recording setups, and laptop performance rigs. Pro Tools LE systems use the computer's processing power to mix and process audio. Pro Tools LE has the same look and feel and nearly all of the same features as Pro Tools HD, but with fixed input and output capability and lower track count. You can extend the capabilities of Pro Tools LE by purchasing Toolkit software options that offer increased track count and advanced functionality.

Pro Tools M-Powered runs with a variety of M-Audio hardware. Like Pro Tools LE, Pro Tools M-Powered relies on the computer's processing power to do its work. With a few exceptions, Pro Tools M-Powered software has the same capabilities as Pro Tools LE; however, M-Powered systems cannot be extended beyond their core capabilities.

Sessions created with one type of Pro Tools system can be opened with the other types, after taking into account track limitations, available plug-ins, and processing capacity. And even if you encounter these limitations on a smaller system, nothing is lost from the session; all elements are available again when you return to the original system. This flexibility makes it possible to start a project at home and then bring it to a professional system for mixing, or to take a session home from the studio to do some editing.

The Many Uses of Pro Tools

Pro Tools can be used in many different ways.

◆ Some engineers use Pro Tools primarily as an audio recorder and editor, connecting its inputs and outputs to an external mixing console. Others mix entirely "in the box," creating a final mix directly from Pro Tools.

◆ Songwriters use Pro Tools as a compositional tool, constructing pieces with MIDI and virtual instruments, arranging materials, and creating a score.

◆ Editors for video and film use Pro Tools as a post-production tool for tasks such as replacing dialogue, spotting sound effects, and mixing music.

◆ Sound designers use Pro Tools to manage sample and sound effects libraries and to create new sounds for use in games, video, or film.

◆ Broadcasters use Pro Tools as a portable recording and editing rig, and as an editing tool in the studio.

◆ Performing musicians use Pro Tools as an instrument, using virtual instruments or real-time processing, often in conjunction with other software.

These are just a few of the possibilities with Pro Tools and its vast set of features—people are still finding new and creative ways to use them.

In recent years, digital technology has changed the way audio is created, distributed, and consumed. Pro Tools has undoubtedly played a large part in this transformation. It has also changed the way people work, blurring the boundaries between the tasks of recording, editing, arranging, and mixing.

INTRODUCTION

Who Should Use This Book?

Pro Tools 8 for Mac OS X and Windows: Visual QuickStart Guide is for anyone new to Pro Tools who wants to get up and running quickly. Its task-oriented, visual approach takes you step by step through the fundamentals of using the program to record, edit, and mix audio and MIDI. This book can also serve as a quick reference for intermediate users who want to explore new ways of working.

This book assumes some familiarity with audio signal flow, MIDI communication, and musical terminology. If you're not familiar with basic concepts of audio and MIDI production, you can refer to one of the many excellent books and online resources on recording techniques, MIDI equipment, and music theory.

What Do You Need to Use This Book?

The book requires a basic installation of Pro Tools LE 8 software and a compatible Pro Tools LE audio interface. The only optional software mentioned is the MP3 Export Option, which is required to create MP3 versions of final mixes. This option can be purchased and downloaded from the Digidesign Web site.

The Toolkit Software options for Pro Tools LE (Complete Production Toolkit, DV Toolkit 2, and Music Production Toolkit) are beyond the scope of this book and are not required for any of the procedures contained within.

If you have a different type of Pro Tools system, you can still get full benefit from this book. Nearly all of the tasks covered here involve core Pro Tools functions, so they are applicable on Pro Tools HD systems and also possible on Pro Tools M-Powered systems.

INTRODUCTION

Additional Resources

The Pro Tools 8 installer DVD set includes a disc of demo sessions, sounds, and audio loops that you can use to start exploring Pro Tools. To get started with them, copy the contents of the disc to your audio drive, and then locate and open a session that interests you. The installer set also comes with an instructional DVD that surveys the features of Pro Tools.

Don't forget the documentation that comes with your system—the full set of Pro Tools guides, in PDF format, is automatically installed on your computer when you install Pro Tools. In addition to the *Pro Tools Reference Guide*, there are handy guides that cover all of the menus, keyboard and right-click shortcuts, and preference settings in Pro Tools.

Finally, the Internet offers an embarrassment of riches regarding Pro Tools and audio production. Start with Digidesign's Web site at www.digidesign.com, where you can watch videos and browse the user forums.

INSTALLING AND SETTING UP PRO TOOLS

This chapter provides an overview of Pro Tools software and hardware installation, and covers the basics of connecting studio equipment to a Pro Tools system.

While the steps for installing Pro Tools software are slightly different on Mac and Windows computers, the procedures outlined here apply to both platforms, except where noted. For detailed, up-to-date installation instructions, refer to the Setup guides and Read Me files that came with your system.

Pro Tools LE hardware gives you many options for connecting the audio and MIDI devices in your studio.

System Requirements for Pro Tools

Recording, editing, and mixing with Pro Tools LE places special demands on computer processing power, memory usage, data transfer, and hard drive operation. This section covers just some of the factors to consider when building a Pro Tools system.

Computer processor speed and memory

Pro Tools LE systems use the computer's processing power for all of the digital signal processing tasks associated with recording, playback, mixing, and using real-time plug-ins. Computers with faster processor speeds and sufficient memory yield better performance, allowing higher track counts with more real-time effects.

Hard drive speed and capacity

You should use a dedicated hard drive to record and play back Pro Tools sessions, and avoid recording to your computer's system drive. External FireWire drives are convenient to connect and portable, and make it easy to back up your work.

A hard drive must be fast enough, in terms of data throughput, spin speed, and seek time, to record and play back multiple tracks of audio.

As hard drive sizes continue to increase while the cost per megabyte decreases, drive capacity should not be a problem. You can monitor the available space on your drives from Pro Tools.

System requirements and compatibility information

Digidesign qualifies computer configurations and specifies the minimum requirements for computer processor speed, amount of system RAM, and hard drive specifications needed to run each version of Pro Tools. These system requirements are published in the Support area of Digidesign's Web site at www.digidesign.com.

SYSTEM REQUIREMENTS FOR PRO TOOLS

Installing Pro Tools LE 8 Software

Before you connect Pro Tools LE hardware to your computer, you need to install Pro Tools LE 8 software first.

Upgrading from previous versions of Pro Tools

If you are upgrading to Pro Tools LE 8 from a previous version, you should make note of your Pro Tools preference settings before installation, either by writing them down or by taking screen shots of each preferences page. All preferences are reset to their defaults during installation. Digidesign provides a *Preferences Primer* (available in the Documentation folder on the installer disc) to help you with this process.

Uninstalling previous versions of Pro Tools (Windows only)

On Windows systems, you need to uninstall any previous version of Pro Tools on your computer before you install Pro Tools LE 8.

To uninstall previous versions of Pro Tools:

1. Disconnect any Pro Tools hardware from your computer.

2. Insert the installer disc in your computer.

3. Locate and double-click Uninstall Pro Tools.exe.

4. Follow the onscreen instructions to complete the uninstall process.

5. Restart your computer.

Pro Tools Installation Options

The Pro Tools LE 8 Installer offers a number of software options. The following options are common to both Mac OS and Windows systems:

◆ **Application Files** includes the required files for the Pro Tools application.

◆ **DigiRack Plug-Ins** includes core plug-ins that come free with Pro Tools.

◆ **Pro Tools Creative Collection** includes a set of effects and virtual instrument plug-ins that come free with Pro Tools.

✔ Tip

■ More than 4 GB of samples are included with the installation of the Pro Tools Creative Collection. It can take considerable time to complete this installation.

To install Pro Tools LE 8:

1. Disconnect any Pro Tools hardware from your computer.

2. Make sure you are logged in to an Administrator account on your computer.

3. Insert the installer disc in your computer.

4. Do one of the following:
   ▲ On the Mac OS, locate and double-click the Install Pro Tools LE application.
   ▲ On Windows, locate and double-click Setup.exe.

5. Follow the onscreen instructions to install the software on your system drive.

   On Windows, the installer will prompt you to connect your Pro Tools LE hardware.

6. Restart the computer.

   On the Mac OS, connect your Pro Tools LE hardware after the computer has restarted.

Connecting Pro Tools Hardware to the Computer

Pro Tools LE 8 supports USB- and FireWire-based Digidesign Pro Tools LE hardware, including:

◆ **003-series interfaces:**
003 (FireWire) (**Figure 1.1**)
003 Rack (FireWire) (**Figure 1.2**, **1.3**)
003 Rack+ (FireWire)

◆ **002-series interfaces:**
002 (FireWire)
002 Rack (FireWire)

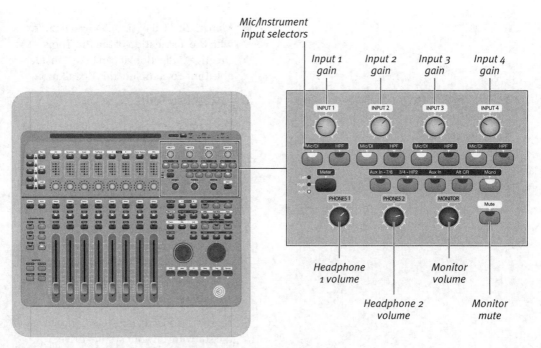

Figure 1.1 Top panel of the 003, showing the location of the input controls.

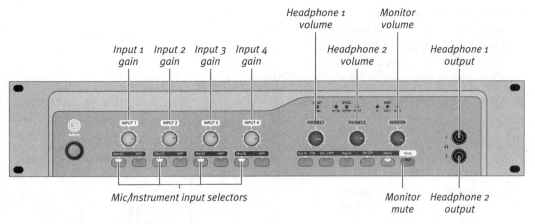

Figure 1.2 Front panel of the 003 Rack.

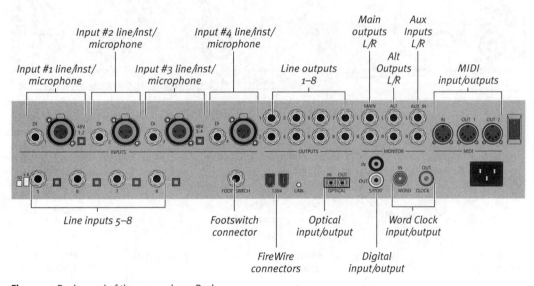

Figure 1.3 Back panel of the 002 and 003 Rack.

CONNECTING PRO TOOLS HARDWARE

◆ **Mbox 2-series interfaces:**
   Mbox 2 Pro (FireWire) (**Figure 1.4**, **1.5**)
   Mbox 2 (USB) (**Figure 1.6**, **1.7**)
   Mbox 2 Mini (USB) (**Figure 1.8**, **1.9**)
   Mbox 2 Micro (USB)

◆ **Mbox interface** (USB)

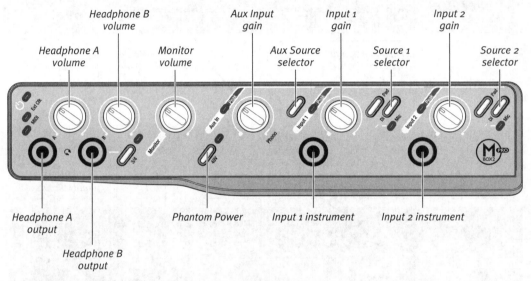

Figure 1.4 Front panel of the Mbox 2 Pro.

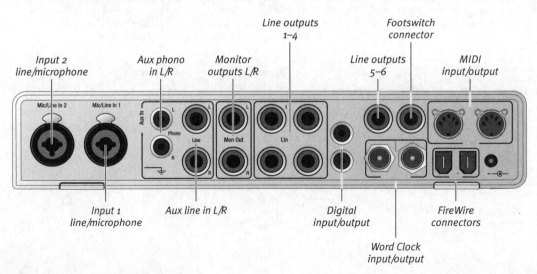

Figure 1.5 Back panel of the Mbox 2 Pro.

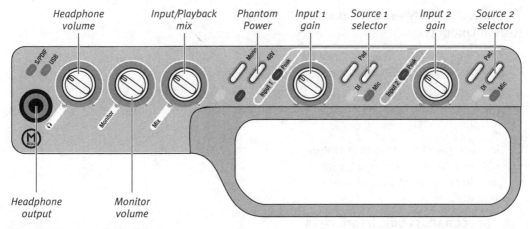

Headphone volume · Input/Playback mix · Phantom Power · Input 1 gain · Source 1 selector · Input 2 gain · Source 2 selector

Headphone output · Monitor volume

Figure 1.6 Front panel of the Mbox 2.

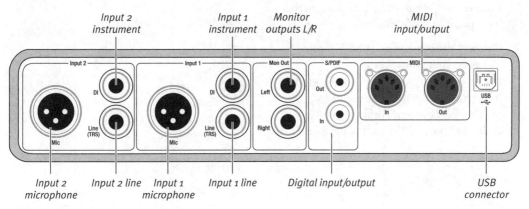

Input 2 instrument · Input 1 instrument · Monitor outputs L/R · MIDI input/output

Input 2 microphone · Input 2 line · Input 1 microphone · Input 1 line · Digital input/output · USB connector

Figure 1.7 Back panel of the Mbox 2.

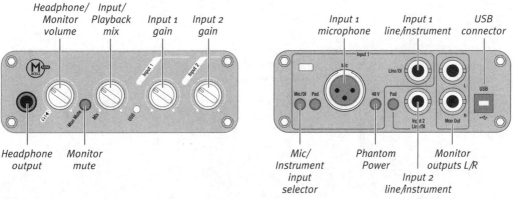

Headphone/ Monitor volume · Input/ Playback mix · Input 1 gain · Input 2 gain

Headphone output · Monitor mute

Figure 1.8 Front panel of the Mbox 2 Mini.

Input 1 microphone · Input 1 line/instrument · USB connector

Mic/ Instrument input selector · Phantom Power · Monitor outputs L/R · Input 2 line/instrument

Figure 1.9 Back panel of the Mbox 2 Mini.

To connect a FireWire audio interface to your computer:

1. Connect a FireWire cable to a FireWire port on the back panel of the interface.

2. Connect the other end of the FireWire cable to a FireWire port on your computer.

   or

   Connect the other end of the FireWire cable to a FireWire port on a FireWire hard drive that is connected to your computer.

To connect a USB audio interface to your computer:

1. Connect a USB cable to a USB port on the back panel of the interface.

2. Connect the other end of the USB cable to a port on your computer.

   Note: Use of a USB hub is not supported. If you have a USB hub, connect it to another port on your computer and use a dedicated port for the audio interface.

CONNECTING PRO TOOLS HARDWARE

Connecting Audio Sources to Pro Tools LE Hardware

Pro Tools LE hardware can accommodate a wide variety of audio inputs. Most audio sources fall into one of the following categories:

Microphones can be any of several types, including *dynamic, condenser,* or *ribbon* microphones. Certain microphones (usually condenser mics) require phantom power to operate. Pro Tools LE interfaces can provide phantom power to microphone inputs.

Instruments can be any low-level analog audio source, but usually include electric guitar or electric bass. Inputs for this type of audio signal are also called direct inputs (DIs).

Line-level analog devices can include mixers, preamplifiers, or certain instruments (such as some keyboards) that output higher-level signals. Typical nominal operating levels of such devices include –10 dBV (for consumer equipment) and +4dBu (for professional equipment).

Digital devices include DAT machines or CD recorders with S/PDIF connections, or modular digital multitrack machines with S/PDIF or Optical connections.

To connect a microphone:

1. Make sure phantom power to the microphone input is turned off.

2. Connect an XLR cable from a microphone to an available microphone connector on the audio interface.

3. Make sure the corresponding input selector is set to Microphone.

4. If the microphone requires phantom power, press the appropriate 48V switch to apply power.

5. Adjust the gain of the input.

To connect an instrument:

1. Connect a ¼-inch cable from the instrument output to a DI connector on the audio interface.

2. Make sure the corresponding input selector is set to DI.

3. Adjust the gain of the input.

To connect a line-level device:

1. Connect a ¼-inch cable from the device output to any line-level input on the audio interface.

2. If the line-level input has an operating level switch, set the switch to match the level of the device (–10 dBV or +4 dBu).

3. Adjust the gain of the input.

To connect a S/PDIF digital audio device:

1. Connect a S/PDIF cable from the output of the device to the S/PDIF input of the audio interface.

2. If you want to record from Pro Tools to the device, connect a second S/PDIF cable from the interface S/PDIF output to the S/PDIF input of the device.

To connect an optical digital audio device:

1. Connect an optical cable from the output of the device to the ADAT/Optical input of the audio interface.

2. If you want to record from Pro Tools to the device, connect a second optical cable from the interface ADAT/Optical output to the optical input of the device.

Connecting MIDI Devices

The 003-series, 002-series, and the Mbox 2 Pro and Mbox 2 include MIDI ports for connecting MIDI devices directly to the system. These ports appear in the Audio MIDI Setup (Mac) and the MIDI Studio Setup (Windows) when connected.

With other LE hardware, you will need to use the USB ports on your computer or an external MIDI interface to connect MIDI gear.

To connect a MIDI device to LE hardware:

1. Using a standard 5-pin MIDI cable, connect the MIDI Out port on the device to the MIDI In port on the LE hardware.

2. Using a second 5-pin MIDI cable, connect the MIDI In port on the device to a MIDI Out port on the LE hardware.

CONNECTING MIDI DEVICES

Connecting Monitoring Equipment

Your options for monitoring the audio output of Pro Tools depend on the hardware you are using.

◆ The 003-series and 002-series interfaces have two pairs of monitor outputs (Main and Alt) allowing you to connect two contrasting sets of monitor speakers to the system.

◆ The Mbox 2 Pro and Mbox 2 each provide one pair of dedicated monitor outputs.

◆ The Mbox 2 Mini has a pair of monitor outputs that share a gain control with the headphone outputs.

To connect a monitoring system to LE hardware:

1. Make sure the monitoring system is turned off before making any connections.

2. Connect ¼-inch TRS cables to the monitor outputs on the back of the LE interface.

3. Connect the other end of the TRS cables to the inputs on a power amplifier or powered speakers.

THE PRO TOOLS WORKSPACE

This chapter takes you on a tour of the Pro Tools workspace and shows you some ways to customize its appearance.

The two main Pro Tools windows show tracks in a session in complementary ways:

◆ The Edit window displays tracks on a timeline, where you can edit and arrange media.

◆ The Mix window displays tracks as mixer channel strips, where you can set signal routing and adjust mixing controls.

The MIDI Editor and Score Editor windows offer enhanced editing capabilities:

◆ MIDI Editor windows let you edit one or more tracks of MIDI data in both piano roll and notation views.

◆ The Score Editor window lets you edit one or more tracks of MIDI notes as music notation in full score view.

The Transport window displays controls for navigating sessions, choosing record and playback settings, and working with MIDI.

Plug-In windows give you access to controls and presets for a variety of effects and virtual instruments.

Pro Tools browser windows let you search, audition, import, and manage media files.

The Edit Window

The Edit window displays track material on a horizontal timeline. In this window you can navigate, play back, record, edit, and arrange audio, MIDI, and video.

The Edit window (**Figure 2.1**) consists of the Toolbar, the Ruler area, and the Tracks area, plus the Tracks, Groups, and Regions lists.

To display the Edit window:

◆ Choose Window > Edit.

✔ Tip

■ To alternately display the Edit window and the Mix window, press Command-Equal (Mac) or Ctrl-Equal (Windows). This is probably the most frequently used keyboard shortcut in Pro Tools.

Figure 2.1 The main areas of the Edit window: the Toolbar, the Ruler area, the Tracks area, and the Tracks, Groups, and Regions lists.

THE EDIT WINDOW

The Edit window Toolbar

The Edit window Toolbar (**Figure 2.2**) includes the following controls:

◆ **Edit Mode selectors (Figure 2.3)** affect the behavior of regions and the operation of Edit tools and commands in the Tracks area.

◆ **Zoom controls (Figure 2.4)** let you zoom in and out on material in the Tracks area, both horizontally and vertically.

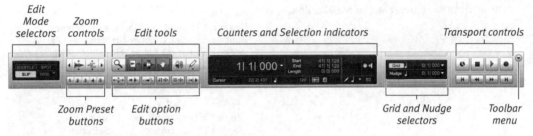

Figure at top, labels: Edit Mode selectors | Zoom controls | Edit tools | Counters and Selection indicators | Transport controls | Zoom Preset buttons | Edit option buttons | Grid and Nudge selectors | Toolbar menu

Figure 2.2 The Edit window Toolbar.

Labels: Shuffle mode button | Spot mode button | Slip mode button | Grid mode menu

Figure 2.3 The Edit Mode selectors let you switch between Shuffle, Slip, Grid, and Spot modes.

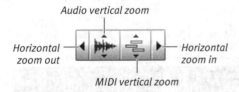

Labels: Audio vertical zoom | Horizontal zoom out | Horizontal zoom in | MIDI vertical zoom

Figure 2.4 The Zoom controls have separate vertical zoom buttons for audio waveforms and MIDI notes.

◆ **Zoom Preset buttons** (**Figure 2.5**) let you store and recall zoom levels for material in the Tracks area.

◆ **Edit tools** (**Figure 2.6**) are used to view, select, move, and modify material in the Tracks area.

◆ **Edit option buttons** (**Figure 2.7**) let you control cursor behavior when selecting, editing, and playing back track material.

◆ **Counters and Selection indicators** (**Figure 2.8**) show information about the cursor location, the current selection, and the attributes of any selected MIDI notes.

Figure 2.5 The Zoom Preset buttons let you switch between five different zoom levels with a single click.

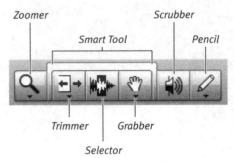

Figure 2.6 The Edit tools include the Zoomer, Trimmer, Selector, Grabber, Scrubber, and Pencil tools, as well as the Smart Tool, which combines the functions of multiple tools.

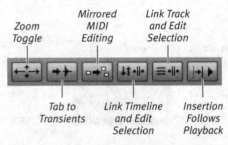

Figure 2.7 The Edit option buttons include Tab to Transient, Link Timeline and Edit Selection, Link Track and Edit Selection, and Insertion Follows Playback.

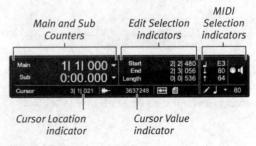

Figure 2.8 The Main and Sub counters can show the cursor location in two different time scales. The cursor location and edit selection indicators follow the Main counter.

Grid Value selector

Grid Display button

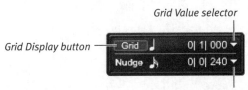

Nudge Value selector

Figure 2.9 The Grid and Nudge values used to move regions can be set independently from the Main and Sub counters.

Online Stop Play Record

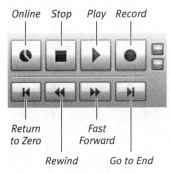

Return
to Zero

Fast
Forward

Rewind

Go to End

Figure 2.10 You can display Transport and MIDI controls in the Edit window Toolbar as an alternative to the Transport window.

Figure 2.11 To show or hide controls in the Toolbar, select them from the menu at the top right of the Toolbar area.

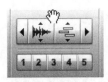

Figure 2.12 To rearrange controls in the Toolbar, press Command (Mac) or Ctrl (Windows) and drag the controls to another location.

◆ **Grid and Nudge selectors** (**Figure 2.9**) let you constrain edit selections and the movement of regions when working in Grid mode.

◆ **Transport controls** (**Figure 2.10**) make it possible to navigate, play back, and record in a session without leaving the Edit window.

◆ **Toolbar menu** (Figure 2.2) lets you customize the appearance of the Toolbar.

Customizing the Toolbar

You can show, hide, and rearrange groups of controls in the Edit window Toolbar.

To show controls in the Toolbar:

◆ Click the Toolbar menu button (**Figure 2.11**) and select the items to display in the Toolbar.

To rearrange controls in the Toolbar:

1. Hold down Command (Mac) or Control (Windows) and position the pointer over the controls so that it turns into a hand (**Figure 2.12**).

2. Click the controls and drag them to another location in the Toolbar.

The Edit window Rulers area

The Rulers area (**Figure 2.13**) across the top of the Edit window shows the time location of material and events in the Tracks area.

There are two types of rulers:

◆ **Timebase rulers** provide a continuous time scale for placing material (such as audio or MIDI regions) in the session. Available Timebase rulers include Minutes:Seconds, Bars|Beats, and Samples.

Any of the Timebase rulers can be set as the Main ruler, which automatically sets the corresponding Main Time Scale.

◆ **Conductor rulers** show the time location of certain types of events in the session, such as tempo or meter changes. Available Conductor rulers include Tempo, Meter, Key, Chords, and Markers.

You can add or change events directly from Conductor rulers.

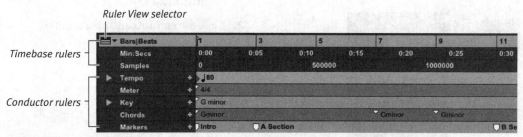

Figure 2.13 The rulers at the top of the Edit window show a variety of time scales, including Minutes:Seconds, Bars|Beats, and Samples.

Figure 2.14 To show or hide rulers in the Edit window, click the Ruler View selector at the top left of the Ruler area.

Figure 2.15 To rearrange rulers, drag the name of a ruler to a new location in the Ruler area.

Figure 2.16 To set any of the Timebase rulers to be the Main ruler, click the name of the ruler so that it is highlighted.

Displaying rulers

You can display rulers in any combination or order in the Edit window.

To display rulers:

◆ Choose View > Rulers and select the rulers to display.

or

Click the Ruler View selector at the top left of the Ruler area and select the rulers to display from the pop-up menu (**Figure 2.14**).

To rearrange rulers:

◆ Click the name of a ruler in the Ruler area and drag it up or down in the list (**Figure 2.15**).

To set a Timebase ruler as the Main ruler:

◆ Click the name of the ruler in the Ruler area (**Figure 2.16**).

The ruler highlights to indicate that it is the Main ruler. The Main Time Scale in the Counters area (Figure 2.8) changes to match this setting.

THE EDIT WINDOW

The Universe view

The Universe view (**Figure 2.17**) shows an overview of the entire session at the top of the Edit window. You can use this view to navigate quickly to different parts of the session.

The visible area in the Edit window appears as a framed area in the Universe view.

To display the Universe view:

◆ Click the Toolbar menu button (**Figure 2.18**) at the top right of the Edit window and select Universe from the pop-up menu.

or

At the top right of the Ruler area, click the vertical arrow (**Figure 2.19**).

To change the Edit window display from the Universe view:

◆ In the Universe view, drag the framed area to reveal different parts of the Edit window.

Figure 2.17 The Universe view shows an overview of all visible audio and MIDI tracks in the session.

Figure 2.18 To show or hide the Universe view, select Universe from the Toolbar menu.

Figure 2.19 To display the Universe view, click the arrow at the top right of the Rulers area.

The Edit window Tracks area

The Tracks area of the Edit window (**Figure 2.20**) is where audio, MIDI, video, and automation data are displayed horizontally in tracks along the timeline. The vertical order of tracks in this area corresponds to the left-to-right order of channel strips in the Mix window.

Basic controls for each track (such as Record Enable, Solo, and Mute) are displayed at the left side of the Tracks area.

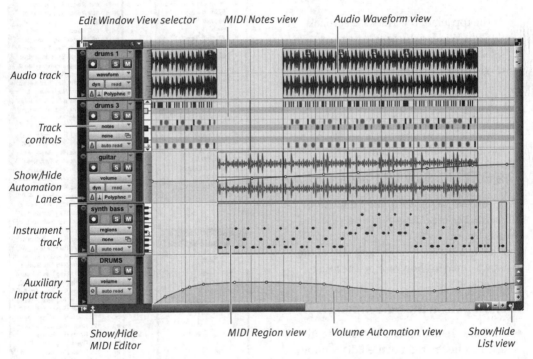

Figure 2.20 The Tracks area in the Edit window, showing different types of track material.

Displaying Edit window views

In addition to basic track controls, you can display views with signal routing and mixing controls in the Tracks area. These views correspond to views available in the Mix window, making it possible to do much of your work without having to leave the Edit window.

To display views in the Edit window:

◆ Choose View > Edit Window Views and select the view.

or

At the top left of the Tracks area, click the Edit Window View selector and select a view from the pop-up menu (**Figure 2.21**).

✔ Tip

■ To hide a view in the Edit window, Option-click (Mac) or Alt-click (Windows) the name of the view column.

The Edit window List areas

There are two List areas in the Edit window (**Figure 2.22**), including the Tracks list and Groups list (on the left side of the window) and the Regions list (on the right side of the window). You can show or hide these list areas independently.

To show lists in the Edit window:

◆ Click the Toolbar menu button (Figure 2.18) at the top right of the Edit window and choose the list to view.

or

At the bottom left or bottom right of the Edit window, click the horizontal arrow (**Figure 2.23**).

Figure 2.21 To display signal routing and mixer controls in the Edit window, click the View selector at the top left of the Tracks area. Available views include track inputs and outputs, inserts, sends, and Instrument track controls.

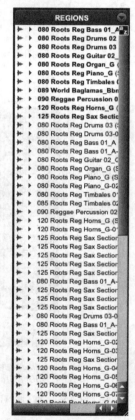

Figure 2.22 The List areas in the Edit window include the Tracks list, Groups list, and Region list.

Figure 2.23 To show or hide List areas, click the horizontal arrow at the bottom left or right of the Edit window.

Tracks list

Groups list

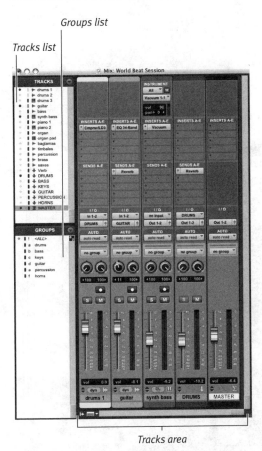

Tracks area

Figure 2.24 The Mix window includes the Tracks area, the Tracks list, and the Groups list.

The Mix Window

The Mix window shows tracks as vertical channel strips with standard signal routing and mixing controls. From this window, you can assign inputs, outputs, inserts, and sends to tracks, and adjust the volume, pan, solo, or mute status of each track.

The Mix window (**Figure 2.24**) consists of two main areas: the Tracks area and the List area, which includes the Tracks list and the Groups list.

To display the Mix window:

◆ Choose Window > Mix.

✔ Tip

■ To alternately display the Mix window and the Edit window, press Command-Equal (Mac) or Ctrl-Equal (Windows).

The Mix window Tracks area

The Tracks area of the Mix window
(**Figure 2.25**) is where tracks are displayed
as vertical channel strips. The horizontal
order of tracks in this area corresponds to
the top-to-bottom order of tracks in the
Edit window.

THE MIX WINDOW

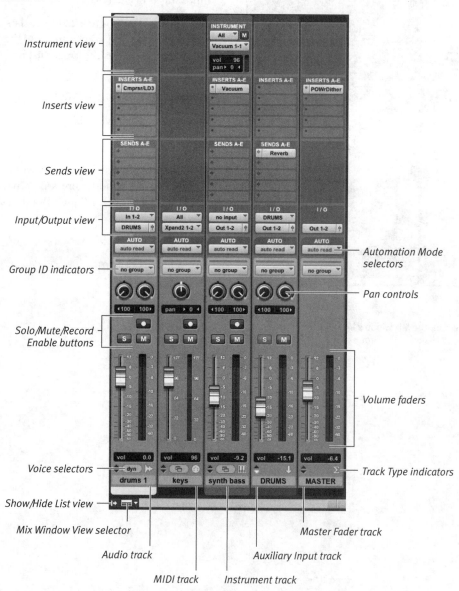

Instrument view

Inserts view

Sends view

Input/Output view

Group ID indicators

Solo/Mute/Record
Enable buttons

Voice selectors

Show/Hide List view

Mix Window View selector

Audio track

MIDI track

Instrument track

Auxiliary Input track

Master Fader track

Automation Mode
selectors

Pan controls

Volume faders

Track Type indicators

Figure 2.25 The Tracks area in the Mix window, showing tracks as mixer channel strips.

Figure 2.26 To display additional signal routing controls in the Mix window, use the View selector at the bottom left of the Tracks area.

Figure 2.27 To show more tracks in the Mix window, you can display channel strips in Narrow view.

Displaying Mix window views

In addition to the basic mixing controls in the Tracks area, you can display views with signal routing and instrument controls for each track.

To display views in the Mix window:

◆ Choose View > Mix Window Views and select the view.

or

At the bottom left of the Tracks area, click the Mix Window View selector and select a view from the pop-up menu (**Figure 2.26**).

✔ Tip

■ To hide a view in the Mix window, Option-click (Mac) or Alt-click (Windows) the name of the view in any track.

Displaying channel strips in Narrow view

To fit more tracks onscreen in the Mix window, you can display channel strips in Narrow view (**Figure 2.27**).

To display narrow channel strips in the Mix window:

◆ Choose View > Narrow Mix.

or

Press Option-Command-M (Mac) or Ctrl-Alt-M (Windows).

The Mix window List area

The List area in the Mix window (**Figure 2.28**) includes the Tracks list and Groups list.

To show lists in the Mix window:

◆ At the bottom left of the Mix window, click the horizontal arrow (**Figure 2.29**).

Figure 2.28 The List area in the Mix window includes the Tracks list and Groups list.

Figure 2.29 To show or hide the List area, click the horizontal arrow at the bottom left of the Mix window.

The MIDI Editor

While you can edit MIDI in individual tracks in the Edit window, Pro Tools also provides a separate MIDI Editor window that lets you edit MIDI data on one or more MIDI or Instrument tracks simultaneously.

You can open a MIDI Editor view at the bottom of the Edit window, or open separate MIDI Editor windows to focus on different parts of a session at the same time.

Like the Edit window, the MIDI Editor (**Figure 2.30**) consists of four main areas: the Toolbar, the Ruler area, the Tracks area, and the List area.

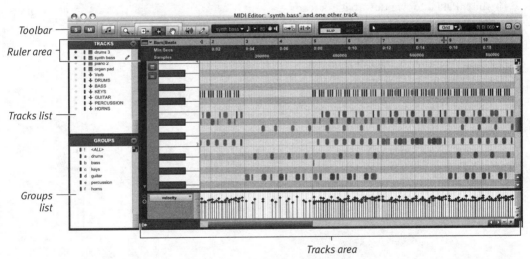

Figure 2.30 The main areas of the MIDI Editor window: the Toolbar, the Ruler area, the Tracks area, and the List area.

To open a MIDI Editor window:

◆ To open the MIDI Editor view in the Edit window, click the vertical arrow at the bottom left of the Edit window (**Figure 2.31**).

   or

   To open a separate MIDI Editor window, choose Window > MIDI Editor.

✔ Tip

■ If you select MIDI notes in one or more tracks and then open a new MIDI Editor window, those notes are selected and zoomed in the new window.

To open additional MIDI Editor windows:

1. In the MIDI Editor window that is already open, click the Target button (**Figure 2.32**) so that it is not highlighted.

2. Choose Window > MIDI Editor to open another window.

Figure 2.31 To open the MIDI Editor view that is docked to the Edit window, click the vertical arrow at the bottom left of the Edit window.

Figure 2.32 To open more than one MIDI Editor window, first deselect the Target button in the previously opened MIDI Editor.

The MIDI Editor Toolbar

The MIDI Editor Toolbar (**Figure 2.33**) has some of the same controls as the Edit window Toolbar. The MIDI Editor Toolbar controls include:

◆ **Solo and Mute buttons** let you control playback of the tracks displayed in the MIDI Editor.

◆ **Notation view button** displays MIDI notes in the form of musical notation along the timeline.

◆ **Edit tools** are used to view, select, move, and modify material in the MIDI Editor.

◆ **Note attributes** shows default attributes for new MIDI notes.

◆ **Edit option buttons** let you control selection and MIDI editing behavior in the session.

◆ **Edit Mode selectors** affect the behavior of Edit tools in the MIDI Editor.

◆ **Cursor Location indicator** shows the cursor location.

◆ **Grid and Nudge selectors** constrain selections and regions in the MIDI Editor.

◆ **Selection display** shows the attributes of any selected MIDI notes.

◆ **Target button** sets the MIDI Editor window to follow edit selections made in the main Edit window.

◆ **Toolbar menu** lets you customize the appearance of the Toolbar.

THE MIDI EDITOR

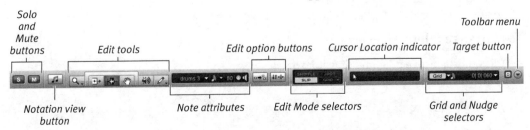

Figure 2.33 The MIDI Editor Toolbar has some of the same controls as the Edit window Toolbar.

Customizing the MIDI Editor Toolbar

You can show, hide, and rearrange controls in the MIDI Editor Toolbar.

To show controls in the MIDI Editor Toolbar:

◆ Click the MIDI Editor Toolbar menu button (**Figure 2.34**) and select the items to display in the Toolbar from the pop-up menu.

Figure 2.34 To show or hide controls in the MIDI Editor Toolbar, select them from the menu at the top right of the Toolbar area.

To rearrange controls in the MIDI Editor Toolbar:

1. Press Command (Mac) or Ctrl (Windows) and position the pointer over the controls so that it turns into a hand (**Figure 2.35**).

2. Drag the controls to another location in the Toolbar.

Figure 2.35 To rearrange controls in the MIDI Editor Toolbar, press Command (Mac) or Ctrl (Windows) and drag the controls to another location.

The MIDI Editor Ruler area

The rulers in the MIDI Editor (**Figure 2.36**) work in the same way as the rulers in the Edit window.

Displaying rulers

You can display rulers in any combination or vertical order in the MIDI Editor window.

To display rulers:

◆ Choose View > MIDI Editor Rulers and select the rulers to display.

or

Click the Ruler View selector at the top left of the Ruler area and select the rulers to display (Figure 2.14).

To rearrange rulers:

◆ Click the name of a ruler and drag it up or down in the list (Figure 2.15).

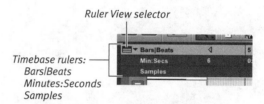

Figure 2.36 The rulers at the top of the MIDI Editor window mirror the rulers in the main Edit window.

Color Code Notes by Track   MIDI notes

Color Code Notes by Velocity

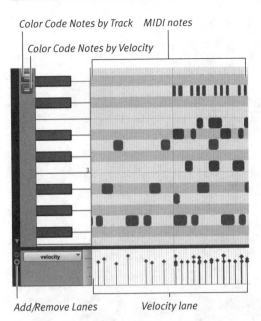

Add/Remove Lanes   Velocity lane

Figure 2.37 The Tracks area in the MIDI Editor window, showing superimposed MIDI notes from multiple MIDI and Instrument tracks.

Figure 2.38 The List area in the MIDI Editor window includes the Tracks list and Groups list.

Figure 2.39 To show or hide the List area, click the horizontal arrow at the bottom left of the MIDI Editor window.

To set a Timebase ruler as the Main ruler:

◆ Click the name of the ruler (Figure 2.16).

The ruler highlights to indicate that it is the Main ruler. The Main ruler in the Edit window changes to match this setting.

The MIDI Editor Tracks area

The Tracks area of the MIDI Editor (**Figure 2.37**) has two parts. The top part shows MIDI notes; the bottom part shows velocity information for the displayed MIDI.

When multiple tracks are displayed in the MIDI Editor, their notes are superimposed in the top part of the Tracks area, and their corresponding velocities are superimposed in the velocity lane at the bottom.

The MIDI Editor List area

The List area in the MIDI Editor window (**Figure 2.38**) includes the Tracks and Groups lists.

To show lists in the MIDI Editor:

◆ At the bottom left of the MIDI Editor window, click the horizontal arrow (**Figure 2.39**).

THE MIDI EDITOR

The Score Editor

Pro Tools lets you view MIDI in the form of musical notation in the Score Editor window.

Like the MIDI Editor, the Score Editor lets you edit one or more MIDI or Instrument tracks simultaneously. However, in the Score Editor, notes are not arranged against a timeline. Instead, they are shown in a page layout that can be printed from Pro Tools.

The Score Editor (**Figure 2.40**) consists of three main areas: the Toolbar, the Score area, and the Tracks list.

To open the Score Editor window:

◆ Choose Window > Score Editor.

✔ Tip

■ If you select MIDI notes in one or more tracks and then open the Score Editor window, those notes are selected in the new window.

Figure 2.40 The main areas of the Score Editor window: the Toolbar, the Score area, and the Tracks list.

The Score Editor Toolbar

The Score Editor Toolbar (**Figure 2.41**) has many of the same controls as the MIDI Editor Toolbar. The Score Editor Toolbar controls include:

◆ **Edit tools** are used to view, select, move, and modify notes in the Score Editor.

◆ **Note attributes** shows default attributes for new MIDI notes.

◆ **Edit option buttons** let you control selection and MIDI editing behavior in the session.

◆ **Grid selector** constrains selections in the Score Editor.

◆ **Selection display** shows the attributes of any selected MIDI notes.

◆ **Cursor Location indicator** shows the current cursor location.

◆ **Target button** sets the Score Editor window to follow edit selections made in the main Edit window.

◆ **Toolbar menu** lets you customize the appearance of the Toolbar.

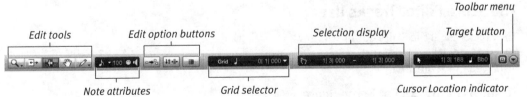

Figure 2.41 The Score Editor Toolbar has many of the same controls as the MIDI Editor window.

THE SCORE EDITOR

Customizing the Score Editor Toolbar

You can show, hide, and rearrange controls in the Score Editor Toolbar.

To show controls in the Score Editor Toolbar:

◆ Click the Score Editor Toolbar menu selector (**Figure 2.42**) and choose the items to display in the Toolbar from the pop-up menu.

To rearrange controls in the Score Editor Toolbar:

1. Press Command (Mac) or Ctrl (Windows) and position the pointer over the controls so that it turns into a hand (Figure 2.35).

2. Drag the controls to another location in the Toolbar.

The Score Editor Score area

The Score area (**Figure 2.43**) shows MIDI notes as musical notation, arranged in page layout. You can edit MIDI by directly manipulating the notation in the Score area, using the same tools that you use in the Edit window.

The Score Editor Tracks list

The Tracks list in the Score Editor window (**Figure 2.44**) lets you select the tracks to display in the Score area.

To show the Tracks list in the Score Editor:

◆ At the bottom left of the Score Editor window, click the horizontal arrow (**Figure 2.45**).

Figure 2.42 To show or hide controls in the Score Editor Toolbar, select them from the pop-up menu at the top right of the Toolbar area.

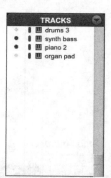

Figure 2.43 The Score area in the Score Editor window shows MIDI as musical notation in page layout.

Figure 2.44 The Tracks list in the Score Editor window.

Figure 2.45 To show or hide the Tracks list, click the horizontal arrow at the bottom left of the Score Editor window.

THE SCORE EDITOR

The Transport Window

The Transport window (**Figure 2.46**) lets you locate and audition material in your session, choose settings and select ranges for recording and playback, and adjust MIDI controls.

✔ Tip

- The Transport window will remain in front of the main windows in your session, providing quick access to recording and playback functions.

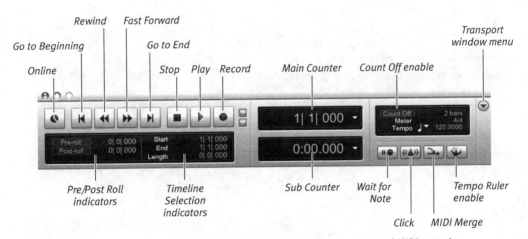

Figure 2.46 The Transport window showing Expanded Transport controls, counters, and MIDI controls.

To display the Transport window:

◆ Choose Window > Transport.

Displaying Transport window views

The Transport window has several views including transport controls, pre/post-roll settings and selection indicators, MIDI controls, and a counter display.

To display views in the Transport window:

◆ Choose View > Transport and select the view.

or

At the top right of the Transport window, click the Transport Window View selector and choose a view from the pop-up menu (**Figure 2.47**).

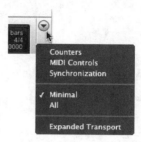

Figure 2.47 To show or hide controls in the Transport window, select them from the pop-up menu at the top right of the window.

Plug-In Windows

Pro Tools lets you use a wide range of software modules called *plug-ins* that include audio processors (such as equalizers or compressors) and virtual instruments (such as synthesizers or samplers). Real-time plug-ins are inserted on a track and used to process or create sound on that track.

Plug-in controls are displayed in floating windows (**Figure 2.48**) that you can show onscreen or hide.

Figure 2.48 A Plug-In window (Digidesign EQ III shown).

All plug-ins have a standard set of controls (**Figure 2.49**) that appear in the header area of the window:

◆ **Track controls** let you choose which plug-in to display by selecting its track and insert position.

◆ **Plug-In Preset controls** let you select presets or create new settings for the currently displayed plug-in.

◆ **Plug-In Automation controls** let you enable plug-in controls for mix automation in the session.

◆ **Plug-In Bypass button** lets you disable the plug-in to hear the track output without the effect.

◆ **Plug-In Target button** sets the Plug-In window to update when a different insert is selected in the Edit or Mix windows (see Chapter 16, "Using Plug-In Effects," for more on this).

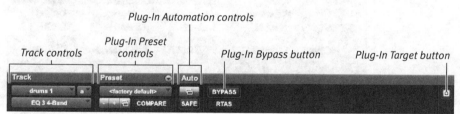

Figure 2.49 All Plug-In windows have a header area at the top with standard controls for controlling presets, automation, and bypass status.

Pro Tools Browsers

Pro Tools provides a set of browser utilities that let you search, audition, and import Pro Tools data and media files, as well as manage background tasks on your system.

Browsers are especially useful for managing large sessions or when working with collections of samples, loops, or sound effects.

The main browser windows include:

◆ **Workspace browser** lets you view and search across the entire system, including all mounted volumes (such as hard drives, CDs, or network storage devices).

◆ **Volume browsers** limit the view to individual volumes (such as a single hard drive).

◆ **Project browser** limits the view to files referenced by the current session, so you can quickly find its associated media, regardless of its location.

All Pro Tools browser windows use similar layouts and display similar types of data (**Figure 2.50**). All browser windows include:

◆ **Toolbar** has Search and View Preset buttons, Preview controls, and the Browser menu.

◆ **Column headers** show the type of data displayed. Columns can be reordered by dragging their headers.

◆ **List area** shows the media contents and metadata in fixed and scrolling panes that can be resized by dragging their borders.

To display a browser window:

◆ Choose Window > Workspace.

◆ In the Workspace browser, double-click a volume or folder to open it in a Volume browser.

◆ Open a Pro Tools session and choose Window > Project.

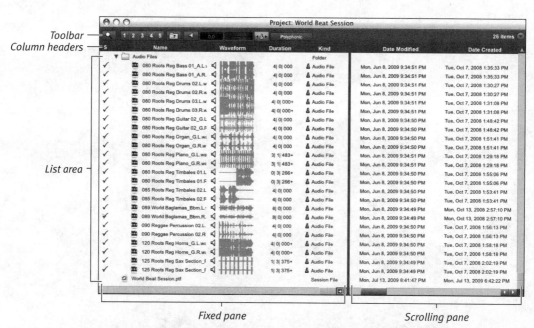

Figure 2.50 The Project browser window for a session, showing the session file and its associated audio files.

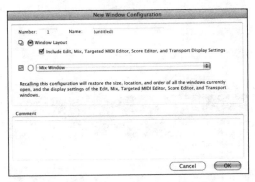

Figure 2.51 To save the arrangement of windows onscreen, choose Window > Configurations > New Configuration.

Organizing Your Workspace

With all of the available windows and views in Pro Tools, you can spend a lot of time moving windows around onscreen.

The Window Configuration feature lets you save arrangements of windows, so you can quickly recall favorite configurations or switch between views. You can also save display settings for the Edit, Mix, MIDI Editor, Score Editor, and Transport windows.

To save a Window Configuration:

1. Open and arrange the windows to include in the configuration.

2. Choose Window > Configurations > New Configuration.

   The New Window Configuration dialog appears (**Figure 2.51**).

3. Select Window Layout to save the arrangement of windows onscreen.

   or

   Select a window from the pop-up menu to save its display settings.

4. Enter a number for the configuration.

5. Click OK.

To recall a Window Configuration:

1. Choose Window > Configurations > Window Configuration List.

2. In the Window Configurations list (**Figure 2.52**), click the configuration name in the list.

To update a Window Configuration:

1. Recall the Window Configuration to be updated.

2. Change the arrangement of windows onscreen.

3. In the Window Configurations list, click the Window Configuration menu button (**Figure 2.53**) and choose Update "*configuration name*" from the pop-up menu.

To delete a Window Configuration:

1. In the Window Configurations list, select the configuration to be deleted.

2. Click the Window Configuration menu button and choose Clear for the configuration name.

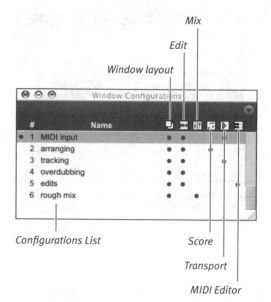

Figure 2.52 To recall a Window Configuration, click its name in the Window Configurations list.

Figure 2.53 To update a Window Configuration, choose Update from the Window Configuration menu.

Working
with Sessions

3

When you work with Pro Tools, you start by creating a *session*. Each session is represented by a file with a .ptf (Pro Tools File) extension. Session files are documents that store information about your work in Pro Tools, but they do not contain any media themselves. Instead, session files refer to other elements of a session, such as audio files and video files.

This chapter shows you how to create new sessions, how to choose session parameters for recording audio, how to back up your work, and how to create custom templates for your sessions.

Using the Quick Start Dialog

When you first launch Pro Tools, it opens a Quick Start dialog that you can use to create or open sessions (**Figure 3.1**).

When creating a new session, the Quick Start dialog works in the same way as the New Session dialog. When opening an existing session, the Quick Start dialog works in the same way as the Open Session dialog or the Open Recent command.

You can choose whether or not to see the Quick Start dialog each time you launch Pro Tools.

To enable the Quick Start dialog:

1. Choose Setup > Preferences.
   The Preferences dialog appears.

2. Click Operation.

3. Under Misc, select "Show Quick Start dialog when Pro Tools starts" (**Figure 3.2**).

4. Click OK.

Figure 3.1 The Quick Start dialog gives you several options to start working: creating a session from a preconfigured session template, creating an empty session without any tracks, opening a session that you worked on recently, or locating a particular session on your system.

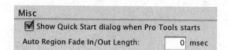

Figure 3.2 The Quick Start dialog option in the Operation Preferences determines whether the dialog is displayed each time Pro Tools is launched.

About the Session Folder

When you create a session, a folder with the session name is created automatically. All the elements of the session are stored in the session folder.

Session folders can contain the following files and folders (**Figure 3.3**):

Figure 3.3 The session folder contains the session file (with the .ptf extension) and its associated files and folders. When you create a session, Pro Tools automatically creates a session folder and stores the elements of the session in the folder.

◆ The session file, which stores information about the editing, mixing, and processing in the session.

◆ An Audio Files folder that contains all of the audio that is recorded, imported, or created in the session.

◆ A Fade Files folder that contains information about fades created in the session. If a session's fade files are missing, Pro Tools can regenerate them.

◆ A Region Groups folder that stores information about any exported region groups.

◆ A Video Files folder that contains any video that is imported into the session.

◆ A Plug-In Settings folder that contains information about any plug-in presets created in the session.

◆ A Session File Backups folder that contains automatically generated session file backups.

◆ A WaveCache file that stores waveform display information for audio in the session. If a session's WaveCache file is missing, Pro Tools can re-create audio waveforms.

Creating a Session

When you create a session, you need to choose the audio file type, sample rate, and bit depth that will be used for the session. These choices will apply to any audio that you record or import into the session.

To create a new session:

1. Choose File > New Session (**Figure 3.4**).

2. In the New Session dialog (or the Quick Start dialog), select Create Blank Session (**Figure 3.5**).

3. Select an audio file type for the session from the Audio File Type pop-up menu (**Figure 3.6**).

    In most cases, you will want to use BWF (.WAV) format.

4. Select a sample rate for the session (**Figure 3.7**).

    See the sidebar "Sample Rate and Frequency Response" for more information on choosing a sample rate.

5. Select a bit depth for the session (**Figure 3.8**).

    See the sidebar "Bit Depth and Dynamic Range" for more information on choosing a bit depth.

Figure 3.4 To create a new session, choose File > New Session.

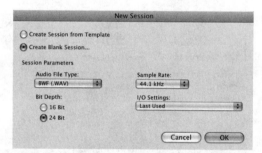

Figure 3.5 To create an empty session without any tracks, select Create Blank Session.

Figure 3.6 Select the audio file type to be used in the session.

Figure 3.7 Select the sample rate for the session.

Figure 3.8 Select the bit depth for the session.

Figure 3.9 Select the I/O Setting that you want to use for your session.

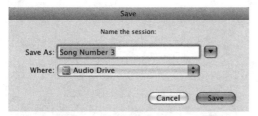

Figure 3.10 Name your session and choose a destination for the session in the Save dialog.

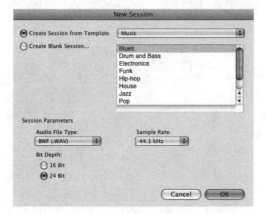

Figure 3.11 To create a session based on a preconfigured session template, select Create Session from Template.

6. Select the I/O Setting (input and output configuration) that you want to use for the session (**Figure 3.9**).

In most cases, Stereo Mix is a good starting point.

7. Click OK.

The Save dialog appears (**Figure 3.10**).

8. Type a name for the session.

9. Choose a destination for the session.

It is best to save sessions on an external hard drive and not your system drive.

10. Click Save.

Creating a session from a template

Pro Tools provides session templates with a variety of mixer configurations, effects routing, and instrument setups that you can use to start working right away.

To create a new session from a template:

1. Choose File > New Session (Figure 3.4).

2. In the New Session dialog (or the Quick Start dialog), select Create Session from Template (**Figure 3.11**).

3. Choose a template category from the pop-up menu.

4. Select a template from the list.

5. Select an audio file type for the session from the Audio File Type pop-up menu (Figure 3.6).

In most cases, you will want to use BWF (.WAV) format.

continues on next page

CREATING A SESSION

6. Select a sample rate for the session (Figure 3.7).

   See the sidebar "Sample Rate and Frequency Response" for more information on choosing a sample rate.

7. Select a bit depth for the session (Figure 3.8).

   See the sidebar "Bit Depth and Dynamic Range" for more information on choosing a bit depth.

8. Select the I/O Setting that you want to use for the session (Figure 3.9).

   In most cases, Stereo Mix is a good starting point.

9. Click OK.

   The Save dialog appears (Figure 3.10).

10. Type a name for the session.

11. Choose a destination for the new session.

12. Click Save.

Sample Rate and Frequency Response

Sample rate is the number of times an analog audio signal is measured each second in order to create a digital representation of that signal. Expressed in *kilohertz* (kHz, or thousands of cycles per second), the sample rate determines the accuracy, or frequency response, of a digital recording (**Figure 3.12**).

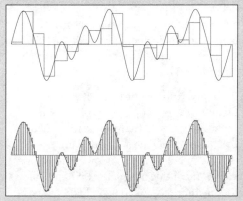

Figure 3.12 Sampling a signal at a lower sample rate (top) and a higher sample rate (bottom). The higher sample rate captures high-frequency information in the signal with greater accuracy.

According to the Nyquist-Shannon sampling theorem, in order to accurately reproduce an analog signal in a digital system, the sample rate must be more than twice the highest frequency of that signal. CD-quality audio, which has a sample rate of 44.1 kHz, was designed to represent the frequencies within the range of human hearing, which extends to about 20 kHz.

Higher sample rates are used to achieve more accurate reproduction of a signal's high-frequency content.

With Pro Tools LE, you can record at sample rates of 44.1, 48, 88.2, and 96 kHz, depending on your system hardware.

When choosing a sample rate, consider the following:

◆ The sample rate setting for a session affects hard disk usage. For example, recording at 88.2 kHz uses twice as much disk space as recording at 44.1 kHz.

◆ A sample rate of 44.1 kHz is sufficient for most music applications, such as CD or high-quality MP3 release.

◆ A sample rate of 48 kHz is often used for video, DVD, and professional broadcast applications.

◆ A sample rate of 88.2 kHz can be used can be used for high-quality music recording if you plan to release on CD at 44.1 kHz.

◆ A sample rate of 96 kHz is supported by several DVD audio formats.

CREATING A SESSION

Bit Depth and Dynamic Range

Bit depth is the length of the digital word used for each sample of an analog audio signal. Expressed simply as the number of bits, bit depth describes the precision, or resolution, of a digital recording (**Figure 3.13**).

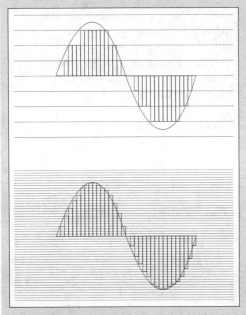

Figure 3.13 Sampling a signal at a lower bit depth (top) and a higher bit depth (bottom). The higher bit depth captures the amplitude of the signal with greater precision.

Bit depth is a factor in determining the *headroom* or potential dynamic range of a recording. Dynamic range is the ratio (expressed in decibels, or dB) of the loudest and softest sounds that can be accurately reproduced by a system.

In theory, 16-bit recording can yield a dynamic range of up to 96 dB, and 24-bit recording can yield a dynamic range of up to 144 dB. While the actual dynamic range of digital audio systems is lower than these values, recording at a higher bit depth allows for greater precision in digital processing.

With Pro Tools LE, you can record audio at either 16-bit or 24-bit resolution.

When choosing the bit depth, consider the effect on hard disk usage. Recording at a bit depth of 24 bits uses 50 percent more disk space than recording at a bit depth of 16 bits.

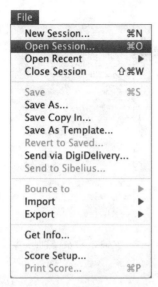

Figure 3.14 To open an existing session, choose File > Open Session.

Figure 3.15 Select a session file and click Open.

Opening a Session

You can open an existing session by double-clicking the session file, or by opening it from within Pro Tools.

To open a session:

1. Choose File > Open Session (**Figure 3.14**).

   or

   In the Quick Start dialog, select Open Session and click OK.

2. In the Open dialog, select a session file and click Open (**Figure 3.15**).

To open a recent session:

◆ Choose File > Open Recent and select a session file (**Figure 3.16**).

or

1. In the Quick Start dialog, select Open Recent Session (**Figure 3.17**).

2. Select a session file.

3. Click OK.

Closing a session

Only one session can be open at a time. Pro Tools will prompt you to save any changes before closing a session.

To close a session:

◆ Choose File > Close Session.

✔ Tip

■ A session can still be open, even if all of its windows are closed. Use the Close Session command to close a session before creating or opening another one.

Figure 3.16 To open a recent session, choose File > Open Recent.

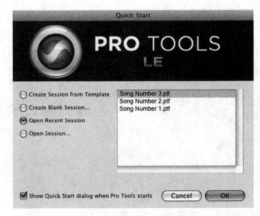

Figure 3.17 To open a recent session from the Quick Start dialog, select Open Recent Session and select a session from the list.

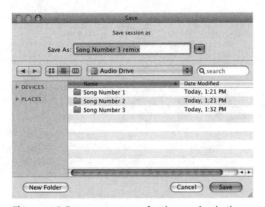

Figure 3.18 Enter a new name for the session in the Save dialog.

Saving a Session

When you save a session, you are saving the Pro Tools session file, but not any of its associated files. All other elements of a session, including audio files, fade files, region group files, and video files, are saved automatically when they are created.

To save a session:

◆ Choose File > Save.

Reverting to the last saved session

While working on a session, you can choose to discard all the changes you made since you last saved the session. This lets you start over from the previously saved version.

To revert to the last saved version of a session:

◆ Choose File > Revert to Saved.

Renaming a session

If you want to save different versions of the session you are working on, you can save the current session with a different name using the Save As command. This lets you save intermediate steps of a project and go back to them if necessary.

To rename a session:

1. Choose File > Save As.

   The Save dialog appears (**Figure 3.18**).

2. Type a name for the session.

3. Click Save.

The original session is closed and the newly renamed session remains open for you to continue working. Subsequent automatic session file backups will use the new session name.

Backing Up a Session

By default, Pro Tools automatically saves backups of your session file at 5-minute intervals; it keeps the ten most recent backups in the Session File Backups folder (**Figure 3.19**). Each backup session filename includes the suffix .bak and a number indicating its position in the backup sequence.

To enable automatic backup of sessions:

1. Choose Setup > Preferences.

2. Select Operation in the Preferences window.

3. Under Auto Backup, select Enable Session File Auto Backup (**Figure 3.20**).

4. Type the number of backup files to be kept and the backup interval.

5. Click OK.

Figure 3.19 The Session File Backups folder resides in the session folder. A backup session filename includes the suffix .bak and a number indicating its position in the backup sequence.

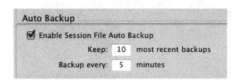

Figure 3.20 The Auto Backup option in Operation Preferences determines how frequently the session file is backed up and the number of backup files kept.

Figure 3.21 Select which elements of the session to copy in the Save Session Copy dialog.

Figure 3.22 To save the session to an earlier version of Pro Tools, choose the version from the Session Format pop-up menu.

Figure 3.23 Select the audio file type, sample rate, and bit depth of the copied session.

Saving a Copy of a Session

You can save a copy of an entire session, including the session file and all of its associated files. This is useful if you want to back up your work or move a session to another Pro Tools system.

While saving a copy of a session, you can also convert the session to a different audio file type, sample rate, or bit depth.

To save a copy of a session:

1. Choose File > Save Copy In.

   The Save Session Copy dialog appears (**Figure 3.21**).

2. If you need to copy the session for use with a version of Pro Tools earlier than 7.0, choose the version from the Session Format pop-up menu (**Figure 3.22**).

   If you will be working with Pro Tools 7.0 or later, you can leave this option set to Latest.

3. Under Session Parameters, select the audio file type, sample rate, and bit depth for the copied session (**Figure 3.23**).

continues on next page

4. Under Items To Copy, select the session elements that you want to copy to the new folder by doing one of the following (**Figure 3.24**):

If you plan to move the entire session to another system, select All Audio Files, Session Plug-In Settings Folder, Root Plug-In Settings Folder, and Movie/Video Files.

If you plan to use the copied session on the same Pro Tools system, select All Audio Files and Session Plug-In Settings Folder.

5. Click OK.

The Save dialog appears (**Figure 3.25**).

6. Type a name for the copied session.

7. Choose a destination for the copied session.

8. Click Save.

The session and its associated files are copied to the destination, and the original session remains open for you to continue working.

Figure 3.24 Select which elements of the session to copy.

Figure 3.25 Name the copied session and choose a destination for the session in the Save dialog.

Figure 3.26 The Save As Template command lets you save sessions as templates for reuse in later projects. You can include your templates in the Quick Start dialog.

Working with Session Templates

In addition to using the session templates that come with Pro Tools, you can also create your own session templates for reuse in later projects. You can also make your new templates available in the Quick Start dialog.

Pro Tools session templates have a .ptt (Pro Tools Template) filename extension.

To create a session template:

1. Open or create a session that you want to use as a template for future projects.

2. Choose File > Save As Template.
   The Save Session Template dialog appears (**Figure 3.26**).

3. Select the Select Location for Template option.

4. Select Include Media to include the session's audio, MIDI, or video content in the template.

5. Click OK.
   The Save dialog appears.

6. Type a name for the copied session.

7. Choose a destination for the copied session.

8. Click Save.

To create a session template and place it in the Quick Start dialog:

1. Open or create a session that you want to use as a template for future projects.

2. Choose File > Save As Template.

   The Save Session Template dialog appears (Figure 3.26).

3. Select "Install template in .system."

4. Choose a category for the template from the Category pop-up menu.

5. Type a name for the template.

6. Select Include Media to include the session's audio, MIDI, or video content in the template.

7. Click OK.

The new template is stored in the Session Templates folder inside the Pro Tools folder on your system.

Creating a new session from a session template

To create a new session from a session template, you can select a template from the Quick Start dialog, or open the template file directly.

To create a new session directly from a session template:

1. Double-click the session template file.

   The New Session From dialog appears (**Figure 3.27**).

2. Select an audio file type, sample rate, and bit depth for the new session.

3. Click OK.

   The Save As dialog appears.

4. Type a name for the session.

5. Click Save.

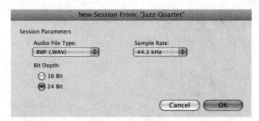

Figure 3.27 When you create a new session from a template file, Pro Tools prompts you to save the session.

WORKING WITH TRACKS

After you create a Pro Tools session, you add tracks to it. Tracks are the staging areas for the media in a session, including audio, MIDI, and video; tracks also include automation and controller data.

Tracks provide controls for routing inputs and outputs, inserting effects, playing software-based instruments, and mixing.

This chapter explains the track types available in Pro Tools, and shows you how to create and name tracks, assign track inputs and outputs, and organize tracks in a session.

About Track Types

Pro Tools LE 8 has six track types: Audio, Auxiliary Input, MIDI, Instrument, Master Fader, and Video. The types of tracks you use depends on the kind of material you want to include in your session.

Audio tracks

Audio tracks are used for recording or importing audio into a session, and then editing, arranging, and playing back that audio.

In the Mix window (see Figure 2.24), Audio track channel strips include controls for volume, pan, record enable, solo, mute, and group ID; plus selectors for automation mode, audio input paths, and audio output paths (**Figure 4.1**). You can also show Inserts and Sends views.

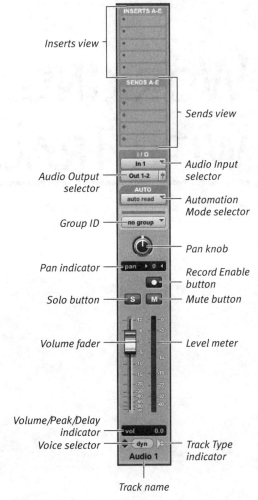

Figure 4.1 An Audio track channel strip in the Mix window.

In the Edit window (see Figure 2.1), Audio tracks include controls for record enable, solo, and mute; plus selectors for automation mode, track timebase, and Elastic Audio processing (**Figure 4.2**). You can also show Inserts, Sends, and I/O views on Audio tracks.

The playlist area is where the track's audio and its associated automation are displayed on the session timeline. The Track Height, Track View, and Playlist selectors affect the appearance of the playlist.

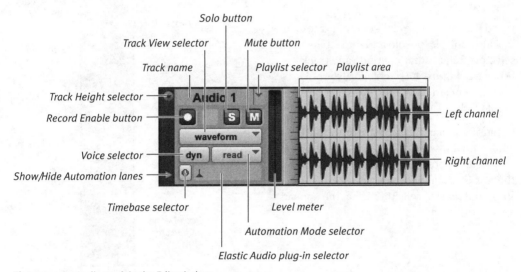

Solo button
Track View selector
Mute button
Track name
Playlist selector   Playlist area
Track Height selector
Record Enable button
Left channel
waveform
Voice selector   dyn   read
Right channel
Show/Hide Automation lanes
Timebase selector
Level meter
Automation Mode selector
Elastic Audio plug-in selector

Figure 4.2 An Audio track in the Edit window.

Auxiliary Input tracks

Auxiliary Input tracks are used to bring audio signals into a session from an internal bus, an external input, or a virtual instrument plug-in inserted on the track.

In the Mix window, Auxiliary Input track channel strips include controls for volume, pan, solo, mute, and group ID; plus selectors for automation mode, audio input paths, and audio output paths (**Figure 4.3**). As with Audio tracks, you can also show Inserts and Sends views.

In the Edit window, Auxiliary Input tracks include controls for solo and mute, plus selectors for automation mode and track timebase (**Figure 4.4**). You can also show Inserts, Sends, and I/O views on Auxiliary Input tracks.

Because Auxiliary Input tracks only route audio into a session and do not record it, the playlist area shows only track automation on the session timeline. The Track Height, Track View, and Playlist selectors affect the appearance of the playlist.

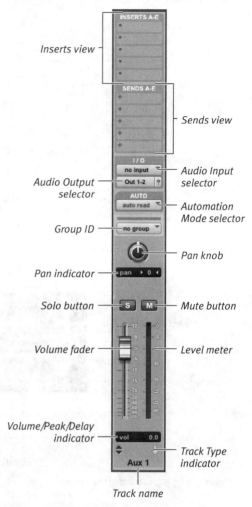

Figure 4.3 An Auxiliary Input track channel strip in the Mix window.

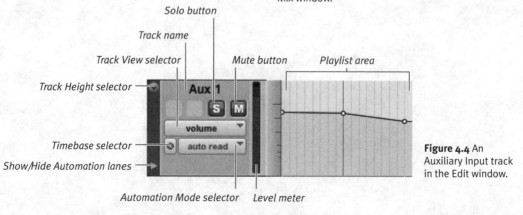

Figure 4.4 An Auxiliary Input track in the Edit window.

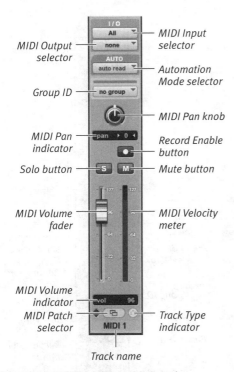

MIDI Output selector
MIDI Input selector
Automation Mode selector
Group ID
MIDI Pan knob
MIDI Pan indicator
Record Enable button
Solo button
Mute button
MIDI Volume fader
MIDI Velocity meter
MIDI Volume indicator
MIDI Patch selector
Track Type indicator
Track name

Figure 4.5 A MIDI track channel strip in the Mix window.

MIDI tracks

MIDI tracks are used for recording MIDI data into a session and playing it back through an external device. You can also use MIDI tracks to send multiple channels of MIDI to a single virtual instrument plug-in inserted on an Auxiliary Input track.

In the Mix window, MIDI track channel strips (**Figure 4.5**) have many of the same controls as Audio and Auxiliary Input tracks, including volume, pan, solo, mute, and group ID, plus selectors for automation mode and MIDI input and output. However, on MIDI tracks, the volume and pan controls affect MIDI controller values, and the input and outputs are MIDI channels.

In the Edit window (**Figure 4.6**), MIDI tracks include controls for MIDI record enable, solo, and mute; plus selectors for automation mode, MIDI patch, and track timebase. You can also show the I/O view on MIDI tracks. (MIDI tracks don't have Inserts or Sends.)

The playlist area displays MIDI notes in piano roll format on the session timeline, along with associated MIDI controller data. The Track Height, Track View, and Playlist selectors affect the appearance of the playlist.

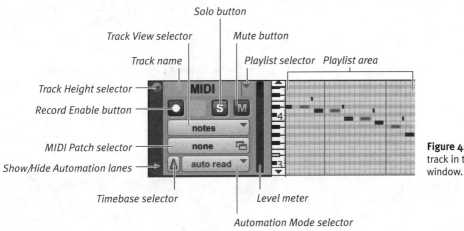

Solo button
Track View selector
Mute button
Track name
Playlist selector   Playlist area
Track Height selector
Record Enable button
MIDI Patch selector
Show/Hide Automation lanes
Timebase selector
Level meter
Automation Mode selector

Figure 4.6 A MIDI track in the Edit window.

Instrument tracks

Instrument tracks combine features of MIDI tracks and Auxiliary Input tracks, so that you need only a single track to use a virtual instrument. Instrument tracks are used to record MIDI and play it back through a virtual instrument plug-in inserted on the same track.

In the Mix window, Instrument track channel strips (**Figure 4.7**) have the same controls as Auxiliary Input tracks: audio volume, pan, solo, mute, and group ID; plus selectors for automation mode, audio input paths, and audio output paths. You can also show Inserts and Sends views. The Record Enable button in this section is for recording MIDI, not audio.

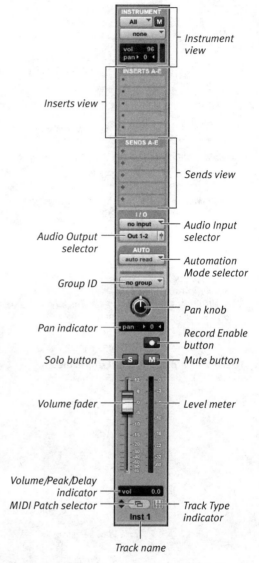

Figure 4.7 An Instrument track channel strip in the Mix window.

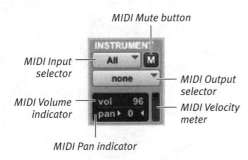

MIDI Mute button

MIDI Input selector

MIDI Output selector

MIDI Volume indicator

MIDI Velocity meter

MIDI Pan indicator

Figure 4.8 The MIDI controls for an Instrument track in the Mix window.

In addition to these controls, Instrument tracks also have MIDI controls (**Figure 4.8**), available in the Instrument view: MIDI input and output selectors, MIDI volume and pan, and MIDI mute.

In the Edit window (**Figure 4.9**), Instrument tracks include controls for record enable, solo, and mute; plus selectors for automation mode, MIDI patch, and track timebase. You can also show the I/O view on Instrument tracks.

The playlist area displays the same information as MIDI tracks: MIDI notes and controller data. The Track Height, Track View, and Playlist selectors affect the appearance of the playlist.

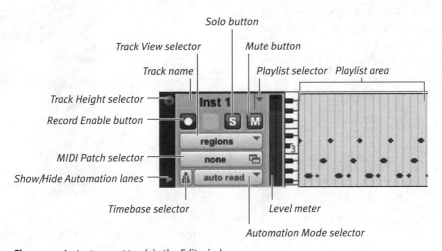

Solo button

Track View selector

Mute button

Track name

Playlist selector   Playlist area

Track Height selector

Record Enable button

MIDI Patch selector

Show/Hide Automation lanes

Timebase selector

Level meter

Automation Mode selector

Figure 4.9 An Instrument track in the Edit window.

Master Fader tracks

Master Fader tracks are used to control the audio outputs of a session. They are most commonly used on the outputs for a session's main mix.

In the Mix window, Master Fader track channel strips (**Figure 4.10**) include track controls for volume and group ID, plus selectors for automation mode and the audio output path. You can also show Inserts view.

In the Edit window (**Figure 4.11**), Master Fader tracks include selectors for automation mode and track timebase. You can also show automation lanes, Inserts, and I/O views.

Because Master Fader tracks only control audio outputs and do not record audio, the playlist area shows only track automation on the session timeline. The Track Height and Track View selectors affect the appearance of the playlist.

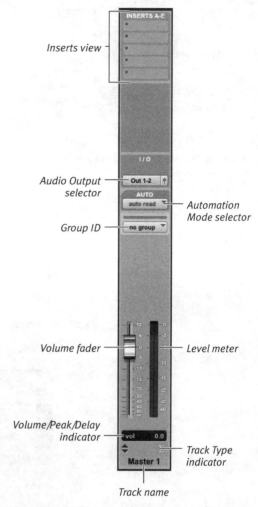

Figure 4.10 A Master Fader track channel strip in the Mix window.

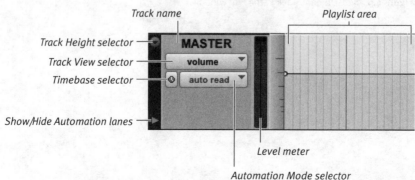

Figure 4.11 A Master Fader track in the Edit window.

Video tracks

Video tracks display imported video in the session timeline, allowing you to edit sound to picture.

Video tracks are displayed in the Edit window only (**Figure 4.12**). Edit window controls include Video Online button and Track View selector. You can also show the I/O view on Video tracks.

The playlist area shows video regions as frames or solid blocks. You can adjust the size of the video track with the Track Height selector.

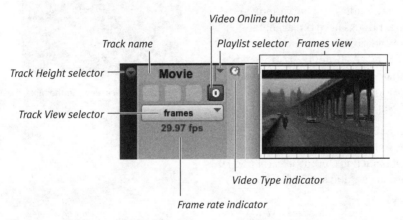

Figure 4.12 A Video track in the Edit window.

About Track Views

Tracks have a common set of available views, most of which are accessible from both the Mix and Edit windows. In the Mix window, views are displayed vertically (**Figure 4.13**), and in the Edit window, views are displayed horizontally (**Figure 4.14**).

- ◆ **Inserts view.** Audio, Auxiliary Input, Instrument, and Master Fader tracks have ten available inserts, displayed in two groups of five (labeled Inserts A–E and F–J). Insert selectors at each position let you choose software plug-ins or hardware inserts.

- ◆ **Sends view.** Audio, Auxiliary Input, and Instrument tracks have ten available sends, displayed in two groups of five (labeled Sends A–E and F–J). The Sends view can be set to show Send selectors at each position, or to show the controls for a single Send position.

- ◆ **Instrument view.** Instrument tracks have a separate view with MIDI controls, including MIDI Input and Output selectors, MIDI Volume and Pan, and MIDI Mute.

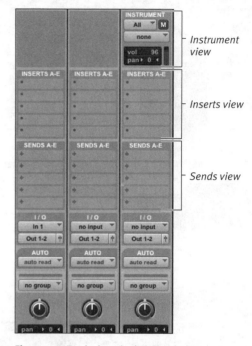

Figure 4.13 Track views in the Mix window.

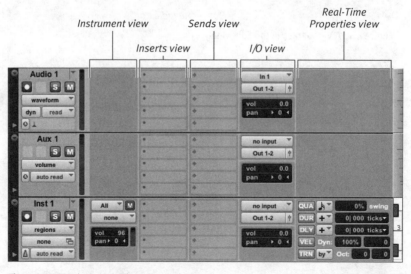

Figure 4.14 Track views in the Edit window.

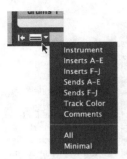

Figure 4.15 To show or hide Mix window track views, click the Mix window View selector.

Figure 4.16 To show or hide Edit window track views, click the Edit window View selector.

◆ **I/O view (Edit window only).** Audio, Auxiliary Input, MIDI, Instrument, and Master Fader tracks have an Edit window I/O view that lets you show track input and output paths, as well as volume and pan indicators. (These controls are always visible in the Mix window, so it does not have a selectable I/O view.)

◆ **Real-Time Properties view (Edit window only).** MIDI and Instrument tracks have a Real-Time Properties view that provides access to any MIDI Real-Time Properties settings that are applied to the entire track.

◆ **Track color view.** All track types can display color coding in the Mix window, Edit window, or both.

◆ **Comments view.** All track types have an area for comments about the track.

To show or hide track views:

◆ Choose View > Mix Window Views or View > Edit Window Views and select the views to display.

◆ In the Mix window, click the View selector at the bottom left of the Tracks area (**Figure 4.15**) and select the views to display from the pop-up menu.

    or

    In the Edit window, click the View selector at the top left of the Tracks area (**Figure 4.16**) and select the views to display from the pop-up menu.

To show all track views:

◆ Click the View selector and choose All.

To hide all but the basic track views:

◆ Click the View selector and choose Minimal.

ABOUT TRACK VIEWS

About Track Controls

Tracks have common controls for recording, playing back, and mixing track material; writing and playing back mix automation; and viewing track attributes. Most controls are available in both the Mix and Edit windows.

Figure 4.17 To view Input and Output selectors in the Edit window, choose the I/O view from the Edit window View selector.

Figure 4.18 To view Pan controls in the Edit window, choose the I/O view from the Edit window View selector, then click the Pan indicator (left) to make the Pan controls appear (right).

◆ **Input and Output path selectors.** Audio, Auxiliary Input, and Instrument tracks have Input and Output path selectors for choosing audio paths. Master Fader tracks have Output selectors only. MIDI tracks have Input and Output selectors for choosing MIDI channels.

   To view Input and Output path selectors in the Edit window, show the I/O view (**Figure 4.17**).

◆ **Automation Mode selector.** All track types (except Video tracks) allow controls to be automated so that you can reproduce mix moves in your session. The Automation Mode selector determines how track automation is written and played back.

◆ **Pan controls.** Audio, Auxiliary Input, MIDI, and Instrument tracks have Pan controls and indicators to position the track output in the stereo field.

   To view Pan controls in the Edit window, show the I/O view and click the Pan indicator (**Figure 4.18**).

◆ **Record Enable button.** Audio tracks have a Record Enable button to arm the track for recording audio inputs. MIDI and Instrument tracks have a Record Enable button to arm the track for recording MIDI input.

Figure 4.19 To view the Volume fader in the Edit window, choose the I/O view from the Edit window View selector, then click the Volume indicator (left) to make the Volume controls appear (right).

◆ **Solo button.** Audio, Auxiliary Input, MIDI, and Instrument tracks have a Solo button that mutes all other tracks so the soloed track's output can be auditioned independently.

◆ **Mute button.** Audio, Auxiliary Input, MIDI, and Instrument tracks have a Mute button that silences the track's output. When a track is soloed, other tracks are implicitly muted.

◆ **Volume fader.** All track types (except Video tracks) have a Volume fader that controls the track output level.

To view the Volume fader in the Edit window, show the I/O view and click the Volume indicator (**Figure 4.19**).

◆ **Level meter.** All track types (except Video tracks) have a Level meter. On Audio tracks, the Level meter shows the audio signal coming from the hard drive, not the track output level.

On Auxiliary Input, Instrument, and Master Fader tracks, the Level meter shows the output level of the track.

On MIDI tracks, the Level meter shows the velocity value of MIDI events on the track.

◆ **Volume/Peak/Delay indicator.** Audio, Auxiliary Input, Instrument, and Master Fader tracks have indicators that can show the current Volume fader level or the recent peak playback level. In addition, this indicator shows the amount of delay (in samples) incurred by any plug-ins inserted on the track. To toggle display among volume, peak volume, and delay, Command-click (Mac) or Ctrl-click (Windows) the indicator.

continues on next page

ABOUT TRACK CONTROLS

◆ **Timebase selector (Edit window only).**
All track types (except Video tracks) have
a timebase selector that lets you change
the timebase setting (Samples or Ticks) of
the track. See the sidebar "Timebases and
Track Display," later in this chapter, for
more information.

◆ **Voice selector.** Audio tracks have a Voice
selector that lets you turn the track's voice
assignment on or off. See the sidebar
"Track Order and Voice Allocation," later
in this chapter, for more information.

◆ **Track Type indicator.** In the Mix window, each track has a small icon that
indicates the track type. With Audio,
Auxiliary Input, Instrument, and Master
Fader tracks, you can deactivate the track
by clicking the Track Type indicator.

◆ **Track name.** You can select a track by
clicking its name in the Mix or Edit window. You can rename a track by double-
clicking its name.

Figure 4.20 The Pan control for a mono Audio track with its output set to a stereo output path.

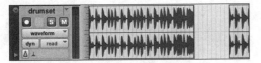

Figure 4.21 The Edit window playlist for a mono Audio track.

Figure 4.22 The Pan controls for a stereo Audio track with its output set to a stereo path.

Figure 4.23 The Edit window playlist for a stereo Audio track.

Setting the Track Format

When you create an Audio, Auxiliary Input, Instrument, or Master Fader track, you choose a format for the track. In Pro Tools LE 8, you can choose between mono and stereo formats.

◆ **Mono tracks.** When the output of a mono track is set to a stereo output path, a pan control is available to position the track output in the stereo field (**Figure 4.20**).

A mono Audio track shows a single lane of audio in its Edit window playlist (**Figure 4.21**).

Mono tracks are used for single input sources, such as a vocal or solo instrument microphone.

◆ **Stereo tracks.** When the output of a stereo track is set to a stereo output path, two pan controls are available to position each channel independently in the stereo field (**Figure 4.22**). All other controls on a stereo track affect both channels in tandem, including the Volume fader, the Record Enable, Solo, and Mute buttons.

Stereo Audio tracks show two channels of audio in the Edit window Track area (**Figure 4.23**). Any selections or edits to material in a stereo track affect both channels simultaneously.

Stereo tracks are used for dual input sources, such as left and right drum overhead microphones or dual piano microphones.

If you want to edit or adjust the controls for a specific channel in a stereo track, you need to split the stereo track into two mono tracks.

To split a stereo track into mono tracks:

1. Click the name of the stereo track to select it (**Figure 4.24**).

2. Choose Track > Split into Mono.

   The stereo track is split into two mono tracks with independent controls (**Figure 4.25**).

Figure 4.24 Selecting a stereo track.

Figure 4.25 Splitting a stereo into two mono tracks.

Timebases and Track Display

Pro Tools displays time in two fundamental ways: *absolute time* and *relative time*.

When events are displayed in absolute time, their location is expressed as *minutes and seconds* (or as the *number of samples*) after the beginning of the session. Tracks that handle audio material (Audio, Auxiliary Input, and Master Fader tracks) are *sample-based* by default.

When a tempo change is applied to a sample-based track, the track material does not move in time, even though its bar and beat label changes.

When events are displayed in relative time, their location is expressed in terms of bar and beat numbers (or in terms of MIDI *ticks*). Tracks that handle MIDI data (MIDI and Instrument tracks) are *tick-based* by default.

When a tempo change is applied to a tick-based track, the track material moves earlier or later in time, maintaining its relative bar and beat location.

The Edit window provides two ways of displaying the relationship between sample-based and tick-based tracks on the timeline:

◆ Linear Sample Display keeps Minutes:Seconds (or Samples) view constant and shrinks or expands the view of tick-based material in response to tempo changes.

◆ Linear Tick Display keeps the Bars|Beats view constant and shrinks or expands the view of sample-based material in response to tempo changes.

Setting the Track Timebase

When you create a new track (for all track types except Video tracks), you can choose one of two timebase settings for the track: Samples or Ticks. The timebase setting determines how events in the track are located on the timeline. See the sidebar "Timebases and Track Display" for more information.

By default, Audio, Auxiliary Input, and Master Fader tracks are set to Samples; MIDI and Instrument tracks are set to Ticks. For straightforward audio or MIDI recording, the default timebase setting for each track type is usually best.

However, you may want to use alternate timebase settings for certain workflows. For example, when working with audio loops, to make the location of audio regions conform to the session tempo, you can set an Audio track timebase to Ticks. Conversely, when spotting sound effects to picture, to have MIDI events always occur at the same time, regardless of session tempo, you can set a MIDI track to Samples.

To change the timebase of a track:

◆ In the Edit window, click the Timebase selector at the lower left of the track controls and select the timebase setting from the pop-up menu (**Figure 4.26**).

To change the timebase display:

◆ In the Edit window, click the Linearity Display selector at the top right of the track controls and select the display setting from the pop-up menu (**Figure 4.27**).

Figure 4.26 To change the timebase of a track, click its Timebase selector in the Edit window.

Figure 4.27 To change the timebase display for a session, click the Linearity Display selector in the Edit window.

Figure 4.28 To create a new track, choose Track > New.

Figure 4.29 Select the Track Type for the new track.

Figure 4.30 Select the format for the new track.

Figure 4.31 To create multiple track types, click the plus sign to add rows to the New Track dialog.

Adding Tracks to a Session

When you first set up a session, you will often want to add more than one track. You can use the New Tracks dialog to create multiple tracks of different types.

To create a new track:

1. Choose Track > New.
   The New Tracks dialog appears (**Figure 4.28**).

2. Select a track type from the Track Type pop-up menu (**Figure 4.29**).

3. Select a format for the track from the Track Format pop-up menu (**Figure 4.30**). MIDI and Video tracks do not have a format choice.

4. Type the number of tracks to create.

5. Click Create.

To create multiple track types:

1. Choose Track > New.
   The New Tracks dialog appears (Figure 4.28).

2. Click the plus sign to add rows to the dialog (**Figure 4.31**).

3. In each row, select the track type and track format from the corresponding pop-up menus.

4. Click Create.
   The tracks are added to the session in the order they were designated in the New Tracks dialog.

✔ Tip

■ To have new tracks appear after an existing track in a session, select the existing track by clicking its name before creating the tracks.

Naming Tracks

When you create a new track, it is automatically given a name based on its track type ("Audio," "Aux," "MIDI," "Inst," "Master," or "Video") followed by a number.

When you record material into a track, Pro Tools uses the track name to automatically name audio files and their associated regions.

✔ Tip

- It's a good idea to rename tracks with more descriptive names before you begin recording. This helps organize your session and ensures that all of the track's files and regions have similar names.

To rename a track:

1. Double-click the track name (**Figure 4.32**).

   The Track Name dialog appears.

2. Type a new track name in the Name area (**Figure 4.33**).

3. Enter any annotations in the Comments area.

4. To rename adjacent tracks in the session, click the Previous or Next button.

5. Click OK.

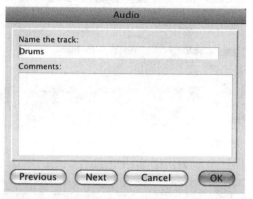

Figure 4.32 To rename a track, double-click the track name.

Figure 4.33 Type a name for the new track.

Figure 4.34 To assign an input path to an audio track, click its Input selector and choose an interface or bus path.

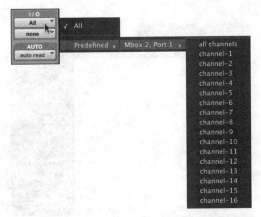

Figure 4.35 To assign an input port/channel to a MIDI track, click its Input selector and choose the MIDI port and channel.

Assigning Track Inputs and Outputs

After you create tracks in your session, you assign inputs and outputs to the tracks in order to record and play back audio and MIDI.

When you create new tracks in a session, input paths are automatically assigned in ascending order, repeating if there are more tracks than available inputs on your Pro Tools LE hardware. Output paths are automatically assigned to the first pair of output paths.

You can assign track inputs and outputs from the Mix window or the Edit window. To view Input and Output selectors in the Edit window, show the I/O view (Figure 4.17).

The audio paths available in Audio, Auxiliary Input, and Instrument track input and output menus are defined in the I/O Setup dialog.

For more information on I/O Setup, see "Configuring Audio Inputs and Outputs" in Chapter 6, "Recording Audio."

The MIDI ports available in MIDI track input and output menus are defined in the Audio MIDI Setup dialog (Mac) or the MIDI Studio Setup dialog (Windows).

For more information on MIDI Setup, see "Configuring MIDI Inputs" in Chapter 7, "Recording MIDI."

To assign a track input:

◆ On Audio, Auxiliary Input, or Instrument tracks, click the Input selector and choose an audio interface or bus path (**Figure 4.34**).

or

On MIDI tracks, click the Input selector and choose the MIDI port and channel (**Figure 4.35**).

To assign a track output:

◆ On Audio, Auxiliary Input, Instrument, or Master Fader tracks, click the Output selector and choose an audio interface or bus path (**Figure 4.36**).

◆ On MIDI tracks, click the Output selector and choose the MIDI port and channel (**Figure 4.37**).

Figure 4.36 To assign an output path to an audio track, click its Output selector and choose an interface or bus.

Figure 4.37 To assign an output port/channel to a MIDI track, click its Output selector and choose the MIDI port and channel.

Figure 4.38 To select a track, click its name in the Tracks list.

Figure 4.39 To select contiguous tracks, click the first track name, then Shift-click the track name at the end of the desired range.

Selecting Tracks

To duplicate, delete, move, group, or deactivate specific tracks in a session, you first need to select the tracks in the Mix or Edit window.

To select a track:

◆ In the Mix or Edit window, click a track name.

or

In the Tracks list, click the track name to select it.

The track name is highlighted to indicate the track is selected (**Figure 4.38**).

To deselect a track:

◆ Command-click (Mac) or Ctrl-click (Windows) the highlighted track name.

To select a range of contiguous tracks:

1. Click the name of the track at one end of the range to be selected.

2. Shift-click the name of the track at the other end of the range to be selected (**Figure 4.39**).

To select noncontiguous tracks:

◆ Command-click (Mac) or Ctrl-click (Windows) the names of the tracks to be selected.

To select all tracks:

◆ Option-click (Mac) or Alt-click (Windows) any track name.

To deselect all tracks:

◆ Option-click (Mac) or Alt-click (Windows) any highlighted track name.

Moving Tracks

You can organize your session by moving tracks in the Mix or Edit windows.

With Audio tracks, the track position in the session determines voice assignment priority. By moving audio tracks relative to each other, you can change their priority. See the sidebar "Track Order and Voice Allocation" for more information.

To move tracks in a session:

1. In the Mix or Edit window, select the track or tracks you want to move.

2. Drag the selected tracks to a different position in the window (**Figure 4.40**).

   or

   In the Tracks list, drag the track name to a new location in the list (**Figure 4.41**).

Figure 4.40 To move tracks in a session, drag them in the Mix or Edit window.

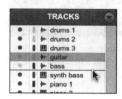

Figure 4.41 To move a track in a session, drag it in the Tracks list.

Track Order and Voice Allocation

In Pro Tools LE 8, the number of available voices (simultaneous channels of recording or playback) is limited to 48. It is possible, however, to have up to 128 tracks in a session. All these tracks are available for editing and mixing, but cannot be recorded or played back at the same time.

Pro Tools LE 8 automatically allocates available voices to the first 48 channels in the session, assigning priority to tracks as follows: in the Edit window, from top to bottom, and in the Mix window, from left to right.

You can change the priority assignments of tracks by moving them in the session, by setting voice selectors to off, or by making tracks inactive.

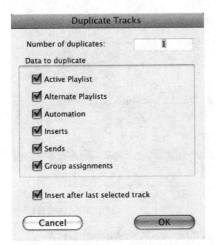

Figure 4.42 To duplicate tracks, choose Track > Duplicate to access the Duplicate Tracks dialog.

Duplicating Tracks

You can create multiple copies of tracks in a session, which lets you use the original as a guide while editing or mixing the copies.

In the Duplicate Tasks dialog, you can choose to copy data associated with the original track, as follows:

◆ **Active Playlist** copies only the Edit playlist currently displayed on the original track.

◆ **Alternate Playlists** copies all Edit playlists in the original track.

◆ **Automation** copies all track automation data from the original track.

◆ **Inserts** copies all insert assignments, associated plug-ins, and plug-in settings from the original track.

◆ **Sends** copies all send assignments and settings from the original track.

◆ **Group assignments** copies all group assignments, which adds the copied track to the same groups as the original track.

To duplicate tracks:

1. Select the track or tracks to duplicate.

2. Choose Track > Duplicate.

   The Duplicate Tracks dialog appears (**Figure 4.42**).

3. Select the attributes you want to include in the duplicate tracks.

4. If you are duplicating more than one track, do one of the following:

   ▲ To locate all duplicate tracks after the last selected track, select "Insert after last selected tracks."

   or

   To locate duplicate tracks next to each selected track, deselect "Insert after last selected tracks."

5. Click OK.

Deleting Tracks

When you delete tracks from a session, any audio files or MIDI data associated with those tracks are retained and remain in the Regions list.

If the track has any alternate playlists associated with it, you can save them.

To delete tracks:

1. Select the track or tracks to delete.

2. Choose Track > Delete.

   A Delete Track warning appears (**Figure 4.43**).

3. Click Delete.

4. If the track has any alternate playlists, choose to keep or delete them (**Figure 4.44**).

   The selected tracks are deleted from the session.

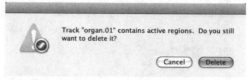

Figure 4.43 Confirm that you want to delete a selected track.

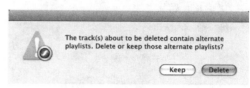

Figure 4.44 If a deleted track has any alternate playlists associated with it, you are prompted to keep or delete them.

Figure 4.45 To hide a track, click its Show/Hide icon in the Tracks list so that the icon is dimmed.

Figure 4.46 To hide or show all tracks, choose Hide All Tracks or Show All Tracks from the Tracks list menu.

Figure 4.47 To show tracks by track type, choose Show Only from the Tracks list menu.

Figure 4.48 To sort tracks in the Tracks list, choose Sort Tracks By from the Tracks list menu.

Showing and Hiding Tracks

Pro Tools lets you temporarily hide tracks in a session, so that you can show only the tracks you need to do your work.

The names of all the tracks in a session appear in the Tracks list, which is on the top left of the Edit and Mix windows. You can show or hide tracks by selecting their names in the Tracks list. In addition, you can sort tracks by track name, track type, or group membership.

Even though hidden tracks do not appear in any Pro Tools window, they play back normally.

To hide tracks:

◆ Click the Show/Hide icon for the track in the Tracks list so that the icon is dimmed (**Figure 4.45**).

To show tracks:

◆ Click the dimmed Show/Hide icon for the hidden track in the Tracks list.

To hide or show all tracks:

◆ Click the Tracks list menu button and select Hide All Tracks or Show All Tracks from the pop-up menu (**Figure 4.46**).

To show tracks by track type:

◆ Click the Tracks list menu button, then from the pop-up menus choose Show Only and the track type to display (**Figure 4.47**).

To sort the display of track names in the Tracks list:

◆ Click the Tracks list menu button, then from the pop-up menus choose Sort Tracks By and the sort term (**Figure 4.48**).

Making Tracks Inactive

If you have Audio, Auxiliary Input, or Master Fader tracks in a session that you don't need to hear, you can mute their output. However, these muted tracks will continue to use available voices and your computer's processing power.

To conserve these resources, you can make tracks inactive. All plug-ins, sends, and automation on inactive tracks are temporarily disabled. Inactive tracks are grayed out in the Mix and Edit windows.

To toggle the active/inactive state of a track:

◆ In the Mix window, Command-Control-click (Mac) or Ctrl-Start-click (Windows) the Track Type indicator (**Figure 4.49**).

To toggle the active/inactive state of multiple tracks:

1. Select the tracks to make active or inactive.

2. Choose Track > Make Inactive (or Make Active).

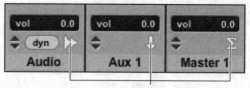

Track Type indicators

Figure 4.49 To make tracks active or inactive, Command-Control-click (Mac) or Ctrl-Start-click (Windows) the Track Type indicator.

NAVIGATING AND PLAYING SESSIONS

When you start to work with audio and MIDI in your session, you'll want to view and audition your material quickly and efficiently.

This chapter shows the main tools for navigating the Pro Tools Edit window, arranging and customizing your view of tracks, and the various ways to play back material.

Adjusting Track Height

You can adjust the display of individual tracks in the Edit window to any of the following preset heights: micro, mini, small, medium, large, jumbo, and extreme. You can also fit tracks to the Edit window.

At track heights smaller than medium, fewer track controls are displayed. Track View and Track Timebase menus become available on the Track Height selector.

To adjust the height of a track:

◆ Do one of the following:

▲ Click the Track Height selector at the top left of a track and choose a setting from the pop-up menu (**Figure 5.1**).

▲ Click in the amplitude scale for Audio, Auxiliary Input, and Master Fader tracks (**Figure 5.2**); for MIDI and Instrument tracks, click the mini key display (**Figure 5.3**). Choose a setting from the pop-up menu.

▲ Resize a track by dragging its bottom edge (**Figure 5.4**).

✔ Tips

■ To adjust all tracks in a session to the same height, hold Option (Mac) or Alt (Windows) while adjusting the height of any track.

■ To adjust only selected tracks to the same height, hold Shift-Option (Mac) or Shift-Alt (Windows) while adjusting the height of a selected track.

■ Controls for adjusting track height are also located on the bottom right of the Edit window (**Figure 5.5**).

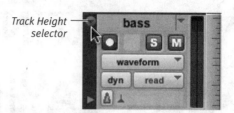

Figure 5.1 To choose a Track Height setting, click the Track Height selector at the left of the track.

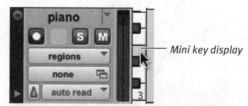

Figure 5.2 To choose a Track Height setting for Audio, Auxiliary Input, and Master Fader tracks, click the amplitude scale to the right of the track's controls.

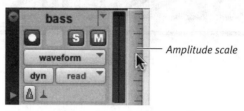

Figure 5.3 To choose a Track Height setting for MIDI and Instrument tracks, click the mini key display to the right of the track's controls.

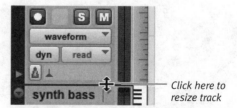

Figure 5.4 To resize a track, drag its bottom edge.

Figure 5.5 Track Height controls in the bottom-right corner of the Edit window.

Figure 5.6 To set the Zoomer tool mode, click the Zoomer tool and choose the mode from the pop-up menu.

Figure 5.7 To zoom in horizontally, click or drag in a track with the Zoomer tool.

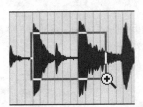

Figure 5.8 To zoom out horizontally, hold Option (Mac) or Alt (Windows) and click with the Zoomer tool.

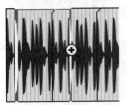

Figure 5.9 To zoom in horizontally and vertically, hold Command (Mac) or Ctrl (Windows) and drag with the Zoomer tool.

Zooming Tracks

Pro Tools provides several ways to zoom in and out on track material in the Edit window: the Zoomer tool, the Zoom controls, Zoom Preset buttons, and the Zoom Toggle button.

Using the Zoomer tool

You can set the Zoomer tool to work in two modes:

◆ **Normal Zoom** remains active so you can continue to use the Zoomer tool.

◆ **Single Zoom** returns you to the previously active Edit tool after you zoom once.

To set the Zoomer tool mode:

◆ Click the Zoomer tool and choose the mode from the pop-up menu (**Figure 5.6**).

To zoom in horizontally:

1. Select the Zoomer tool.

2. Click or drag in a track where you want to zoom in (**Figure 5.7**).

To zoom out horizontally:

◆ Hold Option (Mac) or Alt (Windows) and click with the Zoomer tool.

The Zoomer tool changes to show a Minus sign when zooming out (**Figure 5.8**).

To zoom in horizontally and vertically:

◆ Hold Command (Mac) or Ctrl (Windows) and drag with the Zoomer tool (**Figure 5.9**).

To zoom all the way out and display the entire session:

◆ Double-click the Zoomer tool.

or

Press Option-A (Mac) or Alt-A (Windows).

Using the Zoom controls

The Zoom controls (**Figure 5.10**) let you zoom horizontally or vertically, with separate vertical zoom buttons for audio waveforms and MIDI notes.

To zoom in or out horizontally:

◆ To zoom incrementally, click the left or right Horizontal zoom button.

or

To zoom continuously, drag left or right on either of the Horizontal zoom buttons.

✔ Tip

■ Controls for zooming horizontally are also located in bottom-right corner (**Figure 5.11**) of the Edit window.

To zoom in or out vertically on audio or MIDI:

◆ To zoom incrementally, click the top or bottom of the audio zoom button or the MIDI zoom button.

or

To zoom continuously, drag up or down on the audio zoom button or MIDI zoom button.

✔ Tip

■ Controls for zooming audio and MIDI are also located in the top-right corner (**Figure 5.12**) of the Edit window.

Using Zoom Presets

The Zoom Preset buttons (numbered 1–5) are preprogrammed with increasing horizontal zoom levels. You can jump quickly between zoom levels by clicking the buttons (**Figure 5.13**).

You can also store your own zoom levels and use these buttons to jump to them.

Zoom controls

Figure 5.10 The Zoom controls in the Edit window Toolbar.

Horizontal zoom controls

Figure 5.11 Horizontal Zoom controls in the bottom-right corner of the Edit window.

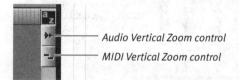

Audio Vertical Zoom control

MIDI Vertical Zoom control

Figure 5.12 Audio and MIDI Vertical Zoom controls in the top right of the Edit window.

Figure 5.13 The Zoom Preset buttons in the Edit window Toolbar.

Zoom Preset buttons

ZOOMING TRACKS

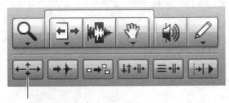

Figure 5.14 To save a Zoom Preset value, choose Save from the Zoom Preset button pop-up menu.

Zoom Toggle button

Figure 5.15 The Zoom Toggle button in the Edit window Toolbar.

To save a Zoom Preset:

1. Zoom in a track to the level you want to save.

2. Command-click (Mac) or Ctrl-click (Windows) a Zoom Preset button (1–5).

   or

   Click and hold a Zoom Preset button, then choose Save Zoom Preset from the pop-up menu (**Figure 5.14**).

Using Zoom Toggle

Zoom Toggle lets you store zoom settings and then toggle between your current view and those settings with a single click.

By default, Zoom Toggle remembers settings for track height and track view, and applies them when zooming in on your edit selection.

To store Zoom Toggle settings:

1. Select material in one or more tracks.

2. Click the Zoom Toggle button (**Figure 5.15**).

   The Zoom Toggle button highlights to indicate that it is enabled. Any previous Zoom Toggle setting is recalled.

3. In the tracks where you selected material, set the track height and track view.

   These settings are stored as the new Zoom Toggle state.

4. Click the Zoom Toggle button to switch back to the previous view.

To use Zoom Toggle:

1. Select the material you want to zoom.

2. Click the Zoom Toggle button (Figure 5.15).

   The Zoom settings are recalled for the selection.

ZOOMING TRACKS

Setting Zoom Toggle preferences

In addition to Track Height and Track View settings, you can configure Zoom Toggle to store specific zoom levels and grid value settings.

To set Zoom Toggle preferences:

1. Choose Setup > Preferences, and click Editing.

2. Under Zoom Toggle, do any of the following (**Figure 5.16**):

   ▲ To set the Vertical MIDI Zoom or Horizontal Zoom to zoom in on the current selection, choose "selection" from the pop-up menu.

   ▲ To set the Vertical MIDI Zoom or Horizontal Zoom to recall the previous Zoom Toggle level, choose "last used" from the pop-up menu.

   ▲ To set the Track Height to a specific value, choose "medium," "large," "jumbo," "extreme," or "fit to window" from the pop-up menu.

   ▲ To set the Track Height to recall the previous Zoom Toggle setting, choose "last used" from the pop-up menu.

   ▲ To set the Track View to a specific setting, choose "waveform/notes" or "warp/notes" from the pop-up menu.

   ▲ To set the Track View to recall the previous Zoom Toggle setting, choose "last used" from the pop-up menu.

   ▲ To save a separate Grid value setting for Zoom toggle, select "Separate Grid Settings When Zoomed In."

3. Click OK.

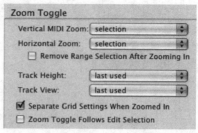

Figure 5.16 The Zoom Toggle preferences.

Click here to resize Universe view

Figure 5.17 To change the size of the Universe view, drag its bottom edge.

Framed area shows Edit window view

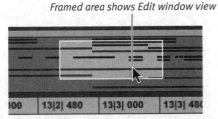

Figure 5.18 To navigate with the Universe window, drag the framed area.

Navigating with the Universe View

The Universe view shows the entire session at the top of the Edit window, representing markers as small yellow areas at the top, and tracks as thin lines within the view.

The framed area in the Universe view represents the currently visible area in the Edit window.

To display the Universe view:

◆ Choose View > Other Displays > Universe.

To change the height of the Universe view:

◆ Drag the bottom edge of the Universe view (**Figure 5.17**).

To navigate with the Universe view:

◆ Drag the framed area to reveal different parts of the Edit window (**Figure 5.18**).

Navigating with Memory Locations

Pro Tools lets you add Memory Locations to a session. Memory Locations (**Figure 5.19**) are useful for marking and navigating to sections of a song, selecting material in a session, and saving track display settings.

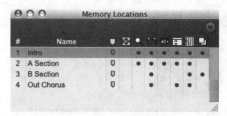

Figure 5.19 The Memory Locations window.

Memory Location properties

Memory Locations have two types of properties: *time properties* and *general properties*.

Time properties of Memory Locations include the following:

◆ **Marker Memory Locations** recall a specific timeline location in a session. Markers appear in the Markers ruler.

◆ **Selection Memory Locations** recall an edit selection that can be set to reference an Absolute (Minutes:Seconds) or Relative (Bars|Beats) scale.

◆ **General Properties Memory Locations** are Memory Locations with time properties that are set to None, These do not recall timeline locations, but are used to store and recall sets of general properties.

General properties include the following:

◆ **Zoom Settings** recall zoom values for Audio, MIDI, and Instrument tracks.

◆ **Pre/Post-Roll Times** recall pre- and post-roll values for a selection.

◆ **Track Show/Hide** recalls which tracks are hidden in a session.

◆ **Track Heights** recalls all of the session's current track heights.

◆ **Group Enables** recalls which Edit and Mix groups are enabled.

◆ **Window Configuration** recalls an available Window Configuration.

Figure 5.20 To create a Marker Memory Location, click the Marker Memory Location button in the Rulers area.

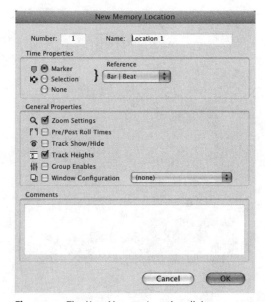

Figure 5.21 The New Memory Location dialog.

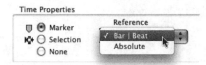

Figure 5.22 To set the reference Timescale for the Memory Location, select it from the Reference pop-up menu.

Figure 5.23 To move a Marker Memory Location, drag it in the Markers ruler.

To create a Marker Memory Location:

1. Configure any settings you want to save along with the Memory Location (such as zoom settings, pre/post-roll times, Show/Hide tracks status, Track Heights, or Group Enables).

2. Choose Options > Link Edit and Timeline Selection. (This makes all selections apply to both Timebase rulers and track playlists.)

3. Choose View > Rulers > Markers.

4. With the Selector tool, click in a track.

5. Click the Marker Memory Location button to the left of the Markers ruler (**Figure 5.20**).

   or

   Press Enter on the numeric keypad.

   The New Memory Location dialog appears (**Figure 5.21**).

6. Select the Marker option.

7. Choose Bar:Beat or Absolute from the Reference pop-up menu (**Figure 5.22**).

8. Enter a name for the new marker and select any general properties you want to save with the marker.

9. Click OK.

   A marker appears at the designated location in the Markers ruler and in the Memory Locations window.

✔ Tip

■ To move a marker to a new location, drag it in the Markers ruler (**Figure 5.23**).

Recalling Memory Locations

You can recall Marker Memory Locations from the Memory Locations window or from the Edit window.

To recall a Memory Location:

1. Choose Window > Memory Locations. The Memory Locations window appears (Figure 5.19).

2. Click the Memory Location you want to recall.

   or

   Click a Marker Memory Location in the Markers ruler.

   The playback cursor moves to the Memory Location and any general properties stored with it are recalled.

To delete a Memory Location:

◆ Option-click (Mac) or Alt-click (Windows) the Memory Location in the Memory Locations window.

   or

   In the Markers ruler, Option-click (Mac) or Alt-click (Windows) the Marker Memory Location you want to delete (**Figure 5.24**).

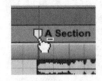

Figure 5.24 To delete a Marker Memory Location, Option-click (Mac) or Alt-click (Windows) the Marker.

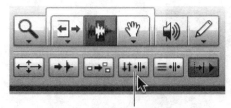

Link Timeline and Edit Selection button

Figure 5.25 To unlink the playback and edit cursors, click the Link Timeline and Edit Selection button so that it is not highlighted.

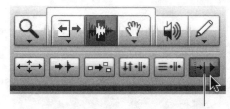

Insertion Follows Playback button

Figure 5.26 To set the play start location to follow play, click the Insertion Follows Playback button so that it is highlighted.

Setting Cursor Behavior

There are two cursors that indicate position in the Edit window:

◆ The **playback cursor** is a solid line that moves across the timeline and tracks during playback or recording.

◆ The **edit cursor** is a flashing line that appears when you use the Selector tool to click in a track.

By default, these cursors are linked, so that playback begins from the edit cursor location.

You can unlink these cursors to allow for editing during playback, or for auditioning material in one location while maintaining a selection in another.

To unlink the playback and edit cursors:

◆ Choose Options > Link Timeline and Edit Selection and deselect the option.

or

In the Edit Toolbar, click the Link Timeline and Edit Selection button so that it is not highlighted (**Figure 5.25**).

Setting the start point to advance with playback

By default, when you stop playback, the playback cursor returns to the start point.

You can set the playback cursor to advance to the point where playback stops, so that when you restart playback, it resumes from where it stopped.

To set the play start location to follow playback:

◆ In the Edit Toolbar, click the Insertion Follows Playback button so that it is highlighted (**Figure 5.26**).

Setting Scrolling Behavior

Pro Tools has the following options for scrolling material in the Edit window during playback or recording:

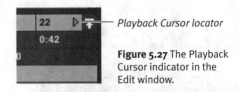

Figure 5.27 The Playback Cursor indicator in the Edit window.

◆ **No Scrolling.** The Edit window does not scroll; the playback cursor appears onscreen when playing displayed material, then moves offscreen.

◆ **After Playback.** The Edit window scrolls to the stop location when playback is stopped.

◆ **Page.** The Edit window scrolls page-by-page during playback so that the playback cursor is always onscreen.

To set the Edit window scrolling behavior:

◆ Choose Options > Scrolling and select the scrolling option.

✔ Tips

■ To play back long sections of a session, enable Link Timeline and Edit Selection and Insertion Follows Playback, and choose Page Scrolling.

■ To focus on a short section of a session, disable Link Timeline and Edit Selection and Insertion Follows Playback and choose No Scrolling.

Finding the playback cursor

When the cursor is offscreen, a Playback Cursor locator appears on the left or right side of the Edit window Main ruler (**Figure 5.27**).

To find the playback cursor:

◆ Click the Playback Cursor locator.
   The display scrolls to show the cursor location in the center of the Edit window.

Figure 5.28 Click the Link Timeline and Edit Selection button so that it is highlighted.

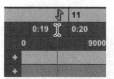

Figure 5.29 Set the playback location by clicking in a track.

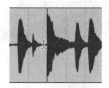

Figure 5.30 Setting the playback location by clicking in a Timebase ruler.

Main Counter

Figure 5.31 Setting the playback location with the Main or Sub counters.

Rewind button

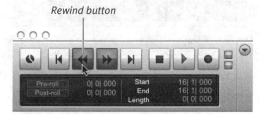

Figure 5.32 Setting the playback location with the Transport controls.

Return to Zero button

Figure 5.33 Setting the playback location to the beginning of the session.

Setting the Playback Location

You can position the playback cursor in the Edit window with the Selector tool, the counters, or the Transport controls.

To set the playback location with the Selector:

1. Click the Link Timeline and Edit Selection button so that it is highlighted (**Figure 5.28**).

2. With the Selector tool, click in a track at the location where you want to start playback (**Figure 5.29**).

   or

   Click in a Timebase ruler (**Figure 5.30**).

To set the playback location using the counters:

1. Click in the Main or Sub counter (**Figure 5.31**).

2. Type a new location and press Return (Mac) or Enter (Windows).

To set the playback location using the Transport controls:

◆ Click and hold the Rewind or Fast Forward button (**Figure 5.32**).

   or

   Repeatedly click the Rewind or Fast Forward button.

   Depending on the Main Time Scale setting, the cursor moves backward or forward in one-bar or one-second increments.

To set the playback location to the beginning of the session:

◆ Click the Return to Zero button in the Transport window (**Figure 5.33**).

   or

   Press Return (Mac) or Enter (Windows).

Playing Back Sessions

Pro Tools has several playback modes: Normal, Half-Speed, Prime for Playback, Loop Playback, and Dynamic Transport.

To start playback:

1. Position the cursor where you want to start playback.

2. Click the Play button in the Transport window (**Figure 5.34**).

   or

   Press the spacebar.

To stop playback:

◆ Click the Stop button in the Transport window (**Figure 5.35**).

   or

   Press the spacebar.

To play back a session at half-speed:

◆ Shift-click the Play button in the Transport window.

   or

   Hold Shift and press the spacebar.

To prime a session for instant playback:

1. Option-click (Mac) or Alt-click (Windows) the Play button in the Transport window.

   The Stop button lights and the Play button flashes to indicate that playback is primed (**Figure 5.36**).

2. Click the Play button to start playback.

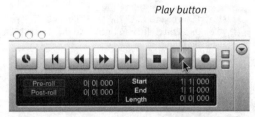

Figure 5.34 Click the Play button or press the spacebar to begin playing back a session.

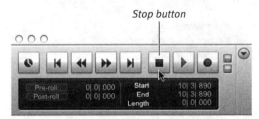

Figure 5.35 Click the Stop button or press the spacebar again to stop playback.

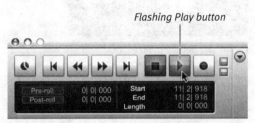

Figure 5.36 Option-click (Mac) or Alt-click (Windows) the Play button to prime a session for instant playback.

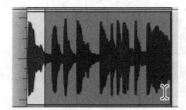

Figure 5.37 Making a selection in a track.

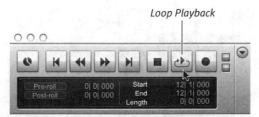

Figure 5.38 The Playback button indicating Loop Playback.

Looping Playback

You can set Pro Tools to repeatedly play back a selection in the Edit window. This is useful when auditioning material for rhythmic flow.

To loop a selection:

1. Click the Link Timeline and Edit Selection button so that it is highlighted (Figure 5.28).

2. With the Selector tool, drag in a track to select the material you want to loop (**Figure 5.37**).

3. Control-click (Mac) or Start-click (Windows) the Play button in the Transport window.

   The Play button displays a loop symbol to indicate Loop Playback mode (**Figure 5.38**).

4. Click the Play button.

5. To stop looped playback, click the Stop button.

Scrubbing Tracks

Scrubbing plays back audio or MIDI track material at variable speed, allowing you to locate edit points by ear. You can audition up to two tracks at a time.

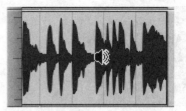

Figure 5.39 Scrubbing tracks with the Scrubber tool.

To scrub a track:

1. Select the Scrubber tool.

2. Drag left or right with the Scrubber over a track (**Figure 5.39**).

   The speed at which you drag determines the speed of playback.

To scrub two tracks simultaneously:

◆ Drag the Scrubber between the two tracks (**Figure 5.40**).

Figure 5.40 Scrubbing two tracks simultaneously.

RECORDING AUDIO

Before you start recording, there are a few things you need to do, such as connecting audio sources, configuring inputs in Pro Tools, and setting levels.

If you're recording music, you may also want to generate a click track, set the session meter and tempo, and configure monitoring so that you can follow the click and do overdubs later.

This chapter covers these necessary steps and takes you from your first recording to recording multiple takes, punching in fixes, and auditioning your takes.

Connecting Audio Input Sources

Before you create a Pro Tools session and start recording, it's helpful to make sure your audio sources are properly connected.

Microphones should be connected to XLR microphone inputs, and phantom power applied to microphones that require it.

Low-level sources requiring preamplification, such as an electric guitar or bass, should be connected to instrument (DI) inputs.

◆ On Mbox Mini, Mbox 2, Mbox 2 Pro, and 003-series interfaces, press the Mic/DI switch to select the input type.

◆ On the 003 Rack+ interface, press the Line/DI switch to select the input type.

Line-level sources, such as a mixer or keyboard, should be connected to line inputs.

◆ On 003 and 003 Rack interfaces, set the line inputs to the correct operating level (line inputs 5–8 on the 003 are switchable between –10 dBV or +4dBu levels).

Digital sources should be connected and powered on so that the clock source can be set correctly.

Figure 6.1 Select the clock source from the Clock Source pop-up menu in the Hardware Setup dialog.

Selecting the Clock Source

After you have connected your audio sources, you will need to configure the system for analog or digital input.

If you are recording an analog source such as a microphone or instrument, set the clock source to Internal.

If you are recording a digital source, such as a CD recorder or portable digital device, set the clock source to the digital inputs you are using.

◆ On Mbox 2 and Mbox 2 Pro interfaces, choose the S/PDIF digital input.

◆ On 003-series and 002-series interfaces, choose between the S/PDIF or Optical digital inputs.

To select the clock source:

1. Choose Setup > Hardware.
   The Hardware Setup dialog appears.

2. Choose the source from the Clock Source pop-up menu (**Figure 6.1**).

3. Click OK.

SELECTING THE CLOCK SOURCE

Configuring Audio Inputs and Outputs

Pro Tools refers to the various ways of routing audio through the system as *paths*. Each system has a default configuration with generic names for all of its available paths; this appears as the "Stereo Mix" I/O Setting in the New Session dialog. In most cases, this default configuration is sufficient for general use.

The I/O Setup Dialog

The I/O Setup dialog shows all of the available audio inputs and outputs on your Pro Tools LE interface across the top of the window, and a list of paths along the left side of the window. The channel grid in the center of the window shows how the interface inputs and outputs are mapped to paths.

Four types of paths are shown in the I/O Setup dialog:

◆ **Inputs** are analog or digital inputs on the audio interface.

◆ **Outputs** are analog or digital outputs on the audio interface.

◆ **Inserts** are pairs of inputs and outputs on the audio interface, used to send and return audio signals to external devices such as effects processors.

◆ **Busses** are internal signal paths in Pro Tools, used to send audio to other tracks, or to external devices such as a studio headphone system.

For each of these path types, the list shows the path names that appear in the Input, Output, Insert, and Send selectors.

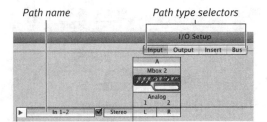

Path name   Path type selectors

Figure 6.2 The I/O Setup dialog shows paths for system inputs, outputs, inserts, and busses.

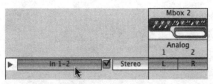

Figure 6.3 Double-click a path name to rename the path.

Customizing I/O Setups

You can rename paths in the I/O Setup dialog so that those names appear in your session.

To turn off inputs or outputs you are not using, but keep all path assignments in Pro Tools, you can make paths inactive in the I/O Setup dialog.

To rename paths:

1. Choose Setup > I/O.

   The I/O Setup dialog appears.

2. Click the Path Type selector for the type of path you want to rename (**Figure 6.2**).

3. Double-click a path name in the Path Name column (**Figure 6.3**).

4. Type a new name for the path.

5. Press Return (Mac) or Enter (Windows) to confirm the name.

   or

   Double-click another path name to rename it.

6. When you are finished renaming paths, click OK.

To restore paths to their defaults:

1. Choose Setup > I/O.

2. Click the Path Type selector for the type of path you want to restore (Figure 6.2).

3. Click the Default button.

   Path names and channel configurations return to their default states.

4. Click OK.

To make paths inactive:

1. Choose Setup > I/O.

2. Click the Path Type selector for the type of path you want to deactivate (Figure 6.2).

3. Deselect the check box next to the name of the path (**Figure 6.4**).

4. Click OK.

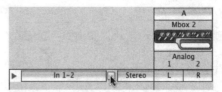

Figure 6.4 To deactivate the path, deselect the check box.

Exporting and importing I/O Setups

After you have customized your I/O Setup, you can save it for use in different sessions. I/O Setup configurations are exported and imported as I/O Settings files with a .pio extension.

To export an I/O Setup configuration:

1. In the I/O Setup dialog, click Export Settings.

2. Type a name for the I/O Settings file (**Figure 6.5**).

3. Click Save.

   The I/O Settings file is saved in the I/O Settings folder for your system, from which it can be imported into other sessions.

To import an I/O Settings file:

1. In the I/O Setup dialog, click Import Settings.

2. Select an I/O Settings file.

3. Click Open.

   A Delete Unused Paths dialog appears.

4. To remap current path definitions to the imported paths, click Yes.

   or

   To add imported paths to the current path definitions, click No.

5. Click OK.

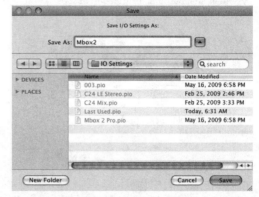

Figure 6.5 You can save I/O Setup configurations as I/O Settings files, and reuse them in other sessions.

Figure 6.6 You can click the plus sign in the Meter ruler to change the meter.

Figure 6.7 You can also click the Meter Value display in the Transport window MIDI controls to change the meter.

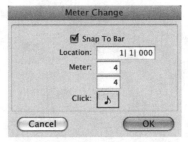

Figure 6.8 Enter the location for the meter change and the time signature in the Meter Change dialog.

Figure 6.9 Click the plus sign in the Tempo ruler to change the tempo.

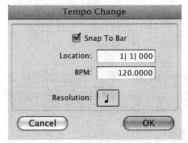

Figure 6.10 Enter the location for the tempo change and the tempo (in beats per minute) in the Tempo Change dialog.

Setting Session Meter and Tempo

If you plan to record to a click, you'll need to set the meter and tempo for your session.

To set the session meter:

1. In the Edit window Meter ruler, click the plus sign (**Figure 6.6**).

   or

   In the Transport window MIDI controls, double-click the Meter Value display (**Figure 6.7**).

2. In the Meter Change dialog, enter the location 1|1|000 (the beginning of the session) (**Figure 6.8**).

3. Enter the time signature in the Meter text boxes (the default meter is 4/4).

4. Choose a beat value for the click from the Click pop-up menu.

5. Click OK.

To set the session tempo:

1. In the Transport window MIDI controls, make sure the Conductor Track button is selected. This enables the Tempo ruler.

2. In the Edit window Tempo ruler, click the plus sign (**Figure 6.9**).

3. In the Tempo Change dialog, enter the location 1|1|000 (the beginning of the session) (**Figure 6.10**).

4. Enter the tempo in the BPM (beats per minute) text box; the default is 120.

5. Choose a note value for the beat.

6. Click OK.

SETTING SESSION METER AND TEMPO

Setting Up a Click Track

If you're recording rhythmic music or will be incorporating MIDI in your session, you'll want to record to a click. This ensures that recorded audio and MIDI will align with the grid, making it much easier to overdub, edit, and arrange with reference to bars and beats.

To set up a click track:

1. Choose Track > Create Click Track.

   Pro Tools automatically creates an Auxiliary Input track with the Click plug-in inserted, and assigned to the main outputs (**Figure 6.11**).

2. In the Transport window MIDI controls, click the Metronome button so that it is highlighted (**Figure 6.12**).

3. To audition the click, press the spacebar to start and stop playback.

4. In the Mix window Inserts area, click the insert named Click (**Figure 6.13**).

   The Click plug-in window opens (**Figure 6.14**).

Click plug-in

Figure 6.11 Choose Track > Create Click Track to create an Auxiliary Input track with the Click plug-in inserted.

Figure 6.12 Click the Metronome button in the MIDI controls area of the Transport window.

Figure 6.13 Click the Insert to open the Click plug-in window.

Plug-In Librarian menu   *Click volume sliders*

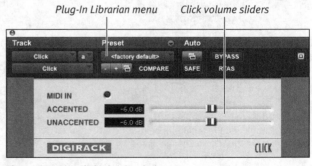

Figure 6.14 The Click plug-in window.

Figure 6.15 Choose a click sound from the Plug-In Librarian menu.

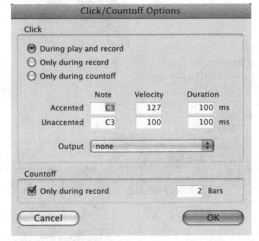

Figure 6.16 Use the Click/Countoff dialog to set preferences for the click.

5. To change the sound of the click, choose a different preset from the Plug-In Librarian menu in the Click plug-in window (**Figure 6.15**).

6. To change the relative levels of the accented and unaccented beats, adjust the sliders in the Click plug-in window.

7. In the Transport window MIDI controls, double-click the Metronome button (Figure 6.12).

   The Click/Countoff Options dialog appears (**Figure 6.16**).

8. Under Click, choose when you want the click to sound: "During play and record," "Only during record," or "Only during countoff."

9. Under Countoff, click the check box to select "Only during record" if you want the countoff to sound only when recording (and not on playback).

10. Type the number of bars for the countoff.

11. Click OK.

Setting Up a Cue Mix

If you are recording a single track and can monitor the click through headphones connected to your audio interface, a click track assigned to the main outputs works well.

If you are overdubbing multiple tracks and want to send the click (or any previously recorded material) to multiple headphones, you can create separate cue mixes to send to an external monitoring system.

To create a cue mix:

1. Connect your monitoring system to available outputs on your audio interface.

2. On each track that you want to send to the cue mix, assign a send to the track by clicking a Send selector and choosing a bus pair (**Figure 6.17**).

   For more information on assigning and adjusting Sends, see Chapter 13, "Mixing."

3. Create a new stereo Auxiliary Input track.

4. Click the Input selector on the Auxiliary Input track and assign the bus pair you chose in Step 2 (**Figure 6.18**).

5. Click the Output selector of the Auxiliary Input track and assign the hardware output for your cue monitoring system (**Figure 6.19**).

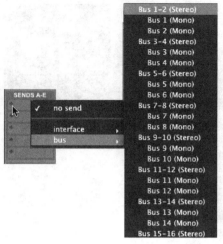

Figure 6.17 Assign sends to the tracks you want to send to the cue mix.

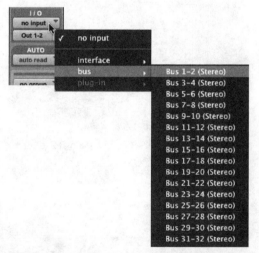

Figure 6.18 Assign the input of the Auxiliary Input track to the bus pair you chose for the cue mix send.

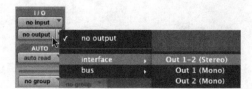

Figure 6.19 Assign the output of the Auxiliary Input track to the input of your cue monitoring system.

Figure 6.20 Click the send to open the Send window.

Figure 6.21 Adjust the send level for each track you are sending to the cue mix.

Figure 6.22 Adjust the Auxiliary Input track output level to the cue monitoring system.

6. Start playback to audition the click and any previously recorded material.

7. In the Mix window Sends area, click the send that you assigned earlier to open the Send window (**Figure 6.20**).

8. In the Send window, adjust the Send level on each of the tracks in the mix to control their relative balance (**Figure 6.21**).

9. In the Auxiliary Input track, adjust the Volume fader to control the overall output to the cue monitoring system (**Figure 6.22**).

Record Modes

Pro Tools LE has four record modes that determine how audio is recorded.

◆ **Normal Record** is the default. In this nondestructive mode, all recorded audio is saved onto the hard disk, even if it doesn't appear as a region in a track. You can record over existing regions without erasing any audio.

◆ **Destructive Record** is a rarely used mode that erases the original audio when you record over existing regions. While this mode can save disk space, in most cases, it's best to use Normal Record mode.

◆ **Loop Record** mode lets you record multiple takes while the same section of audio repeats. This mode is good for recording multiple takes without losing spontaneity. Loop Record mode is nondestructive.

◆ **QuickPunch** mode lets you punch in (start recording) and punch out (stop recording) on a record-enabled audio track at any time during playback.

SETTING UP A CUE MIX

Enabling Audio Tracks for Recording

Once you have the input source connected and the session configured, you're ready to enable Audio tracks for recording.

To enable an Audio track for recording:

1. Click the Input selector on the track and choose the audio input source (**Figure 6.23**).

2. Click the Output selector on the track and choose the output path for monitoring (**Figure 6.24**).

3. Click the Record Enable button on the track (**Figure 6.25**).

   The Record Enable button flashes and the track's Volume fader turns red to indicate that the track is enabled for recording.

✔ Tips

■ To enable all audio tracks for recording, Option-click (Mac) or Alt-click (Windows) the Record Enable button on an audio track.

■ To enable all selected audio tracks for recording, Shift-Option-click (Mac) or Shift-Alt-click (Windows) the Record Enable button on any selected audio track.

To prevent an Audio track from being record enabled:

◆ Command-click (Mac) or Ctrl-click (Windows) the Record Enable button.

   This puts the track in Record Safe mode, preventing any recording on the track. The track's Record Enable button grays out to indicate that it is in Record Safe mode.

Figure 6.23 Select the input path for the audio source, such as a microphone or instrument connected to your audio interface.

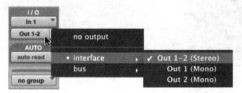

Figure 6.24 Select the output path to your studio monitors.

Figure 6.25 Record enable the track by clicking its Record Enable button. The button flashes to indicate the track is record enabled.

A Practical Approach to Setting Levels

The setting of recording levels in the digital domain is much discussed. Some people advocate recording at the highest possible levels without *clipping* (distortion from overloading the system's inputs), in order to take full advantage of the system's dynamic range. Others suggest a more moderate approach, recording at lower levels to allow headroom for signal peaks and for mixing and processing.

You can get the benefits of full dynamic range *and* avoid the nastiness of digital distortion by keeping input levels high but still giving yourself some headroom.

Pro Tools track meters show levels in four distinct zones (**Figure 6.26**): green, –Infinity to –12 dB; yellow, –12 dB to –3 dB; orange, –3 dB to 0 dB or "full code"; and red, "over" or "clipping."

When you set recording levels, try to keep signal peaks at the top of the yellow zone and out of the orange zone. Inevitably, the performance will be a little more energetic than the level check, and a few peaks will extend into the orange zone—and your track will sound just fine.

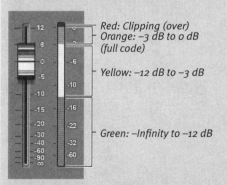

Red: Clipping (over)
Orange: –3 dB to o dB (full code)

Yellow: –12 dB to –3 dB

Green: –Infinity to –12 dB

Figure 6.26 A Pro Tools track meter, showing the green, yellow, orange, and red level zones.

Setting Audio Input Levels

Once a track is record enabled, you can see the input level in its meter. You can then play the audio source to check levels before you start recording.

Analog audio input level

To achieve the proper input level, you need to adjust the level from the audio interface, not onscreen in Pro Tools. The red Volume fader on a record-enabled Audio track changes the record monitoring volume only, not the input level.

The preamplifiers built into the 003-series, 002-series, Mbox2 Pro, Mbox 2, and Mbox 2 Mini interfaces let you adjust the level of analog audio inputs.

✔ Tip

■ The 003-series and 002-series interfaces have additional line-level inputs without preamplifiers; levels to these inputs must be adjusted at the source.

Digital audio input level

When recording a digital audio source into Pro Tools, the level of the digital source is copied exactly. You cannot adjust levels with the audio interface or onscreen in Pro Tools. If your digital device has output gain controls, you can adjust level at the source.

Monitoring Audio While Recording

Pro Tools provides two modes for monitoring audio input when recording:

◆ **Auto Input Monitoring** is useful when punching in on a track. Pro Tools switches automatically between monitoring recorded material and live input. In this mode, existing audio on record-enabled tracks is played until the punch-in point, then the input signal is monitored until the punch-out point, when existing audio plays again.

◆ **Input Only Monitoring** mode monitors only live input on record-enabled tracks, and does not play back any existing audio on the tracks.

In most recording situations, Auto Input Monitoring mode works well.

To toggle the Input Monitoring mode:

◆ Choose Track > Auto Input Monitoring (or Input Only Monitoring).

Setting monitoring levels

Pro Tools lets you set independent track monitoring levels for recording and playback. When a track is record enabled, its Volume fader is red; when it is not record enabled, its Volume fader is gray.

You can unlink these two fader displays so that that you can set independent monitoring levels for recording and playback.

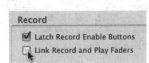

Figure 6.27 To set separate levels for playback and recording, deselect the Link Record and Play Faders option in Operation preferences.

Figure 6.28 Set the hardware buffer size in the Playback Engine dialog.

To unlink record and playback faders:

1. Choose Setup > Preferences and click Operation.

2. Deselect the Link Record and Play Faders check box (**Figure 6.27**).

3. Click OK.

Reducing monitoring latency when recording

It takes time for Pro Tools to convert an incoming analog signal to a digital signal, apply processing, and send it to the outputs for monitoring. This delay, or *monitoring latency*, though relatively small, can be noticeable when recording or overdubbing tracks.

Because Pro Tools LE uses the computer's processor for all recording, mixing, and playback functions, it introduces an amount of delay related to the Hardware Buffer Size. You can adjust the Hardware Buffer Size to suit your current task.

◆ Larger buffer sizes allow for higher track counts and more plug-in processing, but introduce more latency. Use higher settings for editing and mixing, when monitoring latency is not an issue.

◆ Smaller buffer sizes introduce less latency, but reduce track count and processing capacity. Use lower settings for recording, and deactivate tracks or plug-ins as necessary to optimize performance.

To set the Hardware Buffer Size:

1. Choose Setup > Playback Engine.
   The Playback Engine dialog appears.

2. Choose a setting from the H/W Buffer Size pop-up menu (**Figure 6.28**).

3. Click OK.

Recording Audio

With inputs configured, tracks record enabled, and levels set, you're ready to record a take.

To record audio:

1. Create an Audio track.

2. Assign the audio input source to the track input.

3. Record enable the track.

4. Play the audio source and set the audio input level.

5. To start recording from the beginning of the session, click the Return to Zero button in the Transport window (**Figure 6.29**).

   or

   To resume recording at the end of the session, click the Go to End button in the Transport window (Figure 6.29).

6. Click the Record button in the Transport window to ready Pro Tools for recording (Figure 6.29).

7. Click the Play button to start recording.

   If you enabled Countoff, the Record and Play buttons flash during the countoff.

8. Click the Stop button when you are finished recording.

   The recorded audio appears as a new region in the track playlist (**Figure 6.30**) and in the Regions list (**Figure 6.31**).

Figure 6.29 In the Transport window, click Return to Zero to start recording from the beginning of the session; click Go to End to resume recording at the end of the session; and click Record to ready Pro Tools for recording.

Figure 6.30 Newly recorded audio appears as a region in the track playlist.

Figure 6.31 Audio regions appear in the Regions list.

To cancel a take while recording:

◆ Press Command-Period (Mac) or Ctrl-Period (Windows) during recording.

To discard a take after recording:

◆ Choose Edit > Undo Record.

To play back a take:

1. Click the Record Enable button to disable the track for recording.

2. Move the playback cursor to the beginning of the take.

3. Click the Play button in the Transport window to start playback.

4. Click the Stop button when you are finished.

✔ Tip

■ If your system is set to Auto Input Monitoring mode, you can audition audio on a track while it is still record enabled.

Recording additional takes

If you are recording in a nondestructive mode, you can record additional takes on the same track. While each additional take replaces the previous take in the track's main playlist, it does not erase it. Each take appears in the Regions list and remains available for use in the session.

Instead of recording additional takes to the same playlist, you can create new playlists for the track, and record a new take onto each playlist.

To record to a new playlist on a track:

1. In the Edit window, click the track's Playlist selector and choose New (**Figure 6.32**).

2. Type a new name for the playlist (**Figure 6.33**).

3. Click OK.

   A new, empty playlist appears in the track, and the track name changes to reflect the name of the new playlist (**Figure 6.34**).

4. Record enable the track.

5. Click the Record button in the Transport window to ready Pro Tools for recording.

6. Click the Play button to start recording.

7. Click the Stop button when you are finished recording.

   The recorded audio appears as a new region in the track playlist and in the Regions list (**Figure 6.35**).

Figure 6.32 Click a track's Playlist selector to add a new playlist to the track.

Figure 6.33 Name the new playlist. The new, active playlist name appears as the track name.

Figure 6.34 The new empty playlist, ready for recording.

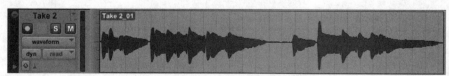

Figure 6.35 Newly recorded audio in the new playlist.

RECORDING AUDIO

Figure 6.36 Click the pre-roll or post-roll value in the Transport window to change the value.

Figure 6.37 Click the pre-roll or post-roll button to enable pre-roll or post-roll.

Punch Recording Audio

If you want to fix a take instead of rerecording it, you can *punch in* on a track to record just the part you want to fix.

Pro Tools makes it possible to punch record with precision. Select the track material you want to fix, and Pro Tools will automatically punch in at the selection start and punch out at the selection end.

You can set Pro Tools to play a set amount of track material before (pre-roll) and after (post-roll) your record selection, to provide a cue reference.

To enable pre-roll or post-roll:

1. In the Expanded view of the Transport window, click the pre-roll or post-roll value (**Figure 6.36**).

2. Type a new pre-roll or post-roll value and press Return (Mac) or Enter (Windows).

   The displayed units for pre- and post-roll match the currently selected Main Time Scale.

3. Click the pre-roll or post-roll button so that it is highlighted (**Figure 6.37**).

To punch record audio:

1. Make sure Link Timeline and Edit Selection is enabled (**Figure 6.38**).

2. Record enable the track you want to punch.

3. With the Selector tool, drag to select the time range where you want to punch in (**Figure 6.39**).

4. Set the pre- and post-roll amounts.

5. Click the Record button in the Transport window to ready Pro Tools for recording.

6. Click the Play button to start recording.

   If pre- and post-roll are enabled, the track plays up to the punch-in point, records until the punch-out point, plays to the end of the post-roll, then stops.

Figure 6.38 Click the Link Timeline and Edit Selection button so that it is highlighted.

Figure 6.39 Drag with the Selector tool to define the range to punch record.

Figure 6.40 The Record Button in the Transport window displays a loop icon to indicate Loop Record mode.

Loop Recording Audio

You can record multiple takes over the same section of a track using Loop Record mode. This lets you record continuously without interrupting the flow of a performance to start each new take.

If you enable pre-roll, it will be used only before the first looped pass, and will be not be applied to successive passes.

To loop record audio:

1. Make sure Link Timeline and Edit Selection is enabled (Figure 6.38).

2. Choose Options > Loop Record.
   The Record button in the Transport window displays a loop icon to indicate Loop Record mode (**Figure 6.40**).

3. Record enable the track on which you want to loop record.

4. With the Selector tool, drag to select the time range where you want to loop (**Figure 6.41**).

continues on next page

Figure 6.41 Drag with the Selector tool to define the range to loop record.

5. Set the pre-roll amount.

6. Click the Record button in the Transport window to ready Pro Tools for recording.

7. Click the Play button to start recording.

If pre-roll is enabled, the track plays up to the loop start point, records until the loop end point, and then returns to the beginning of the loop to continue recording.

8. Click the Stop button when you are finished.

All looped takes appear in the Regions list, numbered in sequence (**Figure 6.42**). The final take also appears as a region in the track playlist.

Figure 6.42 Looped takes appear in the Regions list, in numerical sequence.

LOOP RECORDING AUDIO

Auditioning Alternate Takes

When you have recorded multiple takes by recording to multiple playlists, punching in, or loop recording, you can view and audition those takes in several ways: from the Regions list, from the track, or by expanding takes to new playlists.

Auditioning takes from the Regions list

An easy way to audition a single alternate take is to drag it from the Regions list onto the track.

To audition a take from the Regions list:

1. In the track use the Grabber tool to select the region for the current take (**Figure 6.43**).

2. Command-drag (Mac) or Ctrl-drag (Windows) the region for the alternate take from the Regions list onto the selected region.

    The region for the alternate take replaces the selected region in the track.

3. Play the session to audition the alternate take in place.

Figure 6.43 Select the region for the current take with the Grabber tool.

Auditioning takes from the track

You can audition multiple takes from punch or loop recording directly from the track using the Alternate Takes pop-up menu.

To audition takes from the track:

1. Select the region for the current take in the track.

2. With the Selector tool, Command-click (Mac) or Ctrl-click (Windows) the selected region and choose the alternate take from the pop-up menu (**Figure 6.44**).

   The region for the alternate take replaces the selected region in the track.

3. Play the session to audition the alternate take in place.

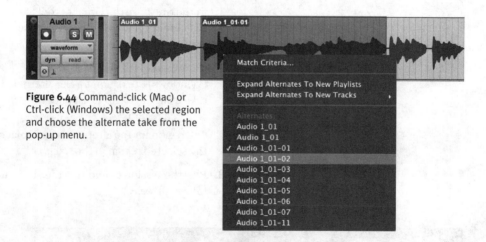

Figure 6.44 Command-click (Mac) or Ctrl-click (Windows) the selected region and choose the alternate take from the pop-up menu.

Auditioning takes by expanding to alternate playlists

Pro Tools lets you expand alternate takes onto alternate playlists and display them in a track's Playlist view. From this view, you can audition the takes and assemble them on the main playlist.

To audition takes with alternate playlists:

1. Select the region for the current take in the track.

2. With the Selector tool, Command-click (Mac) or Ctrl-click (Windows) the selected region and choose Expand Alternates to New Playlists from the pop-up menu (**Figure 6.45**).

continues on next page

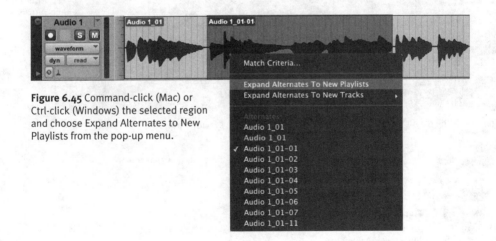

Figure 6.45 Command-click (Mac) or Ctrl-click (Windows) the selected region and choose Expand Alternates to New Playlists from the pop-up menu.

The track switches to Playlist view and displays each alternate take in its own playlist lane (**Figure 6.46**).

3. Start playback.

4. In the track's Playlist view, click the solo button for the playlist with the take that you want to hear (**Figure 6.47**).

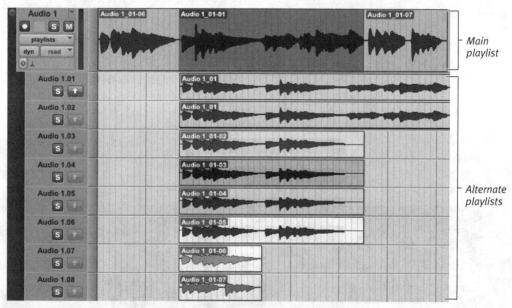

Figure 6.46 The playlist view, showing each alternate take on a separate playlist.

Figure 6.47 To audition an alternate take, click its Solo button in Playlist view.

AUDITIONING ALTERNATE TAKES

Figure 6.48 The Record Button in the Transport window displays the letter *P* to indicate QuickPunch mode.

QuickPunch

Figure 6.49 Click the Record button to punch in and out during playback.

Using QuickPunch

Instead of selecting a single area and punching in once, you can use the QuickPunch feature to punch in and out of recording multiple times during a single playback pass.

When you use QuickPunch, Pro Tools is actually recording continuously in the background during playback, but revealing recorded regions only when you punch in. Because of this, there are limits to the number of tracks you can record in QuickPunch mode.

To punch in and out with QuickPunch:

1. Make sure Link Timeline and Edit Selection is enabled (Figure 6.38).

2. Choose Options > QuickPunch.

   The Record button in the Transport window displays the letter *P* to indicate QuickPunch mode (**Figure 6.48**).

3. Record enable the track you want to punch.

4. In the Transport window, click the Play button to start playback.

5. When you reach a punch-in point, click the Record button (**Figure 6.49**).

6. To punch out, click the Record button a second time.

   While Pro Tools plays back, you can continue to punch in and punch out, up to 200 times in a single pass.

continues on next page

USING QUICKPUNCH

7. When you are finished, click the Stop button.

The regions created by QuickPunch appear in the track and in the Regions list (**Figure 6.50**).

Figure 6.50 A track showing regions created by punching in and out with QuickPunch.

RECORDING MIDI

To record a MIDI performance, you need to establish communication with your external MIDI gear, configure MIDI inputs and outputs, and set options for recording.

As with audio recording, you may want to record live MIDI input with a click track so that recorded MIDI data aligns with bar and beat boundaries, making it easier to edit and arrange.

This chapter covers setting up MIDI devices; setting the session meter, tempo, and key; using virtual instruments; choosing a MIDI recording mode; and punch and loop recording.

Connecting Your MIDI Studio

To record MIDI, you need to set up communication with your MIDI devices so that Pro Tools can receive and send MIDI data.

Connecting MIDI devices

MIDI devices can be connected to a Pro Tools system in any of the following ways:

◆ Many MIDI devices connect directly to a USB port on the computer, and do not need to be connected to an external MIDI interface.

◆ If you have a Pro Tools LE interface with built-in MIDI In and MIDI Out ports, you can connect MIDI devices using standard 5-pin MIDI cables.

◆ If your Pro Tools LE interface does not have built-in MIDI ports, you can add a USB MIDI interface to your system and connect to its MIDI In and MIDI Out ports using standard 5-pin MIDI cables.

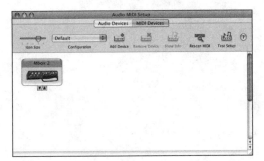

Figure 7.1 The MIDI Devices page in the Audio MIDI Setup window (Mac OS X).

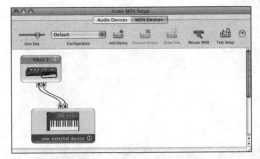

Figure 7.2 Configuring a MIDI device in Audio MIDI Setup.

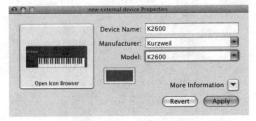

Figure 7.3 Naming a device in Audio MIDI Setup.

✔ **Tip**

■ When you name a device in Audio MIDI Setup, that name will appear in MIDI input and output selectors in Pro Tools.

MIDI Setup in Mac OS X

In Mac OS X, you use the Audio MIDI Setup (AMS) application to identify MIDI devices connected to your system.

To set up a MIDI device on Mac OS X:

1. In Pro Tools, choose Setup > MIDI > MIDI Studio.

   The Audio MIDI Setup window opens.

2. In the Audio MIDI Setup window, click MIDI Devices.

   Connected MIDI interfaces or devices appear in the MIDI Devices page (**Figure 7.1**).

   If your MIDI device is an input device such as a keyboard controller, it will automatically be available in Pro Tools; your setup is complete.

   If your MIDI device is a MIDI interface or an LE interface with MIDI ports (such as an Mbox 2), you will need to add any MIDI devices that are connected to it.

3. Click Add Device.

4. In the Audio MIDI Setup window, connect the new device to the MIDI interface by dragging a connection from the input and output of the Interface icon to the output and input of the New External Device icon (**Figure 7.2**).

5. Double-click the New External Device icon to access the Properties window.

6. Name the device, then select or type names for the manufacturer and model of the device (**Figure 7.3**).

7. Click Apply.

8. Quit Audio MIDI Setup.

   The device is now available in Pro Tools.

CONNECTING YOUR MIDI STUDIO

MIDI Setup in Windows

In Windows, you use the MIDI Studio Setup (MSS) application to configure MIDI devices connected to your system.

To set up a MIDI device in Windows:

1. In Pro Tools, choose Setup > MIDI > MIDI Studio.

   The MIDI Studio Setup window opens.

2. Click Create to add a new device.

3. Enter a name for the device in the Instrument Name field.

4. Choose the Input and Output ports that you used to connect your MIDI device (**Figure 7.4**).

5. Close the MIDI Studio Setup window.

   The device is now available in Pro Tools.

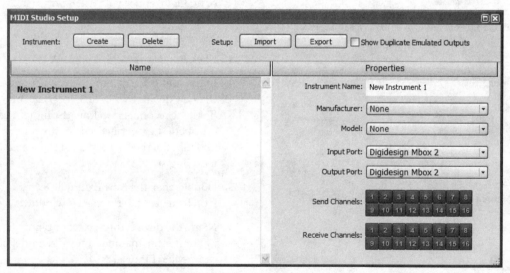

Figure 7.4 Configuring a MIDI device in MIDI Studio Setup (Windows).

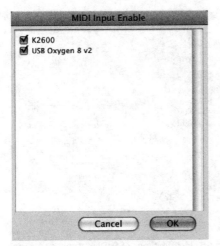

MIDI Input Enable

☑ K2600
☑ USB Oxygen 8 v2

Cancel   OK

Figure 7.5 Select devices in the MIDI Input Enable window to make them available in Pro Tools.

Configuring MIDI Inputs

After you have connected your MIDI devices and identified them in your system, you need to enable them for input in Pro Tools.

In addition to MIDI input devices such as keyboards, MIDI control surfaces (such as the Digidesign Command|8) must also be enabled.

To enable MIDI input devices:

1. Choose Setup > MIDI > Input Devices.

2. In the MIDI Input Enable window, select the check box next to each device that you want to use in Pro Tools (**Figure 7.5**).

3. Click OK.

   Enabled MIDI Input devices appear as available inputs in MIDI and Instrument tracks.

CONFIGURING MIDI INPUTS

Filtering MIDI input

You can set Pro Tools to filter out specific
types of MIDI messages so that they are not
recorded. In most cases, the default filter settings will work.

To filter MIDI input:

1. Choose Setup > Input > MIDI Filter.

   The MIDI Input Filter dialog appears
   (**Figure 7.6**).

2. In the MIDI Input Filter dialog, do one of
   the following:

   ▲ To record all types of MIDI messages,
   select All.

   ▲ To record only selected types of MIDI
   messages, select Only. In the Channel
   Info and Controllers areas, select the
   types of messages you want to record.

   or

   ▲ To exclude selected types of MIDI
   messages, select All Except. In the
   Channel Info and Controllers areas,
   select the types of messages you want
   to exclude from recording.

3. Click OK.

Monitoring MIDI Input

To monitor MIDI input while you are recording, you need to enable MIDI Thru. This
setting mirrors the MIDI messages received
at a channel's input to its output, playing the
output device or virtual instrument.

To enable MIDI Thru:

◆ Choose Options > MIDI Thru.

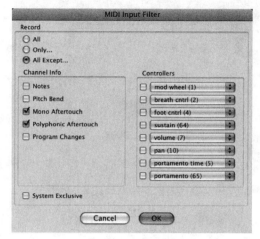

Figure 7.6 Select the types of MIDI messages to filter
in the MIDI Input Filter dialog.

Figure 7.7 You can click the plus sign in the Meter ruler to change the meter.

Figure 7.8 You can also click the Meter Value display in the Transport window MIDI controls to change the meter.

Figure 7.9 Enter the location for the meter change and the time signature in the Meter Change dialog.

Setting Session Meter, Tempo, and Key

If you are recording material based on bars and beats, you'll need to set the meter and tempo for your session.

You can also set the key signature for the session, which is helpful when working with diatonic transpositions or exporting MIDI data to a notation program.

To set the session meter:

1. In the Edit window Meter ruler, click the plus sign (**Figure 7.7**).

    or

    In the Transport window MIDI controls, double-click the Meter Value display (**Figure 7.8**).

2. In the Meter Change dialog, enter the location 1|1|000 (the beginning of the session) (**Figure 7.9**).

3. Enter the time signature in the Meter text boxes (the default meter is 4/4).

4. Choose a beat value for the click from the Click pop-up menu.

5. Click OK.

To set the session tempo:

1. In the Transport window MIDI controls, make sure the Conductor Track button is highlighted. This enables the Tempo ruler.

2. In the Edit window Tempo ruler, click the plus sign (**Figure 7.10**).

3. In the Tempo Change dialog, enter the location 1|1|000 (the beginning of the session) (**Figure 7.11**).

4. Enter the tempo in the BPM (beats per minute) text box; the default is 120.

5. Choose a note value for the beat.

6. Click OK.

To set the session key:

1. In the Edit window Key ruler, click the plus sign (**Figure 7.12**).

2. In the Key Change dialog, enter the location 1|1|000 (the beginning of the session) in the From text box and select "next key signature" (**Figure 7.13**).

3. Select a mode (major or minor), and choose from the list of keys.

4. Click OK.

Figure 7.10 Click the plus sign in the Tempo ruler to change the tempo.

Figure 7.11 Enter the location for the tempo change and the tempo (in beats per minute) in the Tempo Change dialog.

Figure 7.12 Click the plus sign in the Key ruler to change the key signature.

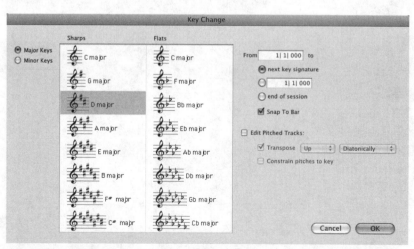

Figure 7.13 Enter the location for the key change, then select the mode and key signature.

Setting Up a Click Track

If you're recording live MIDI input, you'll want to record to a click. This ensures that MIDI notes will align with the grid, making it much easier to overdub, edit, and arrange with reference to bars and beats.

To set up a click track:

1. Choose Track > Create Click Track.

   Pro Tools automatically creates an Auxiliary Input track with the Click plug-in inserted and assigned to the main outputs (**Figure 7.14**).

2. In the Transport window MIDI controls, click the Metronome button so that it is highlighted (**Figure 7.15**).

3. To audition the click, press the spacebar to start and stop playback.

continues on next page

Figure 7.14 Choose Track > Create Click Track to create an Auxiliary Input track with the Click plug-in inserted.

Figure 7.15 The Metronome button in the MIDI controls area of the Transport window.

4. In the Mix window Inserts area, click the insert named Click (**Figure 7.16**).

   The Click plug-in window opens (**Figure 7.17**).

5. To change the sound of the click, choose a different preset from the Plug-In Librarian menu (**Figure 7.18**).

6. To change the relative levels of the accented and unaccented beats, adjust the sliders.

7. Close the plug-in window.

Figure 7.16 Click the insert to open the Click plug-in window.

Figure 7.17 The Click plug-in window.

Figure 7.18 Choose a click sound from the Plug-In Librarian menu.

SETTING UP A CLICK TRACK

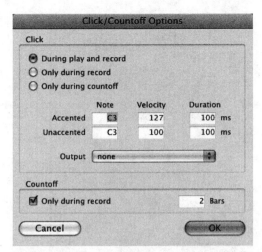

Figure 7.19 Use the Click/Countoff Options dialog to set preferences for the click.

Figure 7.20 Click the Count Off button to enable countoff for recording.

Figure 7.21 The Wait for Note button in the MIDI Controls area of the Transport window.

Using Countoff or Wait for Note

To initiate MIDI recording, you can start recording manually, or you can use Countoff or Wait for Note. The Countoff option counts a specified number of measures before recording begins. The Wait for Note option automatically starts recording when you play the first note. Only one of these features can be used at a time.

To enable Countoff:

1. In the Transport window MIDI controls, double-click the Metronome button (Figure 7.15).

   The Click/Countoff Options dialog appears (**Figure 7.19**).

2. Under Click, choose when you want the click to sound: "During play and record," "Only during record," or "Only during countoff."

3. Under Countoff, if you want the countoff to sound only when recording (and not on playback), select "Only during record."

4. Type the number of bars for the countoff.

5. Click OK.

6. In the Transport window MIDI controls, click the Count Off button so that it is highlighted (**Figure 7.20**).

To enable Wait for Note:

◆ In the Transport window MIDI controls, click the Wait for Note button so that it is highlighted (**Figure 7.21**).

Quantizing MIDI on Input

The operation of *quantizing*, or aligning MIDI data to a grid, is often done during editing. It can also be done automatically during recording, using the Input Quantize feature.

Quantizing MIDI input improves the precision of a performance, but it can also remove musical expression if applied too narrowly.

To quantize MIDI on input:

1. Choose Event > Event Operations > Input Quantize.

   The Input Quantize page of the Event Operations window opens (**Figure 7.22**).

2. Select Enable Input Quantize.

3. Choose the MIDI note attributes to quantize: "Note On," "Note Off," or "Preserve note duration."

4. Set the Quantize Grid to the resolution you want to impose on recorded notes.

   For more information on Quantize options, see Chapter 12, "Editing MIDI."

5. Close the Event Operations window.

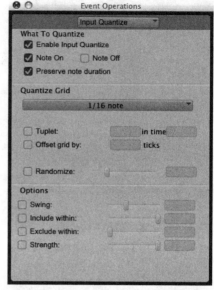

Figure 7.22 The Input Quantize page of the Event Operations window.

QUANTIZING MIDI ON INPUT

Figure 7.23 Click an Insert selector on the Instrument track and choose a virtual instrument plug-in.

Figure 7.24 The MIDI controls in the Instruments view, showing the MIDI output assigned to the virtual instrument.

Using Virtual Instruments

Pro Tools 8 includes a set of software-based synthesizers and samplers in the form of real-time plug-ins. These virtual instruments can be triggered by MIDI data on tracks, or by live input from a MIDI controller. The virtual instruments listed here are included in the Creative Collection package that comes with Pro Tools.

◆ **Mini Grand:** Sampled acoustic piano

◆ **DB-33:** Tonewheel organ emulation

◆ **Vacuum:** Vintage synthesizer emulation

◆ **Xpand**[2]**:** Multitimbral synthesizer/sample player

◆ **Structure Free:** Sample player

◆ **Boom:** Drum machine with pattern sequencer

Virtual instruments can be inserted on Instrument tracks or Auxiliary Input tracks. To play only one channel of MIDI, insert the instrument on an Instrument track. If you want to send more than one channel of MIDI to an instrument, insert it on an Auxiliary Input track and route the output of multiple MIDI tracks to the instrument.

To insert a virtual instrument on an Instrument track:

1. Create a stereo Instrument track.

2. Click an Insert selector on the Instrument track, choose Multi-Channel Plug-In > Instrument, and select a virtual instrument (**Figure 7.23**).

   The MIDI output of the track is automatically assigned to the plug-in (**Figure 7.24**).

3. Click the Output selector and choose the output path for monitoring.

4. If MIDI Thru is enabled, you can play your MIDI controller and hear output from the instrument.

To insert a virtual instrument on an Auxiliary Input track:

1. Create a stereo Auxiliary Input track.

2. Click an Insert selector on the Auxiliary Input track, choose Multichannel Plug-In > Instrument, and select a virtual instrument (Figure 7.23).

3. Click the Output selector on the Auxiliary Input track and choose the output path for monitoring.

4. Create one or more MIDI tracks.

5. On each MIDI track, click the Output selector and assign the output to a MIDI channel for the virtual instrument (**Figure 7.25**).

6. If MIDI Thru is enabled and at least one of the MIDI tracks is record enabled, you can play your MIDI controller and hear output from the instrument.

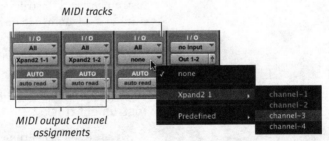

Figure 7.25 Assign the output of each MIDI track to a channel for the virtual instrument.

Figure 7.26 Select the input for the MIDI track.

Figure 7.27 Select the output to monitor the MIDI recording.

Figure 7.28 Record enable the track by clicking its Record Enable button. The button flashes to indicate the track is record enabled.

Enabling Tracks for Recording

When you have established MIDI inputs and configured the session, you're ready to enable MIDI or Instrument tracks for recording.

Each MIDI or Instrument track is capable of recording one channel of MIDI data. If you want to record more than one channel at a time (for example, when a keyboard is split to send to multiple channels), you need to record to multiple tracks.

If you have MIDI Thru enabled, you don't need to record enable MIDI tracks to monitor output.

To enable a MIDI or Instrument track for recording:

1. Click the MIDI Input selector on the track and choose a MIDI input (**Figure 7.26**).

   On MIDI tracks, the Input selector is in the I/O controls; on Instrument tracks, it is in the Instruments view.

   The inputs of MIDI and Instrument tracks are set to All by default. In most cases, this setting is OK, since only one input device is sending at a time. If necessary, set the input to a specific device and MIDI channel.

2. Click the MIDI Output selector on the track and choose a MIDI output (**Figure 7.27**).

   On MIDI tracks, the Output selector is in the I/O controls; on Instrument tracks, it is in the Instruments view.

   The MIDI output of an Instrument track is automatically set to the instrument plug-in on the track.

3. Click the Record Enable button on the track (**Figure 7.28**).

   The Record Enable button flashes and the track's Volume fader turns red to indicate that the track is enabled for recording.

✔ Tips

■ To enable all MIDI or Instrument tracks for recording, Option-click (Mac) or Alt-click (Windows) the Record Enable button on a MIDI or Instrument track.

■ To enable all selected MIDI or Instrument tracks for recording, Shift-Option-click (Mac) or Shift-Alt-click (Windows) the Record Enable button on any selected MIDI or Instrument track.

Record Modes and MIDI

In Pro Tools, MIDI recording is independent of the audio recording mode. MIDI recording is destructive whether you are in Normal Record mode, Destructive Record mode, or QuickPunch mode. In any of these modes, when you record over MIDI data, the original data is replaced.

Unlike audio recording, you can punch record at any time on a MIDI or Instrument track, in any record mode. You do not need to enable QuickPunch to punch record MIDI.

As with audio recording, in Loop Record mode a separate MIDI region is created by each loop and is available from the Regions list.

Two modes determine how MIDI data is recorded:

◆ **Normal MIDI,** or Replace mode, is the default. Newly recorded MIDI data completely replaces existing data.

◆ **MIDI Merge** adds newly recorded MIDI data to existing data, creating a composite of old and new data in the track.

In each of these modes, the modification to the MIDI data is permanent. The only way to revert to previous MIDI data is to undo the recording pass by choosing Edit > Undo.

Return to Zero   *Go to End*   *Record*

Figure 7.29 In the Transport window, click Return to Zero to start recording from the beginning of the session; click Go to End to resume recording at the end of the session; and click Record to ready Pro Tools for recording.

Figure 7.30 Newly recorded MIDI appears as a region in the track playlist.

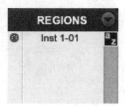

Figure 7.31 The new MIDI region appears in the Regions list.

Recording MIDI

You're ready to record MIDI when you have your MIDI inputs configured; the session meter, tempo, and key set; and tracks record enabled.

To record MIDI:

1. Create a MIDI or Instrument track.

2. Assign the MIDI input for the track.

3. Record enable the track.

4. To start recording from the beginning of the session, click the Return to Zero button in the Transport window (**Figure 7.29**).

   or

   To resume recording at the end of the session, click the Go to End button in the Transport window (Figure 7.29).

5. Click the Record button in the Transport window to ready Pro Tools for recording (Figure 7.29).

6. To start recording when you are using Countoff, click the Play button. The Record and Play buttons flash during the countoff, then recording begins.

   or

   To start recording when you are using Wait for Note, the Record and Play buttons flash until you begin playing. Recording starts when you play the first note.

7. Click the Stop button when you have finished recording.

   The recorded MIDI appears as a new region in the track playlist (**Figure 7.30**) and in the Regions list (**Figure 7.31**).

To cancel a take while recording:

◆ Press Command-Period (Mac) or Ctrl-Period (Windows) during recording.

To discard a take after recording:

◆ Choose Edit > Undo MIDI Recording.

To play back a recording:

1. Press Return (Mac) or Enter (Windows) to move the playback cursor to the beginning of the session.

2. Click the Play button in the Transport window to start playback.

✔ Tip

■ You can leave the track record enabled while playing back a MIDI recording.

Figure 7.32 Click the pre-roll or post-roll value in the Transport window to change the value.

Figure 7.33 Click the appropriate button to enable pre-roll or post-roll.

Punch Recording MIDI

You can punch record MIDI in the same way as audio. Select the data you want to punch, and Pro Tools will automatically punch in and out on the selection.

However, with MIDI you have two options when punch recording: replacing MIDI data (using Normal mode) or adding to the existing MIDI data (using MIDI Merge mode).

You can set Pro Tools to play track material before (pre-roll) and after (post-roll) your record selection.

To enable pre-roll or post-roll:

1. In the Expanded Transport window, click the pre-roll or post-roll value (**Figure 7.32**).

2. Type a new pre-roll or post-roll value and press Return (Mac) or Enter (Windows).

   The displayed units for pre- and post-roll match the currently selected Main Time Scale.

3. Click the Pre-roll or Post-roll button so that it is highlighted (**Figure 7.33**).

To punch record MIDI:

1. Make sure Link Timeline and Edit Selection is enabled (**Figure 7.34**).

2. Record enable the track you want to punch.

3. With the Selector tool, drag to select the time range where you want to punch in (**Figure 7.35**).

4. Set the pre- and post-roll amounts.

5. In the Transport window MIDI controls, click the MIDI Merge button to set the Record mode (**Figure 7.36**).

   ▲ When the MIDI Merge button is highlighted, punched MIDI is added to existing MIDI.

   ▲ When the MIDI Merge button is not highlighted, punched MIDI replaces existing MIDI.

6. Click the Record button in the Transport window to ready Pro Tools for recording.

7. Click the Play button to start recording.

   If pre- and post-roll are enabled, the track plays up to the punch-in point, records until the punch-out point, plays to the end of the post-roll, then stops.

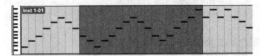

Figure 7.34 Click the Link Timeline and Edit Selection button so that it is highlighted.

Figure 7.35 Drag with the Selector tool to define the range to punch record.

Figure 7.36 Click the MIDI Merge button in the MIDI Controls area of the Transport window.

Figure 7.37 The Play button in the Transport window displays a loop icon to indicate Loop Playback mode.

Figure 7.38 The single looped region appears in the track playlist.

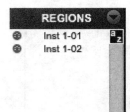

Figure 7.39 The single looped region appears in the Regions list.

Loop Recording MIDI

Pro Tools provides two methods for loop recording MIDI:

◆ Using Loop Playback with MIDI Merge mode lets you add individual parts or notes to a looped section, building a full MIDI part over many passes. This method is commonly used to program drum parts by adding one part of a drum kit at a time.

◆ Loop Record is similar to loop recording audio: a selection in a track is looped, and each pass becomes its own MIDI region. This method is used to capture multiple takes of a passage.

To build a part using Loop Playback and MIDI Merge mode:

1. Make sure Link Timeline and Edit Selection is enabled (Figure 7.34).

2. Select Options > Loop Playback.

   The Play button in the Transport window displays a loop icon to indicate Loop Playback mode (**Figure 7.37**).

3. In the Transport window MIDI controls, click the MIDI Merge button so that it is highlighted (Figure 7.36).

4. Record enable the track on which you want to loop.

5. With the Selector tool, drag to select the time range where you want to loop.

6. Set the pre-roll amount.

7. Click the Record button in the Transport window to ready Pro Tools for recording.

8. Click the Play button to start recording.

9. Click the Stop button when you are finished.

   The single looped region appears in the track playlist (**Figure 7.38**) and in the Regions list (**Figure 7.39**).

To record multiple MIDI takes in Loop Record mode:

1. Make sure Link Timeline and Edit Selection is enabled (Figure 7.34).

2. In the Transport window MIDI controls, make sure the MIDI Merge button is not highlighted (**Figure 7.40**).

3. Select Options > Loop Record.

   The Record button in the Transport window displays a loop icon to indicate Loop Record mode (**Figure 7.41**).

4. Record enable the track on which you want to loop.

5. With the Selector tool, drag to select the time range where you want to loop.

6. Set the pre-roll amount.

7. Click the Record button in the Transport window to ready Pro Tools for recording.

8. Click the Play button to start recording.

9. Click the Stop button when you are finished.

   All looped takes appear in the Regions list, in numerical sequence (**Figure 7.42**). The final take also appears as a region in the track playlist (**Figure 7.43**).

Figure 7.40 Deselect the MIDI Merge button in the MIDI Controls area of the Transport window.

Figure 7.41 The Record button in the Transport window displays a loop icon to indicate Loop Record mode.

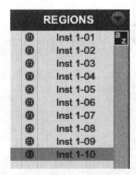

Figure 7.42 Looped takes appear in the Regions list, in numerical sequence.

Figure 7.43 The final looped region appears in the track playlist.

IMPORTING
AUDIO AND MIDI

You can import a variety of media directly into Pro Tools sessions, including audio, MIDI, and video files. In addition, you can import entire tracks from other sessions.

This chapter covers the main methods for importing audio, MIDI, and tracks into a session.

For information on importing video files into a session, see Chapter 17, "Working with Video."

About Audio Files

You can import audio into sessions from a wide range of sources, such as music, sound effects, or sample libraries.

If the file type, sample rate, and bit depth of an audio file match those of the session, the file can be imported directly into the session without any conversion. If any of these attributes is different from the session, conversion is necessary.

To view the file type, sample rate, and bit depth of the current session:

◆ Choose Setup > Session.

The Format section of the Session Setup window shows session attributes (**Figure 8.1**).

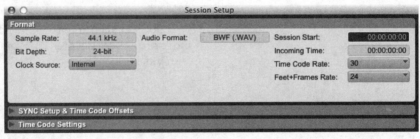

Figure 8.1 The Session Setup window shows session sample rate, bit depth, and audio file type.

Figure 8.2 The Sample Rate Conversion Quality in Processing Preferences.

File type conversion

If the format of an audio file is different from the session format, Pro Tools automatically converts it to the session format.

Pro Tools can import many formats, including the following common formats:

◆ AIFF (Audio Interchange File Format)

◆ WAV/BWF (Waveform Audio File Format)

◆ SD II (Sound Designer II)

◆ MP3 (MPEG-1 Layer-3)

◆ MXF audio (Material Exchange Format)

◆ AAC, Mp4, M4a (Advanced Audio Coding)

◆ WMA (Windows Media Audio)

◆ QuickTime

◆ REX 1 and 2 (ReCycle Export)

◆ ACD (ACID)

Sample rate conversion

If the sample rate of imported audio is different from the session sample rate, Pro Tools converts it to the session sample rate. You can choose the sample rate conversion quality. Settings range from Low (lowest quality, fastest conversion) to TweakHead (highest quality, slowest conversion).

To set the sample rate conversion quality:

1. Choose Setup > Preferences and click Processing.

2. Choose a quality setting from the Sample Rate Conversion Quality pop-up menu (**Figure 8.2**).

3. Click OK.

ABOUT AUDIO FILES

Bit depth conversion

If the bit depth of imported audio is different from the session bit depth, Pro Tools converts it to the session bit depth.

◆ When the bit depth of the imported audio is lower than the session bit depth (for example, importing 16-bit audio into a 24-bit session), the conversion does not change audio quality.

◆ When the bit depth of the imported audio is higher than the session bit depth (for example, importing 24-bit audio into a 16-bit session), Pro Tools applies a noise-shaped dither when converting the file.

Stereo file configurations

Stereo audio files appear in two configurations:

◆ **Split stereo** files are pairs of mono files, one for the left channel (with the suffix .L) and one for the right (with the suffix .R). Pro Tools supports split stereo files.

◆ **Interleaved stereo** files are single files that contain both left and right channel information. Stereo interleaved files are used by CD burning applications and MP3 encoders. When you import a stereo interleaved file, Pro Tools converts it to two split stereo files (**Figure 8.3**).

Figure 8.3 A stereo region in the Regions list, showing the split stereo channels .L and .R.

Importing Audio

Pro Tools lets you import audio files to the Regions list or to new tracks in a session.

If an imported audio file requires conversion, it is automatically copied to the Audio Files folder for the session and the copy is converted.

If an imported audio file does not require conversion, you have the following options:

◆ **Add** the file to the session, which references the file in its original location and does not copy it to the Audio Files folder of the session.

◆ **Copy** the file to the session, which copies the imported file into the session's Audio Files folder and references the copy.

In most cases, it's best to copy the file, ensuring that it will always be available even if the session is moved to another drive or transferred to a different system.

Importing audio with the Import Audio command

The Import Audio command gives you the most flexibility in how you import audio.

To import audio into a session:

1. Choose File > Import > Audio.

   The Import Audio dialog appears (**Figure 8.4**).

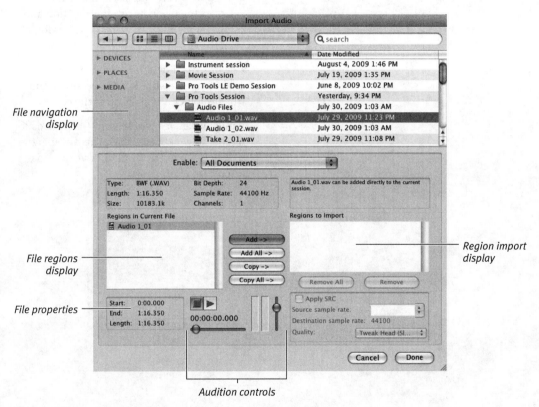

Figure 8.4 The Import Audio dialog.

File navigation display

File regions display

File properties

Region import display

Audition controls

IMPORTING AUDIO

Figure 8.5 The Audio Import Options dialog.

2. In the Import Audio dialog, select an audio file to display its properties.

3. To audition the selected audio file, click the Play and Stop buttons in the dialog.

   Adjust the volume with the vertical slider and set the playback location with the horizontal slider.

4. Do any of the following:
   ▲ To add a file that doesn't require conversion, click Add.
   ▲ To copy a file that doesn't require conversion, click Copy.
   or
   ▲ To copy a file that requires conversion, click Convert.

5. Click Done.

6. Choose a destination folder for any files that are being converted during the import, and click Choose.

7. In the Audio Import Options dialog, select one of the following (**Figure 8.5**):
   ▲ "New track" creates a new track and places the imported audio as a region in the track.
   ▲ "Region list" places the imported audio as a region in the Regions list only.

8. Click OK.

Importing audio from a browser window

You can quickly import audio by dragging it into a session from a Pro Tools browser window. With this method, if an audio file does not require conversion, it will be added to the session and the file will be referenced in its original location.

To import audio from the Workspace browser window:

1. Choose Window > Workspace.

    The Workspace browser opens (**Figure 8.6**).

2. Locate the file you want to import in the browser.

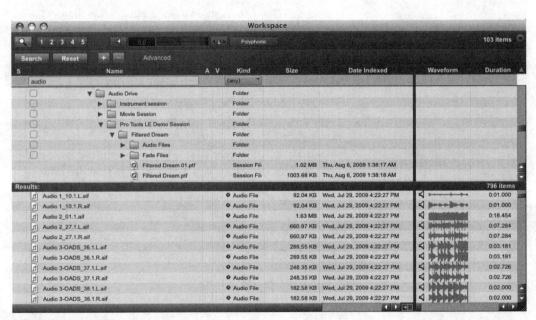

Figure 8.6 The Workspace browser.

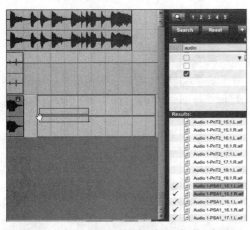

Figure 8.7 Dragging an audio file from the Workspace browser onto a track in the Edit window.

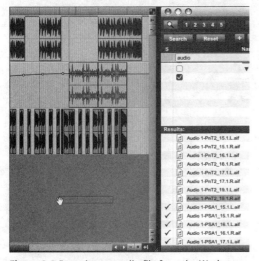

Figure 8.8 Dragging an audio file from the Workspace browser into the Tracks area in the Edit window to create a new track.

Figure 8.9 Dragging an audio file from the Workspace browser into the Regions list.

3. Do one of the following:

▲ To place the imported audio in an existing track in the session, drag the file onto the track in the Edit window (**Figure 8.7**).

▲ To create a new track and place the imported audio as a region in the track, drag the file to an empty space in the Tracks area of the Edit window (**Figure 8.8**).

   or

▲ To place the imported audio as a region in the Regions list only, drag the file onto the Regions list (**Figure 8.9**).

IMPORTING AUDIO

Importing REX and ACID Files

Pro Tools offers several options for handling samples for looping. It supports import of ACID and REX file types.

ACID files, created with Sony ACID software, are audio files with metadata that includes slice information.

REX (ReCycle Export) files, created with Properllerhead ReCycle software, are audio files that are sliced into many small regions.

Both ACID and REX files can be imported into Pro Tools as sample-based regions or as tick-based Elastic audio regions. In addition, when placed as a tick-based region group, the slices in a REX file can adjust to changes in tempo.

To import ACID or REX files as sample-based regions:

1. Choose Setup > Preferences and click Processing.

2. In the Import section, deselect "Import REX files as Region Groups" (**Figure 8.10**).

3. Under "Drag and Drop from Desktop Conforms to Session Tempo," select No Files.

4. Click OK.

5. Import the ACID or REX files using the Import Audio command.

Figure 8.10 Deselect the "Import REX Files as Region Groups" option.

To import ACID or REX files as tick-based Elastic Audio regions:

1. Choose Setup > Preferences and click Processing.

2. In the Import section, deselect "Import REX Files as Region Groups" (Figure 8.10).

3. Under "Drag and Drop from Desktop Conforms to Session Tempo," select REX and ACID Files Only.

4. Click OK.

5. Import the ACID or REX files using the Import Audio command.

To import REX files as tick-based region groups:

1. Choose Setup > Preferences and click Processing.

2. In the Import section, select "Import REX files as Region Groups."

3. Under "Drag and Drop from Desktop Conforms to Session Tempo," select "REX and ACID Files Only."

4. Click OK.

5. Import the ACID or REX files using the Import Audio command.

IMPORTING REX AND ACID FILES

Importing MIDI

Pro Tools lets you import Standard MIDI Files (SMF or .mid files) into sessions. If you want to import MIDI files from other programs, you must first save them as Standard MIDI Files.

Importing MIDI with the Import MIDI command

To import MIDI into a session:

1. Choose File > Import > MIDI.

2. Choose the MIDI file to import.

3. Click Open.

4. In the MIDI Import Options dialog, select one of the following (**Figure 8.11**):

    ▲ To create a new track and place the imported MIDI as a region in the track, select "New track."

    or

    ▲ To place the imported MIDI as a region in the Regions list only, select "Region list."

5. If you selected "New track," do any of the following:

    ▲ To use the tempo information from the MIDI file you are importing, select "Import Tempo Map from MIDI File."

    ▲ To use the key signature from the MIDI file you are importing, select "Import Key Signature from MIDI File."

    ▲ To replace MIDI tracks in the session with the MIDI file you are importing, select "Remove existing MIDI Tracks."

Figure 8.11 The MIDI Import Options dialog.

IMPORTING MIDI

▲ To replace Instrument tracks in the session with the MIDI file you are importing, select "Remove existing Instrument Tracks."

or

▲ To replace MIDI regions in the Regions list with the regions from the MIDI file you are importing, select "Remove existing MIDI Regions."

6. Click OK.

Importing MIDI from a browser window

You can quickly import MIDI by dragging it from a Pro Tools browser window, in the same way as audio.

To import MIDI from the Workspace browser window:

1. Choose Window > Workspace.

   The Workspace browser opens (Figure 8.6).

2. Locate the file you want to import in the browser.

3. Do one of the following:

   ▲ To place the imported MIDI into an existing track in the session, drag the file onto the track in the Edit window.

   or

   ▲ Drag the file to an empty space in the Tracks area of the Edit window or to the Regions list, and choose whether to use the tempo and key signature of the file.

4. Click OK.

Standard MIDI File Types

There are two types of Standard MIDI Files:

◆ **Type 0 MIDI files** combine all MIDI channel data in a single track. When imported into Pro Tools, a Type 0 file appears as a single MIDI track.

◆ **Type 1 MIDI files** save each MIDI channel to a separate MIDI track. When imported into Pro Tools, each channel of a Type 1 file appears as a separate MIDI track.

In most cases, Type 1 MIDI files are best for transferring multitrack MIDI data.

IMPORTING MIDI

Importing Tracks

You can import entire tracks from other sessions, including Audio, MIDI, Auxiliary Input, Instrument, and Master Fader tracks. This is done with the Import Session Data command.

The Import Session Data dialog (**Figure 8.12**) lets you choose how to handle audio files, track information, and ruler information from the source session.

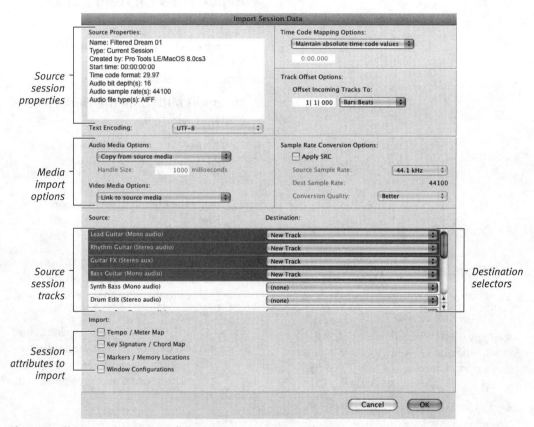

Figure 8.12 The Import Session Data dialog.

The Audio Media Options provide alternatives for copying and consolidating imported audio files, including:

◆ **Consolidate from Source Media** copies only currently used portions of audio files.

◆ **Copy from Source Media** copies all audio files related to the imported tracks from the source media to a new location.

◆ **Link to Source Media** links the current session to the existing audio files.

◆ **Force to Target Session Format** copies and converts any files that do not match the current session's file format, bit depth, and sample rate.

In the Source area, each source track has a corresponding Destination pop-up menu where you choose the track to receive the imported data.

The Import options let you select the tempo, key, and memory location information you want to import from the source session:

Tempo/Meter Map imports meter and tempo maps from the source session.

Key Signature/Chord Map imports key and chord maps from the source session.

Markers/Memory Locations imports markers and Memory Locations from the source session. Markers and Memory Locations in the destination session are retained.

To import tracks from another session:

1. Chose File > Import > Session Data.

2. Select a session and click Open.

   The Import Session Data dialog appears (Figure 8.12).

3. Using the Audio Media Options pop-up menu, choose whether you want to copy or link to the audio files from the source session.

4. Select the tracks to import in the Source Tracks list.

   Selected tracks change to New Track.

5. Do one of the following:

   ▲ To import the configured Tempo and Meter rulers from the source session, select Import Tempo/Meter Map.

   ▲ To import the configured Key and Chord rulers from the source session, select Import Key Signature/Chord Map.

   or

   ▲ To import markers and Memory Locations from the source session, select Import Markers/Memory Locations.

6. Click OK.

7. If you are copying or consolidating media, choose a location to place the media files.

Working with Selections

Making selections is the basis of almost all editing in Pro Tools. You select material in tracks to perform basic editing tasks such as cutting and pasting. You also use selections to create regions, the building blocks of a session.

This chapter shows how to set the time scale and use the grid to help make selections, explains the two types of selections (Timeline selections and Edit selections), and covers the basics of selecting material in the Edit window.

The techniques described here apply to both Audio and MIDI tracks.

Setting the Time Scale

The time scale setting determines the values you see in the counters and selection indicators in the Edit and Transport windows.

When navigating a session, making selections, or moving regions, you use the Main Time Scale to locate material, determine the length of selections, and set Grid and Nudge values. The Sub Counter lets you display a second time scale for reference against the Main Time Scale.

The Main Time Scale and Sub Counter can be set to Bars|Beats, Minutes:Seconds, or Samples.

To set the Main Time Scale:

◆ In the Edit window, click the Main Counter selector and select a Time Scale (**Figure 9.1**).

◆ In the Counters view of the Transport window, click the Main Counter selector and select a Time Scale (**Figure 9.2**).

or

In the Edit window, click the name of a Timebase ruler so that it is highlighted (**Figure 9.3**).

Figure 9.1 Setting the Main Time Scale in the Edit window.

Figure 9.2 Setting the Main Time Scale in the Transport window.

Figure 9.3 Setting the Main Time Scale by clicking a Timebase ruler.

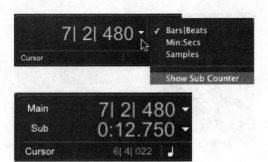

Figure 9.4 Showing the Sub Counter in the Edit window.

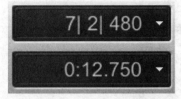

Figure 9.5 Showing the Counters view and the Expanded view in the Transport window lets you see the Main Counter and Sub Counter.

Figure 9.6 Setting the Sub Counter.

To show the Sub Counter:

◆ In the Edit window, click the Main Counter selector and select Show Sub Counter (**Figure 9.4**).

or

In the Transport window, show the Counters view and the Expanded Transport view (**Figure 9.5**).

To set the Sub Counter:

◆ Click the Sub Counter selector in the Edit window or the Transport window and select a Time Scale (**Figure 9.6**).

Setting Grid and Nudge Values

When you are working in Grid mode, the Grid value determines selection boundaries, movement of regions, and placement of MIDI notes in the Edit window.

The Nudge value determines the increment by which a region or MIDI note can be *nudged*, or moved with the Plus and Minus keys on the numeric keypad.

◆ When the Grid is set to Min:Secs, available Grid and Nudge values range from 1 second to 1 millisecond (**Figure 9.7**).

◆ When the Grid is set to Bars|Beats, available Grid and Nudge values range from 1 bar to a 64th note (**Figure 9.8**).

◆ When the Grid is set to Samples, available Grid and Nudge values range from 10,000 samples to 1 sample (**Figure 9.9**).

Figure 9.7 Grid and Nudge values for the Main Time Scale set to Minutes:Seconds.

Figure 9.8 Grid and Nudge values for the Main Time Scale set to Bars|Beats.

Figure 9.9 Grid and Nudge values for the Main Time Scale set to Samples.

Figure 9.10 Selecting a Grid size.

Figure 9.11 Selecting a Nudge amount.

By default, the units for the Grid value and Nudge value follow the Main Time Scale. You can, however, decouple Grid and Nudge values from the Main Time Scale and use a different time scale for each.

To set the Grid value:

◆ In the Edit Toolbar, click the Grid Value selector and select a grid size (**Figure 9.10**).

To set the Nudge value:

◆ In the Edit Toolbar, click the Nudge value selector and select a nudge amount (**Figure 9.11**).

To decouple the Grid or Nudge value from the Main Time Scale:

1. Click the Grid or Nudge value selector and choose a Time Scale.

2. Click the Grid or Nudge value selector again and choose a Grid or Nudge value.

SETTING GRID AND NUDGE VALUES

Using Grid Mode to Make Selections

When selecting in the Timeline or in tracks, you can use Grid mode to constrain selections to Grid boundaries.

With Grid mode enabled, when you click in a track with the Selector tool, the cursor location snaps to the nearest grid line. When you make or modify a selection, the selection boundary snaps to the grid line.

Even if Grid mode is not enabled, you can display grid lines in the Edit window for visual reference.

To enable Grid mode:

◆ In the Edit Toolbar, click the Grid button so that it is highlighted (**Figure 9.12**).

To display grid lines in tracks:

◆ In the Edit Toolbar, click the Grid button so that it is highlighted (**Figure 9.13**).

Figure 9.12 Enable Grid mode by clicking the Grid icon in the Edit Toolbar.

Figure 9.13 Display the Grid by clicking the Grid display icon.

Figure 9.14 Click the Link Timeline and Edit selection icon so that it is not highlighted.

Linking Timeline and Edit Selections

There are two types of selections in Pro Tools:

◆ **Timeline selections** set a range in the Timebase rulers for playback and recording.

◆ **Edit selections** define a range of material in one or more tracks for edit commands.

By default, these two types of selections are linked: Any selection you make in the timeline selects the corresponding material in all tracks; conversely, any selection in a track selects the corresponding playback range in the timeline.

However, you can unlink timeline and edit selections so that you can select separate ranges for playback and for editing. This allows you to audition a range of material while editing other material. For example, you could select a four-bar phrase and set it for loop playback while editing a single bar within the phrase.

To unlink timeline and edit selections:

◆ Choose Options > Link Timeline and Edit Selection and deselect the option.

or

In the Edit Toolbar, click the Link Timeline and Edit Selection icon so that it is not highlighted (**Figure 9.14**).

When timeline and edit selections are unlinked, separate markers are shown for each type of selection: timeline selections are shown with vertical blue arrows, and edit selections are shown with yellow brackets.

LINKING TIMELINE AND EDIT SELECTIONS

177

Making Timeline Selections

Timeline selections define a range for playback or recording. You can make timeline selections by dragging in a Timebase ruler, by moving selection markers in a Timebase ruler, or by entering selection start and end values in the Transport window. You can also modify an existing selection with these same techniques.

To make a timeline selection by dragging in a Timebase ruler:

1. With any Edit tool, move the cursor over a Timebase ruler in the Edit window.

   The cursor changes to the Selector tool.

2. Drag in the Timebase ruler to select an area of the timeline (**Figure 9.15**).

   The boundaries of the selection are indicated by Timeline Selection markers (vertical blue arrows) in the Main ruler.

To modify a timeline selection by dragging in a Timebase ruler:

◆ Shift-click or Shift-drag the start or end of the selection in the Timebase ruler.

To move a timeline selection in a Timebase ruler:

◆ Option-drag (Mac) or Alt-drag (Windows) either of the Timeline Selection markers in the Timebase ruler.

Figure 9.15 Drag in a Timebase ruler to make a timeline selection.

Figure 9.16 A Timeline Selection marker in the Main ruler.

Figure 9.17
Enter values in the Transport window selection indicators to make a timeline selection.

To make or modify a timeline selection by moving selection markers:

1. With any Edit tool, move the cursor over a Timeline Selection marker (vertical blue arrow) in the Main ruler (**Figure 9.16**). The cursor changes to the Grabber tool.

2. Drag the selection start marker (up arrow) and the selection end marker (down arrow) to select an area of the timeline.

To make or modify a timeline selection with the selection indicators:

1. In the Expanded view of the Transport window, click the selection Start value (**Figure 9.17**).

2. Type a new value and press Return (Mac) or Enter (Windows).

3. Click the selection End or Length value.

4. Type a new value and press Return (Mac) or Enter (Windows).

To change the timeline selection to match the edit selection:

◆ Choose Edit > Selection > Change Timeline to Match Edit.

MAKING TIMELINE SELECTIONS

Making Edit Selections

Edit selections define a range of Audio, MIDI, or automation data for editing. You can make edit selections with the Selector tool in a track, by moving selection markers in a Timebase ruler, or by entering selection start and end values in the Edit window. You can also modify an existing selection with these same techniques.

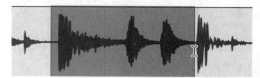

Figure 9.18 Drag in a track with the Selector tool to make an edit selection.

To make an edit selection with the Selector tool:

◆ Drag in a track to select a range of material (**Figure 9.18**).

or

Figure 9.19 An Edit selection marker in the Main ruler.

1. Click in a track to define the selection start.

2. Shift-click to the right in the track to define the selection end.

   The selected material is highlighted in the track, and the boundaries of the selection are indicated by Edit selection markers (yellow brackets) in the Main ruler.

To modify an edit selection with the Selector tool:

◆ Shift-click within the selection.

or

Shift-drag the start or end of the selection.

To make or modify an edit selection by moving selection markers:

1. With any Edit tool, move the cursor over an Edit selection marker (yellow bracket) in the Main ruler (**Figure 9.19**).

   The cursor changes to the Grabber tool.

2. Drag the selection start marker (left bracket) or the selection end marker (right bracket) to select an area of the track.

Figure 9.20 Enter values in the Edit window selection indicators to make an edit selection.

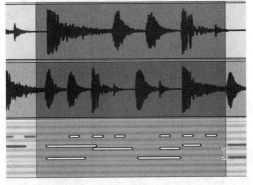

Figure 9.21 Drag vertically and horizontally to make a selection in multiple tracks while selecting the time range.

To make or modify an edit selection with the selection indicators:

1. In the Edit window, click the selection Start value (**Figure 9.20**).

2. Type a new value and press Return (Mac) or Enter (Windows).

3. Click the selection End or Length value.

4. Type a new value and press Return (Mac) or Enter (Windows).

To change the edit selection to match the timeline selection:

◆ Choose Edit > Selection > Change Edit to Match Timeline.

To make an edit selection in multiple tracks:

◆ With the Selector tool, drag vertically to include multiple tracks in the selection; drag horizontally to select the time range (**Figure 9.21**).

   or

1. With the Selector tool, Shift-click vertically to define the selection start in multiple tracks.

2. Shift-click to the right in any of the tracks to define the selection end.

To select all material in a track:

◆ Triple-click in the track with the Selector tool.

   or

   With the Selector tool, click in the track and choose Edit > Select All.

MAKING EDIT SELECTIONS

Making Edit Selections During Playback

Pro Tools lets you select material during playback by marking selection start and end points. You can use this feature in conjunction with commands for separating regions to quickly analyze a take while it plays back.

To make a selection during playback:

1. Make sure Link Timeline and Edit Selection is enabled (Figure 9.14).

2. With the Selector tool, click or Shift-click in one or more tracks just before the location of the selection start.

3. Start playback.

4. When the cursor reaches the point where you want to selection to start, press the Down Arrow key.

5. When the cursor reaches the point where you want to selection to end, press the Up Arrow key.

6. Stop playback.
   The selection is highlighted.

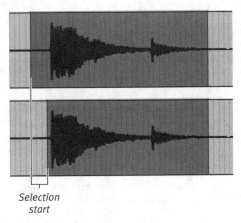

Selection
start

Figure 9.22 Nudging the selection start.

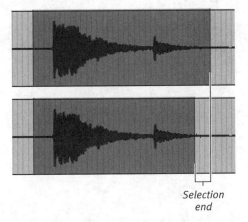

Selection
end

Figure 9.23 Nudging the selection end.

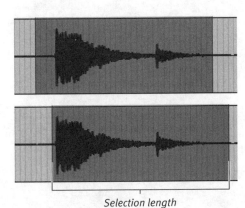

Selection length

Figure 9.24 Nudging a selection range.

Nudging Selections

You can use the Nudge feature to make small adjustments to the start point, end point, or position of a selection, using the Plus and Minus keys on the numeric keypad.

The amount of adjustment is determined by the Nudge setting.

To nudge the start of a selection:

◆ Press Option-Shift-Plus (Mac) or Alt-Shift-Plus (Windows) to move the selection start forward (**Figure 9.22**).

◆ Press Option-Shift-Minus (Mac) or Alt-Shift-Minus (Windows) to move the selection start backward.

To nudge the end of a selection:

◆ Press Command-Shift-Plus (Mac) or Ctrl-Shift-Plus (Windows) to move the selection end forward.

◆ Press Command-Shift-Minus (Mac) or Ctrl-Shift-Minus (Windows) to move the selection end backward (**Figure 9.23**).

To nudge a selection range later or earlier in the timeline:

◆ Press Shift-Plus to move the selection forward (**Figure 9.24**).

◆ Press Shift-Minus to move the selection backward.

Moving the Edit Cursor

When making selections in a track, you can use the Tab key to quickly move the edit cursor to region boundaries.

In audio tracks, you can relocate the edit cursor to *transients*, or peaks in the audio waveform, by enabling the Tab to Transients option.

To move the edit cursor to a region boundary:

1. Make sure the Tab to Transients icon is not highlighted (**Figure 9.25**).

2. To move the cursor to the next region boundary, press Tab (**Figure 9.26**).

   or

   To move the cursor to the previous region boundary, press Option-Tab (Mac) or Ctrl-Tab (Windows).

To move the edit cursor to an audio transient:

1. Make sure Tab to Transients is enabled.

2. In an audio track in waveform view, do one of the following:

   ▲ To move the cursor to the next transient peak, press Tab (**Figure 9.27**).

   or

   To move the cursor to the previous transient peak, press Option-Tab (Mac) or Ctrl-Tab (Windows).

Figure 9.25 The Tab to Transients icon in the Edit Toolbar.

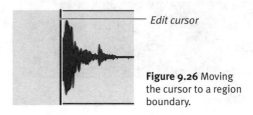

Edit cursor

Figure 9.26 Moving the cursor to a region boundary.

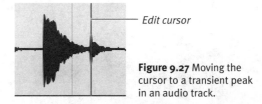

Edit cursor

Figure 9.27 Moving the cursor to a transient peak in an audio track.

MOVING THE EDIT CURSOR

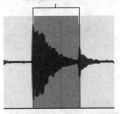

Edit selection

Figure 9.28
Press Shift-
Tab to extend
a selection
to a region
boundary.

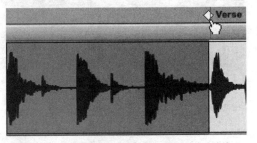

Edit selection

Figure 9.29 Press Shift-
Tab to extend a selection
to a transient peak in an
audio track.

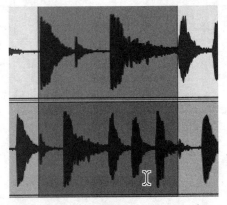

Figure 9.30 Extend a selection to a marker by Shift-
clicking it.

Figure 9.31 Use the Selector tool to extend a
selection to another track.

Extending Selections

You can extend edit selections to region
boundaries, transient peaks, and Memory
Locations in a session.

To extend a selection to a region boundary:

1. Make sure Tab to Transients is disabled.

2. Do one of the following:

   ▲ To extend a selection to the next
   region boundary, press Shift-Tab
   (**Figure 9.28**).

   or

   To extend a selection to the previous
   region boundary, press Option-Shift-
   Tab (Mac) or Ctrl-Shift-Tab (Windows).

To extend a selection to an audio transient:

1. Make sure Tab to Transients is enabled.

2. In an audio track in waveform view, do
   one of the following:

   ▲ To extend a selection to the next
   transient peak, press Shift-Tab
   (**Figure 9.29**).

   or

   To extend a selection to the previous
   transient peak, press Option-Shift-Tab
   (Mac) or Ctrl-Shift-Tab (Windows).

To extend a selection to a marker or Memory Location:

◆ In the Markers ruler, Shift-click a marker
   (**Figure 9.30**).

   or

   In the Memory Locations window,
   Shift-click a Memory Location.

To extend a selection to another track:

◆ With the Selector tool, Shift-click in the
   track where you want to extend the selection (**Figure 9.31**).

Linking Edit Selections and Track Selections

Pro Tools lets you link the selection of individual tracks and the selection of material in the Edit window. By default, these two types of selections are unlinked.

With edit selections and track selections linked, when you make an edit selection in a track, that track is automatically selected. This lets you quickly change the view of material you are editing by carrying out commands for all selected tracks (such as changing track view or track height). Conversely, after you make an edit selection in a track, you can quickly extend that selection to additional tracks.

To link edit selections and track selections:

◆ Select Options > Link Track and Edit Selection.

or

In the Edit Toolbar, click the Link Track and Edit Selection icon so that it is highlighted (**Figure 9.32**).

To extend a selection to additional tracks:

1. Make sure Link Track and Edit Selection is enabled (Figure 9.32).

2. Do one of the following:

   ▲ To extend the selection to contiguous tracks, Shift-click the track names to select them (**Figure 9.33**).

   ▲ To extend the selection to noncontiguous tracks, Command-click (Mac) or Ctrl-click (Windows) the track names to select them (**Figure 9.34**).

Figure 9.32 Click the Link Track and Edit Selection icon so that it is highlighted.

Figure 9.33 Extend a selection to contiguous tracks by Shift-clicking multiple track names.

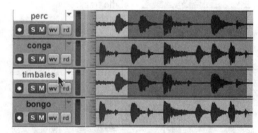

Figure 9.34 You can extend a selection to noncontiguous tracks by Command-clicking (Mac) or Ctrl-clicking (Windows) track names.

Cutting, Copying, Pasting, and Deleting Selections

You can use the Selector tool to perform standard editing commands on track material in Pro Tools. The effect of these commands depends on the current track view.

When editing in any of a track's Master views, cut, copy, paste, and delete operations include all underlying automation or controller data. In all other views, only the data displayed in the view is affected.

The behavior of material surrounding the edit depends on the Edit mode. If you are in Shuffle mode, adjacent material moves to close up any cut material or to accommodate any pasted material. If you are in any other Edit mode, adjacent material does not move.

The Master views for each track type are as follows:

◆ Audio tracks: Waveform view and Block view

◆ MIDI and Instrument tracks: Region view, Block view, and Notes view

CUTTING, COPYING, PASTING, AND DELETING

To cut or copy a selection:

1. Make an edit selection.

2. Do one of the following:
   ▲ To remove the selected material, choose Edit > Cut.

   or

   To leave the selected material in place and copy it, choose Edit > Copy.

   The cut or copied material is moved to the clipboard, ready for pasting.

To paste a selection:

1. Place the cursor where you want to paste the material.

2. Choose Edit > Paste.

To delete a selection:

1. Make an edit selection.

2. Choose Edit > Clear.

WORKING
WITH REGIONS

When you work with audio or MIDI in Pro Tools, a large part of your time will be spent working with regions. Regions are visual representations of material that are placed in tracks, edited, and assembled to construct a session.

Pro Tools offers a wealth of choices for editing—enough to fill an entire book. This chapter covers the main ways to display, move, edit, and manage regions in a session. The features described in this chapter apply to both audio and MIDI regions unless noted otherwise.

About Regions

Regions are segments of audio files or MIDI data that can be arranged in track playlists. A region could represent a recorded take, a punch-in, a loop, or a sound effect.

Figure 10.1 An audio region in a track playlist.

All audio and MIDI regions in a session appear in the Regions list, where they are available for use in tracks.

Audio regions

Audio regions (**Figure 10.1**) in a session are not audio files; they refer to audio files stored on a hard drive. They can also contain automation data associated with the audio.

Figure 10.2 Whole-file audio region names are shown in bold in the Regions list.

Most editing of audio regions is nondestructive. When you create or modify an audio region, you're telling Pro Tools which part of an audio file to play; the original file remains unchanged.

There are several kinds of audio regions, including the following:

Whole-file audio regions represent entire audio files, which are created when you record a take, import an audio file, or process audio in a way that creates a new file. Whole-file audio region names are displayed in bold in the Regions list (**Figure 10.2**).

User-defined regions are the direct results of recording, capturing, separating or trimming regions. This type of region can include whole-file audio regions.

Auto-created regions are generated automatically as a byproduct of editing. For example, when you separate a region in a track, additional regions on either side of the separated region are created.

Figure 10.3 A MIDI region in a track playlist.

Figure 10.4 A region group in a track playlist.

MIDI regions

MIDI regions (**Figure 10.3**) in a session contain MIDI notes and associated MIDI data, such as controller events and program changes. When a MIDI track or an Instrument track is in Regions view, you can edit the regions, but you cannot edit individual notes in the regions.

Some operations on MIDI regions are nondestructive. If you edit a MIDI region without altering the notes in the region, for example, by moving, separating, or trimming it, new regions are created and the original region remains available in the Regions list.

However, if you edit the notes in a MIDI region—for example, by transposing, quantizing or trimming them—the region is permanently altered.

Region groups

Pro Tools lets you group any combination of audio and MIDI regions (**Figure 10.4**) for ease of editing and arranging. You can perform many of the same editing operations on region groups as on individual regions.

Region group information is saved separately in Region group files with an .rgrp suffix.

Setting Region Preferences

Pro Tools lets you set preferences for the display and naming of regions, and for the operation of the Separate Region command on looped takes. These settings apply to all regions in a session.

Setting region information display

Regions can display a wide range of information in the track playlist, including region name, start and end times, sync point, rating, and region overlap. To easily view the contents of regions, you can set them to display only the information you need (**Figure 10.5**).

To set region display options:

◆ Choose View > Region and select the information to display in the region.

Naming newly separated regions

When you create a region with the Separate Region command, Pro Tools automatically names the resulting region by default. New regions are based on the original region name, with a numerical suffix appended (**Figure 10.6**).

You can disable automatic naming of regions so that Pro Tools prompts you for the region name after every Separate Region command.

To disable automatic region naming:

1. Choose Setup > Preferences and click Editing.

2. Under Regions, deselect Auto-Name Separated Regions.

3. Click OK.

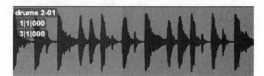

Figure 10.5 A region showing the name, plus start and end times.

Figure 10.6 A newly separated region showing the default names.

Separating regions on multiple takes

When working with multiple takes (for example, from a loop record pass), you can set Pro Tools to separate all related takes when you apply the Separate Region command to a take.

To apply the Separate Region command to all takes:

1. Choose Setup > Preferences and click Editing.

2. Under Regions, select "Separate Region" Operates on All Takes.

3. Click OK.

Edit Tools

The Edit tools in the Edit window toolbar are used to view, select, move, and modify regions (**Figure 10.7**). Several of the tools have multiple modes.

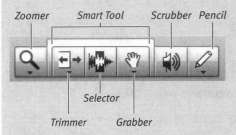

Zoomer Smart Tool Scrubber Pencil

Selector

Trimmer Grabber

Figure 10.7 The Edit tools in the Edit window toolbar.

Figure 10.8 The Zoomer tool is used to zoom views of track material.

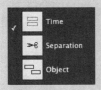

Figure 10.9 The Trimmer tool is used to change the length of regions.

Figure 10.10 The Selector tool is used to place the cursor and make selections.

Figure 10.11 The Grabber tool is used to select and move regions.

The **Zoomer tool** (**Figure 10.8**) is used to zoom in and out on track material, and has the following modes:

◆ Normal Zoom remains active so you can continue to zoom.

◆ Single Zoom returns you to the previously active Edit tool after zooming.

The **Trimmer tool** (**Figure 10.9**) is used to change the length of regions, and has the following modes:

◆ The Standard Trimmer adjusts the boundaries of regions to hide or reveal material in the region.

◆ The TCE (Time Compression/ Expansion) Trimmer compresses or expands material to fit into region boundaries.

◆ The Loop Trimmer creates new region loops and adjusts the boundaries of region loops.

The **Selector tool** (**Figure 10.10**) is used to place the cursor in tracks or rulers, and to make edit and timeline selections.

The **Grabber tool** (**Figure 10.11**) is used to select, move, and separate regions, and has the following modes:

◆ The Time Grabber selects and moves regions in and among tracks.

◆ The Separation Grabber separates selections into new regions and moves them in and among tracks.

◆ The Object Grabber selects noncontiguous regions in and among tracks.

Edit Tools *continued*

Figure 10.12 The Scrubber tool is used to audition material in tracks.

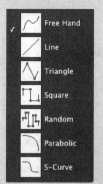

Figure 10.13 The Pencil tool is used to draw MIDI data and edit audio waveforms.

Figure 10.14 The Smart Tool changes depending on its location in a region.

The **Scrubber tool (Figure 10.12)** is used to audition material in regions at variable speed by dragging in tracks.

The **Pencil tool (Figure 10.13)** is used to insert and edit MIDI notes and velocities, draw automation and controller data, and edit audio waveform data. The Pencil tool has several lines shapes available for drawing.

The **Smart Tool (Figure 10.14)** changes function depending on its location in a region, as follows (**Figure 10.15**):

◆ Selector at the top center

◆ Grabber at the bottom center

◆ Trimmer at the center left and right

◆ Fade In/Out at the top left and right

◆ Crossfade at the bottom left and right

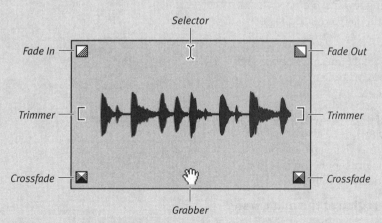

Figure 10.15 The Smart Tool can change to the Selector, Grabber, Trimmer, or to a Fade tool in different parts of a region.

Creating Regions

There are several ways to create audio and MIDI regions. The most common are the Capture Region and Separate Region commands.

Capturing regions

You can select a range of track material and capture it as a region for later reuse. When you capture a region, it is added to the Regions list but is not separated in the track playlist.

To capture a region:

1. With the Selector tool, drag in a track to select a range of material (**Figure 10.16**).

2. Choose Region > Capture.

3. Type a name for the region and click OK. The new region appears in the Regions list (**Figure 10.17**).

Separating regions

Pro Tools provides several different methods for creating regions in tracks. The most common method is to create a region from a selection.

You can also create multiple regions within a selection based on grid lines, or on transients in audio material.

When you separate a region, it is separated in the track playlist and also added to the Regions list. The original region that was in the track before separation also remains available in the Regions list.

To divide a region at the edit cursor:

1. With the Selector tool, click in the region at the point where you want to divide it (**Figure 10.18**).

Figure 10.16 Drag with the Selector tool to select the material to capture to a region.

Figure 10.17 Captured regions appear in the Regions list, available for use in tracks.

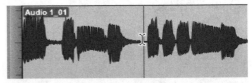

Figure 10.18 Click with the Selector tool to place the cursor at the separation point.

Figure 10.19 A region divided into two regions at the edit cursor.

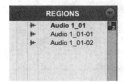

Figure 10.20 The divided regions in the Regions list.

Figure 10.21 Drag with the Selector tool to select the material to separate into a region.

Figure 10.22 A separated region in a track.

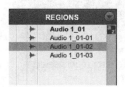

Figure 10.23 The separated region in the Regions list.

2. Choose Edit > Separate Region > At Selection.

or

Press Command-E (Mac) or Ctrl-E (Windows).

The original region is divided into two regions at the edit cursor (**Figure 10.19**). The new regions also appear in the Regions list (**Figure 10.20**).

To create a region from a selection:

1. With the Selector tool, drag in a track to select the range for the region (**Figure 10.21**).

2. Choose Edit > Separate Region > At Selection.

or

Press Command-E (Mac) or Ctrl-E (Windows).

A new region is created from the selection, and regions are created on either side of the separated region (**Figure 10.22**). The new regions also appear in the Regions list (**Figure 10.23**).

To separate material into multiple regions at grid lines or transient points:

1. With the Selector tool, drag in a track to select the range to separate (**Figure 10.24**).

2. Do one of the following:

   ▲ Choose Edit > Separate Region > On Grid

   or

   ▲ Choose Edit > Separate Region > At Transients.

3. In the Pre-Separate Amount dialog, type the amount (in milliseconds) to pad the beginnings of the new regions.

4. Click OK.

   The selected material is divided into regions at each grid line (or audio transient) (**Figure 10.25**). The new regions also appear in the Regions list (**Figure 10.26**).

Restoring separated regions

You can restore separated regions to their original state in a track if their relative positions have not been changed.

To restore separated regions:

1. Select an area in the track that encompasses the separation points on the regions (**Figure 10.27**).

2. Choose Edit > Heal Separation.

   or

   Press Command-H (Mac) or Ctrl-H (Windows).

Figure 10.24 Drag with the Selector tool to select the material to separate into multiple regions.

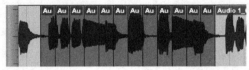

Figure 10.25 Multiple regions separated at grid lines.

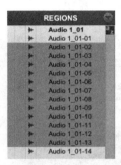

Figure 10.26 The separated regions in the Regions list.

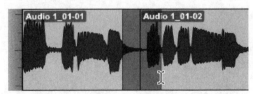

Figure 10.27 Drag with the Selector tool to select across the region separation.

Edit Modes

The behavior of audio and MIDI regions in tracks, the operation of Edit tools, and the effect of Edit commands are controlled by the Edit modes (**Figure 10.28**).

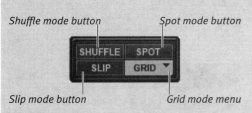

Shuffle mode button   Spot mode button

Slip mode button   Grid mode menu

Figure 10.28 The Edit Mode selectors in the Edit window Toolbar.

In **Shuffle mode**, regions snap end-to-end, shifting to the left (earlier in time) to close up gaps and shifting to the right (later in time) to accommodate insertions. Edits to a region can affect the time placement of surrounding regions in the track. Regions cannot overlap in Shuffle mode.

Shuffle mode is useful for quickly reordering sections of material, such as verses of a song.

In **Slip mode**, regions can be placed and moved freely. Edits to a region do not affect the time placement of surrounding regions in the track. Regions can overlap in Slip mode.

Slip mode is useful for general editing tasks in which you want to preserve the time location of surrounding material.

In **Spot mode**, you specify the location of regions by entering a start time—or if they have a sync point, a sync time. In this mode, locating a region does not affect the placement of surrounding regions. Regions can overlap in Spot mode.

Spot mode is useful for synchronization tasks such as locating (or "spotting") sound effects or music cues to video.

In **Grid mode**, regions snap to grid lines when moved or placed in tracks. Edits to a region are constrained to grid lines, but do not affect the time placement of surrounding regions in the track. Regions can overlap in Grid mode. Grid mode also constrains edit selections to grid lines.

Grid mode has two variants:

◆ **Absolute Grid mode** constrains an edited region to grid lines regardless of its original position relative to the grid. In musical terms, this mode conforms regions to the beat.

◆ **Relative Grid mode** moves an edited region by increments equal to the grid value, preserving the region's position relative to the grid. In musical terms, this mode preserves the region's relationship to the beat.

Grid mode is useful for editing MIDI notes and for quantizing audio and MIDI regions.

Snap to Grid is a hybrid mode that constrains edit selections to the grid, but lets you select Slip, Shuffle, or Spot modes to control the movement of regions.

CREATING REGIONS

Choosing an Edit Mode

You can select the Edit mode with the buttons in the Edit Toolbar or the function keys.

To select Shuffle mode:

◆ Click the Shuffle button.

or

Press the F1 function key.

To select Slip mode:

◆ Click the Slip button.

or

Press the F2 function key.

To select Spot mode:

◆ Click the Spot button.

or

Press the F3 function key.

To select a Grid mode:

◆ Click the Grid button and choose Absolute Grid or Relative Grid from the pop-up menu (**Figure 10.29**).

or

Press the F4 function key to toggle between Absolute and Relative Grid modes.

To enable Snap to Grid operation:

1. Select Shuffle, Slip, or Spot mode.

2. Shift-click the Grid button (**Figure 10.30**) or press Shift-F4.

or

Hold the function key for the mode you want (F1 for Shuffle, F2 for Slip, or F3 for Spot) and press F4.

Figure 10.29 Set the Grid mode to Absolute to constrain regions to the grid, or Relative mode to preserve regions' relationship to the grid.

Figure 10.30 Shift-click the Grid button while in another Edit mode to enable Snap to Grid.

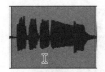

Figure 10.31 Double-click a region with the Selector tool to select it.

Figure 10.32 Click a region with the Grabber tool to select it.

Figure 10.33 The Tab to Transients icon.

Figure 10.34 Moving the cursor to a region boundary.

Figure 10.35 Press Shift-Tab to extend the selection to the next region boundary.

Selecting Regions

There are several ways to select regions in tracks with the Selector tool and the Grabber tool.

To select a single region:

◆ Double-click the region with the Selector tool (**Figure 10.31**).

◆ Click the region with the Grabber tool (**Figure 10.32**).

To select adjacent regions in a track with the Selector tool:

1. Make sure Tab to Transients is disabled (**Figure 10.33**).

2. With the Selector tool, click in a track near the region you want to select.

3. Press Tab to move the cursor forward to the start boundary of the first region you want to select (**Figure 10.34**).

   or

   Press Option-Tab (Mac) or Ctrl-Tab (Windows) to move the cursor back to the end boundary of the last region you want to select.

4. Press Shift-Tab to select adjacent regions from left to right (**Figure 10.35**).

   or

   Press Shift-Option-Tab (Mac) or Shift-Ctrl-Tab (Windows) to select adjacent regions from right to left.

   Adjacent regions, and any time range between those regions, is selected.

SELECTING REGIONS

To select adjacent regions in a track with the Grabber tool:

1. Use the Grabber tool to click the first region.

2. Shift-click successive regions.

   Adjacent regions, and any time range between those regions, are selected (**Figure 10.36**).

To move a selection from a region to an adjacent region in a track:

1. Select a region.

2. Press Control-Tab (Mac) or Start-Tab (Windows) to move the selection to the next region (**Figure 10.37**).

   or

   Press Option-Control-Tab (Mac) or Ctrl-Start-Tab (Windows) to select the previous region.

To select all regions in a track:

◆ Triple-click anywhere in the track with the Selector tool.

To select all regions in all tracks:

1. In the Groups list, click the All group to enable it.

2. Triple-click anywhere in a track with the Selector tool.

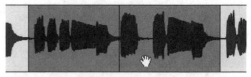

Figure 10.36 Shift-click adjacent regions with the Grabber to select them.

Figure 10.37 Press Control-Tab (Mac) or Start-Tab (Windows) to select the next region in a track.

Figure 10.38 The sync point for a region is indicated by a small triangle at the bottom of the region.

Figure 10.39 Use the Grabber tool to move the sync point in a region.

Setting Region Sync Points

Instead of aligning a region based on its start or end point, you can use a sync point to specify a point within the region for alignment.

Sync points can be useful for aligning notes with different attack characteristics, or for spotting sound effects on the timeline.

To set the sync point for a region:

1. Click the Slip button to enable Slip mode.

2. With the Selector tool, click in the region where you want add the sync point.

3. Choose Region > Identify Sync Point.

or

Press Command-comma (Mac) or Ctrl-comma (Windows).

A small arrow appears at the bottom of the region to indicate the location of the sync point (**Figure 10.38**).

To move a sync point:

◆ With the Grabber tool, click the sync point arrow and drag it to another location within the region (**Figure 10.39**).

To remove a sync point from a region:

1. With the Grabber tool, select the region.

2. Choose Region > Remove Sync Point.

or

Option-click (Mac) or Alt-click (Windows) the sync point with the Grabber tool.

Placing Regions

You can place regions in tracks by dragging
them from the Regions list to the Tracks area
of the Edit window. The Edit mode determines how regions behave when you place
them in tracks.

To place a region in a track:

◆ Drag a region from the Regions list to a
location in the track (**Figure 10.40**).

Placing multiple regions

When placing multiple regions from the
Regions list in the Tracks area, you have the
option of placing each region in its own track,
or putting all regions in a single track.

To set the order in which multiple regions are placed:

◆ Choose Regions list > Timeline Drop
Order and select Top to Bottom or Left
to Right.

To place multiple regions in new tracks:

1. Choose Regions list > Timeline Drop
Order > Top to Bottom.

2. Select multiple regions in the Regions list.

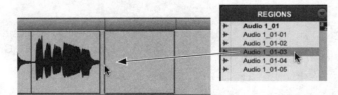

Figure 10.40 Drag a region from the Regions
list to place it in a track.

3. Drag the regions to an empty part of the Tracks area (**Figure 10.41**).

   or

   Drag the regions to the Tracks list.

To place multiple regions in a single new track:

1. Choose Regions list > Timeline Drop Order > Left to Right.

2. Select multiple regions in the Regions list.

3. Drag the regions to an empty part of the Tracks area (**Figure 10.42**).

   or

   Drag the regions to the Tracks list.

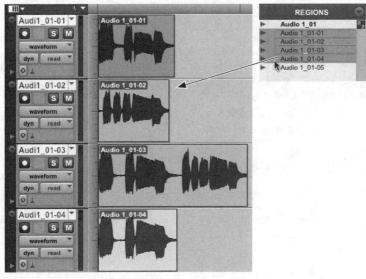

Figure 10.41 Drag multiple regions from the Regions list to the Tracks area to place each region in new tracks.

Figure 10.42 Drag multiple regions from the Regions list to the Tracks area to place the regions sequentially in a new track.

Slipping Regions

In Slip mode, you can move regions freely within and between tracks without causing surrounding material to move.

In this mode, regions can be moved to overlap or to have space between them.

Figure 10.43 In Slip mode, use the Grabber tool to drag a region to a new location.

To slip a region:

1. Click the Slip button to enter Slip mode.

2. With the Grabber tool, drag the region to another location in any track of the same type.

   The region moves to the new location, and a gap is left at the original location (**Figure 10.43**).

To slip a copy of a region:

1. Click the Slip button to enter Slip mode.

2. With the Grabber tool, Option-drag (Mac) or Alt-drag (Windows) the region to another location in any track of the same type.

   A copy of the region is moved to the new location, and the original remains in place.

Figure 10.44
Two overlapping regions, with the top region on the right showing a clipped corner to indicate overlap.

Controlling Region Overlap

In Slip mode, you can position regions so that they overlap. When this occurs, the top region obscures the overlapped audio or MIDI data in the bottom region.

You can set Pro Tools to display a visual indication of region overlap, so you can tell at a glance which region is on top.

You can also change the order of overlapped regions to select which region is on top.

To display region overlap:

◆ Choose View > Region > Overlap.

The top region shows a clipped corner to indicate overlap (**Figure 10.44**).

To change the order of overlapped regions:

1. Select the region to reorder.

2. Choose Region > Bring to Front.
   or
   Choose Region > Send to Back.

Shuffling Regions

In Shuffle mode, when you move a region, it snaps to the boundaries of surrounding regions, causing the other regions to move, or "shuffle."

The relative timing of surrounding regions is preserved, so that any space between regions or overlap is maintained when they shuffle.

To shuffle regions:

1. Click the Shuffle button to enter Shuffle mode.

2. With the Grabber tool, drag a region to the boundary of another region in any track of the same type.

   The region moves to the new location, where later regions move to the right to accommodate it. In the original location, regions move to the left to close up the gap (**Figure 10.45**).

Excluding Shuffle mode

Because even small edits to a region in Shuffle mode can affect the timing of all subsequent regions in a track, it is important to use Shuffle mode with caution.

To avoid inadvertently entering Shuffle mode, you can temporarily lock it out.

To lock out Shuffle mode:

◆ From any other Edit mode, Command-click (Mac) or Ctrl-click (Windows) the Shuffle button.

   The Shuffle button displays a lock icon to indicate that it is locked out (**Figure 10.46**).

To unlock Shuffle mode:

◆ Command-click (Mac) or Ctrl-click (Windows) the locked Shuffle button.

Figure 10.45 In Shuffle mode, use the Grabber to drag a region to another region boundary.

Figure 10.46 Command-click (Mac) or Ctrl-click (Windows) the Shuffle button to lock out Shuffle mode. The Shuffle button displays a lock.

SHUFFLING REGIONS

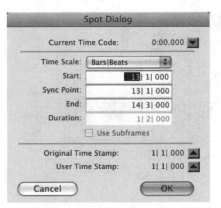

Figure 10.47 In Spot mode, choose a time scale and enter location information for the region.

Spotting Regions

In Spot mode, instead of moving regions in the Edit window with an Edit tool, you enter location information for them. This lets you specify the exact position of regions in relation to a time scale.

To spot a region:

1. Click the Spot button to enter Spot mode.

2. Drag a region from the Regions list into a track.

   or

   With the Grabber tool, click a region in a track.

   The Spot dialog appears (**Figure 10.47**).

3. In the Spot dialog, choose the time scale to use for spotting from the pop-up menu.

4. Enter a value for the Start, Sync Point, or End of the region you are spotting.

   The region moves to the new location.

Restoring regions to their original locations

You can use Spot mode to restore moved regions to their original locations. When a region is created, it is given a permanent time stamp that stores its original location in the session. The Spot dialog lets you locate a region to this location.

To restore a region to its original location:

1. Click the Spot button to enter Spot mode.

2. With the Grabber tool, click the region you want to restore.

3. In the Spot dialog, click the arrow next to the Original Time Stamp value.

   The Start Time updates to the Original Time Stamp value.

4. Click OK.

Aligning Regions

When placing or moving regions in the Edit window, you can align the start, end, or sync point of a region with the start point of a region on another track.

To align a region in a track with the start point of a region in another track:

1. With the Grabber tool, select the region in a track to which you want to align (**Figure 10.48**).

2. Do one of the following:
   - ▲ To align the start point, Control-click (Mac) or Start-click (Windows) the region you want to align (**Figure 10.49**).
   - ▲ To align the end point, Command-Control-click (Mac) or Ctrl-Start-click (Windows) the region you want to align.

     or
   - ▲ To align the sync point, Control-Shift-click (Mac) or Start-Shift-click (Windows) the region you want to align.

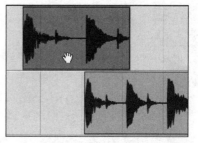

Figure 10.48 Click with the Grabber tool to select the region to which you want to align.

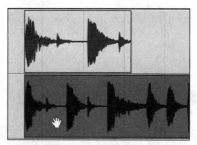

Figure 10.49 Control-click (Mac) or Start-click (Windows) the region whose start point you want to align.

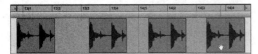

Figure 10.50 Click with the Grabber tool to select the regions to quantize.

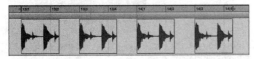

Figure 10.51 Quantized regions move to the nearest grid line.

Quantizing Regions

The Quantize Regions command aligns the start points or sync points of audio and MIDI regions to grid lines.

This command does not quantize the contents of regions, such as MIDI notes or Elastic Audio events. To quantize these elements, use the Quantize page of the Event Operations window. See Chapter 12, "Editing MIDI."

To quantize regions to the grid:

1. With the Selector or Grabber tool, select the regions to quantize (**Figure 10.50**).

2. Choose Region > Quantize to Grid.

   or

   Press Command-0 (zero) (Mac) or Ctrl-0 (zero) (Windows).

   The selected regions move to the nearest grid boundary (**Figure 10.51**).

Nudging Regions

You can use the Nudge feature to move regions in small increments using the Plus and Minus keys on the numeric keypad. For more information on the Nudge feature, see "Setting Grid and Nudge Values" in Chapter 9.

The amount by which regions are nudged is determined by the Nudge setting.

To set the Nudge value:

◆ In the Edit Toolbar, click the Nudge value selector and select an amount (**Figure 10.52**).

To nudge a region:

1. With the Selector tool or the Grabber tool, select the region to nudge.

2. To move the region ahead by the Nudge value, press the Plus key on the numeric keypad (**Figure 10.53**).

   or

   To move the region back by the Nudge value, press the Minus key on the numeric keypad.

Nudging the contents of a region

If the start and end points of a region are located correctly in a track, but the material in the region does not align properly in the session, you can nudge the contents of the region without changing its start and end points.

To nudge the contents of a region:

1. With the Selector tool or the Grabber tool, select the region with content to nudge.

2. To move the contents of the region ahead by the Nudge value, press Control-Plus (Mac) or Start-Plus (Windows) (**Figure 10.54**).

   or

   To move the contents of the region back by the Nudge value, press Control-Minus (Mac) or Start-Minus (Windows).

Figure 10.52 Click the Nudge value selector to select a Nudge amount.

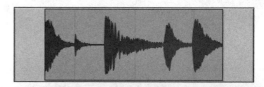

Figure 10.53 Nudging a region.

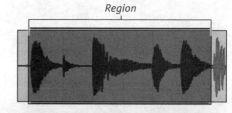

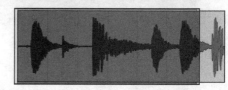

Figure 10.54 Nudging the contents of a region.

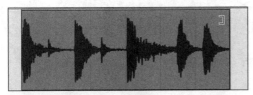

Figure 10.55 With the Standard Trimmer tool, move the cursor over a region boundary.

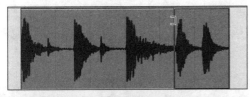

Figure 10.56 Drag with the Standard Trimmer tool to adjust the region boundary.

Trimming Regions

Pro Tools provides powerful features for *trimming* or changing the length of regions. You can trim a region in two ways: by hiding or revealing data, or by time-expanding or time-compressing data.

When you trim a region, the behavior of other regions in the track follows the current Edit mode. In Shuffle mode, other regions move to compensate for the change in region length. In Slip and Spot modes, other regions do not move, but extra space or overlap may result. In Grid mode, the trimmed region boundaries are constrained by the grid.

Trimming regions by hiding or revealing data

The most common method of trimming regions is to adjust region boundaries to hide or reveal data in the track playlist. You can adjust region boundaries with the Standard Trimmer tool or with the Trim Region command.

To trim a region with the Standard Trimmer:

1. Click the Trimmer tool and choose the Standard Trimmer.

2. Move the cursor over the start or end of a region.

   The cursor turns into the Standard Trimmer (**Figure 10.55**).

3. Drag with the Standard Trimmer to move the region boundary.

   The region boundaries move to hide or reveal audio or MIDI data (**Figure 10.56**).

To trim a region to a selection:

1. With the Selector tool, drag to select the part of the region you want to keep (**Figure 10.57**).

2. Choose Edit > Trim Region > To Selection.
   or
   Press Command-T (Mac) or Ctrl-T (Windows).
   Region material outside the selection is trimmed (**Figure 10.58**).

To trim a region to the edit cursor:

1. With the Selector tool, click in the region you want to trim (**Figure 10.59**).

2. Do one of the following:
   ▲ To trim the region from its start point to the edit cursor, choose Edit > Trim Region > Start To Insertion (**Figure 10.60**).
   or
   ▲ To trim the region from the edit cursor to its end point, choose Edit > Trim Region > End to Insertion.

To fill gaps between regions:

1. With the Selector tool, drag to select across the gap between two or more regions (**Figure 10.61**).

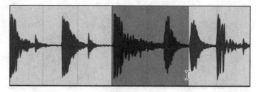

Figure 10.57 Drag with the Selector tool to select the material for the region.

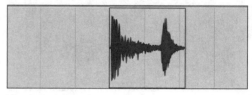

Figure 10.58 A region trimmed from the selection.

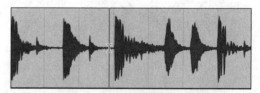

Figure 10.59 Click with the Selector tool to set the trim point.

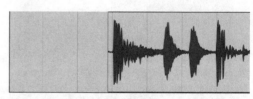

Figure 10.60 A region trimmed from its start point to the Edit cursor.

Figure 10.61 Drag with the Selector tool to select the gap between regions.

Figure 10.62 Regions expanded to fill the gap between them.

Figure 10.63 With the TCE Trimmer tool, move the cursor over a region boundary.

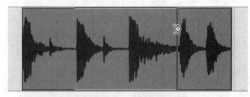

Figure 10.64 Drag with the TCE Trimmer tool to adjust the region boundary.

✔ Tip

■ If you have a third-party Time Compresson/Expansion plug-in installed, you can use it with the TCE Trimmer. Choose Setup > Preferences and click Preferences, then choose a plug-in from the TC/E Plug-In pop-up menu.

2. Do one of the following:

▲ To expand region start points backward, choose Edit > Trim Region > Start to Fill Selection.

▲ To expand region end points forward, choose Edit > Trim Region > End to Fill Selection.

or

▲ To expand both region start and end points, choose Edit > Trim Region > To Fill Selection (**Figure 10.62**).

Trimming regions by time-compressing or time-expanding data

When you trim a region with the Time Compression/Expansion (TCE) Trimmer, you are modifying the displayed audio or MIDI data to fit it within the specified range. The TCE Trimmer automatically invokes the Time Compression/Expansion AudioSuite plug-in to process the trimmed audio.

To trim a region with the TCE Trimmer:

1. Click the Trimmer tool and choose the TCE Trimmer.

2. Move the cursor over the start or end of a region.

The cursor turns into the TCE Trimmer (**Figure 10.63**).

3. Drag with the TCE Trimmer to move the region boundary.

Audio data is time-compressed or expanded, or MIDI note lengths are adjusted to fit the new region length (**Figure 10.64**).

Cutting, Copying, Pasting, and Deleting Regions

You can perform standard editing commands on regions. As with selections in Pro Tools, the effect of these commands depends on the current track view.

When you are editing in any of a track's Master views, cut, copy, paste, and delete operations include all underlying automation or controller data. In all other views, only the data displayed in the view is affected.

The Master views for each track type are as follows:

◆ Audio tracks: Waveform view and Block view

◆ MIDI and Instrument tracks: Region view, Block view, and Notes view

To cut or copy a region:

1. With the Selector or Grabber tool, select the region.

2. Do one of the following:

   ▲ To remove the selected region, choose Edit > Cut.

   or

   ▲ To leave the selected region in place and copy it, choose Edit > Copy.

To paste a region:

1. Click with the cursor where you want to paste the region.

   or

   With the Selector or Grabber tool, select a region to replace.

2. Choose Edit > Paste.

To delete a region:

1. With the Selector or Grabber tool, select the region.

2. Choose Edit > Clear.

   or

   Press Delete.

Duplicating and Repeating Regions

You can quickly copy a region or edit selection and place one or more copies in the track next to the original region or selection.

If you are working with bar- and beat-based material, make sure the Main Time Scale is set to Bars|Beats before you select the material to be copied.

When you duplicate or repeat a region or selection, the behavior of other regions in the track follows the current Edit mode.

To duplicate a selection or region:

1. With the Selector tool, double-click the region you want to duplicate (**Figure 10.65**).

   or

   With the Selector tool, drag to select the material you want to duplicate.

2. Choose Edit > Duplicate.

   or

   Press Command-D (Mac) or Ctrl-D (Windows).

   The duplicate region appears immediately after the original selection or region (**Figure 10.66**).

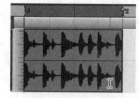

Figure 10.65
Use the Selector tool to select the material to duplicate or repeat.

Figure 10.66 The duplicated region is placed immediately after the original selection in the track.

To repeat a selection or region:

1. With the Selector tool, double-click the region you want to repeat (Figure 10.65).

   or

   With the Selector tool, drag to select the material you want to repeat.

2. Choose Edit > Repeat.

   or

   Press Option-R (Mac) or Alt-R (Windows). The Repeat dialog appears.

3. Type the number of times to repeat the region or selection.

4. Click OK.

   The repeated regions appear immediately after the original selection or region (**Figure 10.67**).

Figure 10.67 The repeated regions are placed immediately after the original selection in the track.

Locking Regions

You can prevent regions from being edited or being moved in the timeline.

Time Locking regions

To prevent a region from being inadvertently moved in the timeline, you can Time Lock the region. This keeps it from being moved as a result of accidental edits or Shuffle mode operations.

To Time Lock a region:

1. With the Grabber tool, select the region to lock.

2. Choose Region > Time Lock/Unlock.

   A hollow lock icon appears in the lower left of the region to indicate that it is Time Locked (**Figure 10.68**).

Edit Locking regions

To prevent a region from being edited in other ways, you can Edit Lock the region. This keeps it from being moved and from being inadvertently cut, separated, or trimmed.

To Edit lock a region:

1. With the Grabber tool, select the region to lock.

2. Choose Region > Edit Lock/Unlock.

   A solid lock icon appears in the lower left of the region to indicate that it is Edit Locked (**Figure 10.69**).

Figure 10.68 A Time-locked region is prevented from being moved in the timeline.

Figure 10.69 An Edit-locked region is prevented from being edited or moved in the timeline.

Figure 10.70 To show the Regions list, click the horizontal arrow at the bottom right of the Edit window.

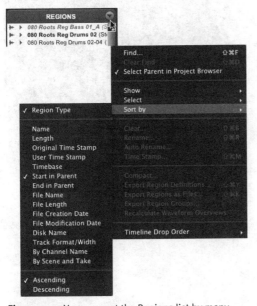

Figure 10.71 You can sort the Regions list by many different criteria such as file type, name, length, and time stamp.

Managing Regions with the Regions List

The Regions list in the Edit window shows all the available Audio regions, MIDI regions, and region groups in the session, even if they are not used in tracks.

The Regions list provides commands for viewing, sorting, and managing regions in the session.

To show the Regions list:

◆ At the bottom right of the Edit window, click the horizontal arrow (**Figure 10.70**).

Sorting regions

You can sort the Regions list by many different criteria, including type (Audio, MIDI, or region group), name, length, and time stamp.

To sort the Regions list:

1. Click the Regions list menu button and choose Sort By (**Figure 10.71**).

2. From the submenu, do any of the following:

   ▲ Choose whether to sort by Region type.

   ▲ Choose whether to list regions in Ascending or Descending order.

   or

   ▲ Choose the criterion for sorting the list.

Showing or hiding regions

You can filter the display of regions in the Regions list by showing or hiding different regions types (Audio, MIDI, or region group), and by showing or hiding auto-created regions.

You can also determine which region attributes to show in the list, including file type, file name, file path name, and processing status.

To show or hide regions in the Regions list:

1. Click the Regions list menu button and choose Show (**Figure 10.72**).

2. From the submenu, do either of the following:

    ▲ Choose to show or hide Audio regions, MIDI regions, region groups, or auto-created regions.

    or

    ▲ Choose to show or hide any of the attributes of regions.

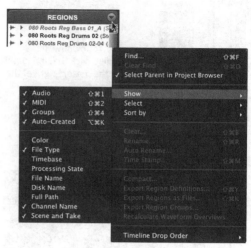

Figure 10.72 You can show or hide region types in the Regions list, and choose to display various attributes in the list.

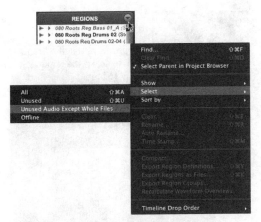

Figure 10.73 To remove unused regions from a session, choose Select > Unused Audio Except Whole Files from the Regions list menu, and click Remove. Be careful not to delete whole-file regions or regions used in tracks.

Removing unused regions

In the course of editing a session, you can accumulate a large number of unused regions in the Regions list. If a region is not used in a track, you can remove it from the session.

◆ Removing a MIDI region permanently deletes the MIDI data from the session, and cannot be undone.

◆ Removing an audio region permanently deletes the region from the session, and cannot be undone. Removing a region does not delete the source audio file from the hard drive.

Note: If you remove a whole-file audio region from a session, Pro Tools gives you the option of deleting the source audio file from the hard drive. Before clicking Delete, make sure you want to erase the source audio.

To remove unused regions in the Regions list:

1. Click the Regions list menu button and choose Select.

2. In the submenu, choose Unused Audio Except Whole Files (**Figure 10.73**).

3. Click the Regions list menu button and choose Clear.

4. Click Remove.

   The unused regions are removed from the Regions list and the session.

Looping Regions

Pro Tools provides a powerful way to work with repeated audio and MIDI regions using *region loops*. Region loops allow more options for editing than using the Repeat command to repeat regions.

There are three main ways to specify region looping: number of loops, overall loop length, or loop to fill a range in the session.

You can loop regions on multiple tracks at the same time. You can also loop region groups.

To loop a region:

1. Use the Grabber tool to select the audio region, MIDI region, or region group to loop (**Figure 10.74**).

2. Choose Region > Loop.

   The Region Looping dialog appears (**Figure 10.75**).

3. In the Region Looping dialog, do one of the following:

   ▲ Select Number of Loops and type the number of times to loop the region.

   ▲ Select Loop Length and type the duration of the loop.

   or

   ▲ Select Loop Until End of the Session or Next Region.

Figure 10.74 Use the Grabber tool to select the region you want to loop.

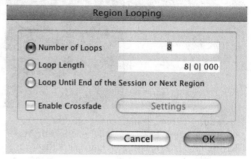

Figure 10.75 Determine how to loop the region with the Region Looping dialog.

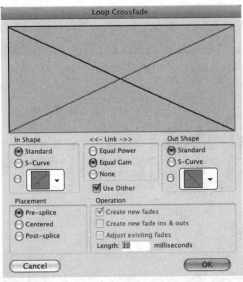

Figure 10.76 Creating crossfades between loops can help smooth the sound of the region loop.

Figure 10.77 A region loop showing the loop icon in each iteration.

4. To add a crossfade between loop iterations, select Enable Crossfade.

For more information on creating crossfades, see Chapter 11, "Editing Audio."

5. In the Loop Crossfade dialog, select crossfade options and click OK (**Figure 10.76**).

6. In the Region Looping dialog, click OK.

The region is looped in the track, with each loop iteration showing a loop icon (**Figure 10.77**).

To unloop regions:

1. Select the region loop.

2. Choose Region > Unloop.

3. Do one of the following:
   ▲ To remove all loop iterations and revert to the original region, click Remove.

   or

   ▲ To convert the loop iterations to individual regions, click Flatten.

Editing Region Loops

Region loops can be edited as a group or as individual regions.

As a group, a region loop can be selected and edited in the same way as a single region, including renaming, cutting, copying and pasting, moving, duplicating, or quantizing.

As individual regions, looped iterations can be edited, but they will no longer remain part of the region loop.

To select an entire region loop:

◆ With the Grabber tool, click in the region loop (**Figure 10.78**).

To select an individual region within the region loop:

◆ With the Grabber tool, click the loop icon of an individual region (**Figure 10.79**).

Figure 10.78 Select an entire region loop by clicking in the region with the Grabber tool.

Figure 10.79 Select an individual region in a region loop by clicking its loop icon with the Grabber tool.

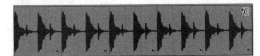

Figure 10.80 With the Standard Trimmer tool, move the cursor over the top half of the region loop boundary, so it turns into the Loop Trimmer.

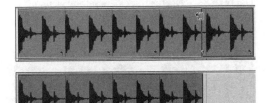

Figure 10.81 Drag with the Loop Trimmer to adjust the region loop boundary.

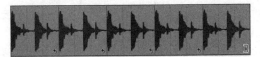

Figure 10.82 With the Standard Trimmer tool, move the cursor over the bottom half of the region loop boundary.

Figure 10.83 Drag with the Trimmer to adjust the size of the individual region.

Trimming region loops

You can trim region loops by changing the overall length of the loop, or by changing the length of the individual regions.

To trim the length of a region loop:

1. Click the Trimmer tool and choose the Standard Trimmer.

2. Move the cursor over the start or end of the region loop, keeping it in the top half of the track.

   The cursor turns into the Loop Trimmer (**Figure 10.80**).

3. Drag with the Loop Trimmer to move the region loop boundary.

   The region loop boundaries move to hide or reveal iterations of the loop (**Figure 10.81**).

To trim the individual regions of a region loop:

1. Click the Trimmer tool and choose the Standard Trimmer.

2. Move the cursor over the start or end of the region loop, keeping it over the bottom half of the track (**Figure 10.82**).

3. Drag with the Trimmer to resize the region.

   All individual regions resize automatically and the number of iterations changes to fill the original region loop (**Figure 10.83**).

EDITING REGION LOOPS

Creating Region Groups

Pro Tools lets you collect audio and MIDI regions together in region groups. You can create region groups across multiple Audio, MIDI or Instrument tracks. This can be helpful for organizing takes or related parts in a session.

Region groups behave just like regions in most situations: You can place, move and edit region groups as if they were single regions. Region groups appear along with regions in the Regions list.

You can select any area to include in a region group, including multiple tracks of different types, empty space between regions, and partial regions. You can also nest region groups by including existing region groups in a new region group.

To create a region group:

1. Select the track material to include in the region group (**Figure 10.84**).

2. Choose Region > Group.

   The selected material appears in the track as a region group, and the region group is added to the Regions list. A region group icon appears in the bottom left of the group (**Figure 10.85**).

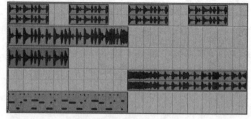

Figure 10.84 Select the track material you want to include in the region group.

Figure 10.85 A region group showing the region group icon to the bottom left of the group.

To ungroup a region group:

1. Select the region group.

2. Choose Region > Ungroup.

   The selected group is removed and its group members are revealed.

To ungroup all region groups in a selection:

1. Select the region group.

2. Choose Region > Ungroup All.

To restore a region group:

1. Select any region that was in the group.

2. Choose Region > Regroup.

Editing Region Groups

Region groups can be edited in the same way as a single region, including renaming, cutting, copying and pasting, moving, duplicating, quantizing, and trimming.

Editing individual regions in a region group

When you trim a region group with the Trimmer tool or a Trim Region command, the region group boundary is trimmed, not individual region boundaries. To trim an individual region, you need to temporarily ungroup the regions.

In addition, certain edit operations will create new regions that will not be included in the region group, including:

◆ Any AudioSuite processing of a grouped region, including use of the TCE Trimmer

◆ Consolidation of any grouped regions

◆ Recording of any new material into a region group

◆ Any redrawing of audio waveforms with the Pencil tool

To keep these edited regions in the region group, you need to temporarily ungroup the regions.

To edit individual regions in a region group:

1. Select the region group.

2. Choose Region > Ungroup.

3. Carry out the edit on the individual region.

4. Choose Region > Regroup.

11

EDITING AUDIO

In addition to the many operations you can perform on all types of regions, Pro Tools offers powerful features specifically for editing audio.

Nearly all audio editing in Pro Tools is non-destructive. When you edit audio regions, the original audio file is unchanged. Only when you edit an audio waveform at the sample level are changes applied permanently.

This chapter covers editing features that are unique to audio, including viewing and editing audio waveforms, creating and editing fades, and track compositing.

Viewing Audio Waveforms

You can display audio tracks in the Edit window in several ways. The most common way to view and work with audio is in Waveform view, in which regions show the amplitude of the audio in graphical form (**Figure 11.1**). You can also view audio in Blocks view, which shows only region information such as name or start time (**Figure 11.2**).

Audio tracks can also show automation views for Volume, Pan, and Mute. For more information on automation, see Chapter 15, "Automating Mix Controls"

To set the track view:

◆ Click the Track View selector and choose a view from the pop-up menu (**Figure 11.3**).

Setting the waveform overview

Waveforms can be displayed in the following ways.

Peak view (**Figure 11.4**) shows the peak level of the audio signal at each sample location, allowing for accurate display of maximum level and any occurrences of clipping. This is the default display setting. Peak view is always shown during recording, and when zoomed in to the sample level.

Power view (**Figure 11.5**) shows the RMS (root mean square) value of the audio signal over time, which can be more predictive of a track's overall level. This view can be useful for visual comparisons of mixdowns. Power view is calculated only after recording is stopped.

To set the waveform overview display:

◆ Choose View > Waveforms and select Peak or Power.

Figure 11.1
A stereo audio region shown in Waveform view.

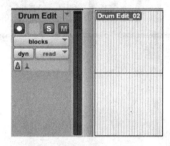

Figure 11.2
A stereo audio region shown in Block view.

Figure 11.3 Click the Track View selector to set the track view.

Figure 11.4
An audio region with the waveform overview set to Peak view.

Figure 11.5
The same audio region with the waveform overview set to Power view.

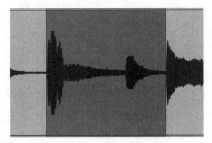

Figure 11.6 Make selections so that they start and end before audio volume peaks.

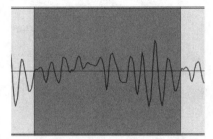

Figure 11.7 Make selections that start and end at zero crossings to prevent pops and clicks. To do this, it's helpful to zoom in to the sample level, as shown here.

Editing Audio Waveforms

When you are editing audio, whether copying and pasting data, creating new regions, or trimming existing regions, the following techniques are helpful for making smooth edits.

When you select audio in Waveform view, it's best to make selections that start and end before volume peaks in the material, at areas of low amplitude (**Figure 11.6**). This can prevent audible changes in sonic character in the middle of notes.

If you are editing rhythmic material, you can use the Tab to Transients feature to make selections that start and end at volume peaks. Regions created in this manner can then be placed at bar and beat boundaries in the session. See "Extending Selections" in Chapter 9.

Also, when selecting audio waveforms, try to make selections that start and end at *zero crossings*, or points where the waveform crosses the center line (**Figure 11.7**). This helps prevent audible clicks or pops at region transitions.

✔ Tip

■ It's often helpful to zoom in to the sample level to choose edit points at zero crossings. The default Zoom Preset number 5 zooms the display to the sample level. See "Zooming Tracks" in Chapter 5.

Repairing Audio Waveforms

Pro Tools let you repair clicks or pops in an audio waveform by redrawing them at the sample level with the Pencil tool.

Waveform editing with the Pencil tool is always destructive, because you are editing the source audio file. Before you attempt a repair, make a backup of the original audio by using the AudioSuite Duplicate plug-in to copy the region you are working in.

Figure 11.8 An audio waveform zoomed in to the sample level, showing a click.

Figure 11.9 Repairing a click with the Pencil tool.

To repair an audio waveform with the Pencil tool:

1. Find the problem area by auditioning the region. Use the Scrubber tool to move back and forth over the area.

2. Zoom in to the sample level, where the waveform changes to a single line (**Figure 11.8**).

   The Pencil tool becomes available for waveform editing.

3. With the Pencil tool, drag over the part of the waveform you want to repair. Try to preserve the slope of the line on either side of the edit (**Figure 11.9**).

4. Audition the edit, and if necessary, choose Edit > Undo and try the edit again.

✔ Tip

■ You should only make small edits with the Pencil tool, and try to maintain the overall shape of the waveform you are modifying. If you redraw a significant portion of a waveform, you will likely introduce noise.

REPAIRING AUDIO WAVEFORMS

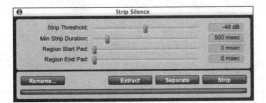

Figure 11.10 The Strip Silence window.

Stripping Silence from Regions

In audio tracks, you will often have regions with large stretches of silence (or low-level noise) in between sections of audio program material. Pro Tools lets you use the Strip Silence command to automatically remove these areas of silence. This process divides the original regions into smaller regions that can be moved, quantized, or edited separately.

To strip silence from an audio selection:

1. Select the area where you want to remove silence.

2. Choose Edit > Strip Silence.

   The Strip Silence window appears (**Figure 11.10**).

3. Adjust the Strip Threshold control to determine the signal level (from −96 to 0 dB) below which audio is considered silence.

   As Pro Tools detects audio above this threshold, it is indicated by rectangles within the selection (**Figure 11.11**).

continues on next page

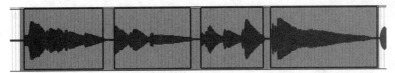

Figure 11.11 Audio above the Strip Silence threshold is indicated in tracks by rectangles in the selection.

4. Adjust the Minimum Strip Duration control to determine the minimum length of audio events (from 0 to 4,000 milliseconds), below which they are considered silence.

As this duration is adjusted, the number and size of the rectangles changes.

5. Adjust the Region Start Pad or Region End Pad controls (Figure 11.10) to fine-tune the rectangles and preserve the attack or decay of sounds.

As these controls are adjusted, the size of the rectangles changes.

6. Click Strip.

New audio regions are created from the material indicated by the rectangles, and the material outside the rectangles is removed (**Figure 11.12**). The new regions appear in the Regions list.

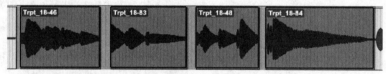

Figure 11.12 The Strip Silence command removes audio below the threshold and creates new audio regions.

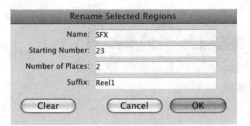

Figure 11.13 Rename audio regions created with the Strip Silence command.

Figure 11.14 Renumbered regions in the Regions list.

Renaming regions created with Strip Silence

The Strip Silence window includes a Rename option that lets you automatically name regions after they have been created with the Strip Silence command.

To rename regions created with Strip Silence:

1. In the Strip Silence window, click Rename.

   The Rename Selected Regions dialog opens (**Figure 11.13**).

2. In the Name field, type the base name to use for all auto-created regions.

3. In the Starting Number field, type the start number for sequential numbering.

4. In the Number of Places field, type the number of digits to be used for sequential numbering.

5. In the Suffix field, type any characters you want to append to each region name, such as a reel or take number.

6. Click OK.

   The regions are renamed, with the Number field incrementing automatically. The new names appear in the Regions list (**Figure 11.14**).

Creating Fades and Crossfades

Pro Tools lets you add fades and crossfades to audio regions. A *fade* is a volume curve that applied to the beginning (fade-in) or end (fade-out) of a region (**Figure 11.15**). A *crossfade* is a simultaneous fade-out of one audio region and fade-in of an adjoining region (**Figure 11.16**). You can add fades and crossfades to audio regions, region groups, and looped regions.

Fades are created as separate files and stored in the Fade Files folder inside the Session folder.

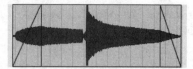

Figure 11.15 A region with a fade-in at its beginning and a fade-out at its end.

Figure 11.16 Two regions with a crossfade between them.

The Fades Dialog

The Fades dialog (**Figure 11.17**) includes the following controls.

Audition lets you preview a fade or crossfade.

Fade Curves Only displays the fade curves without showing the audio waveform.

Fade Curves and Separate Waveforms displays fade curves along with separate views of the fade-in and fade-out waveforms.

Fade Curves and Superimposed Waveforms displays fade curves along with superimposed views of the fade-in and fade-out waveforms.

Fade Curves and Summed Waveform displays fade curves and a single waveform representing a summed version of the cross-faded audio.

Zoom In and **Zoom Out** resize display of the audio waveform.

When you are applying fades to more than one track, or to a stereo track, the following buttons are also available.

View First Track shows the waveform for the first of the two tracks or channels.

View Second Track shows the waveform for the second of the two tracks or channels.

View Both Tracks shows the waveforms for both tracks or channels.

The following fade-in (or fade-out) curve shapes are available. Each of these shapes can be modified by dragging its end points.

Standard is a moderate curve for general-purpose use.

S-Curve inverts at the start and end to make fade-ins faster and fade-outs slower.

Preset Curves lets you choose from seven different curves (**Figure 11.18**).

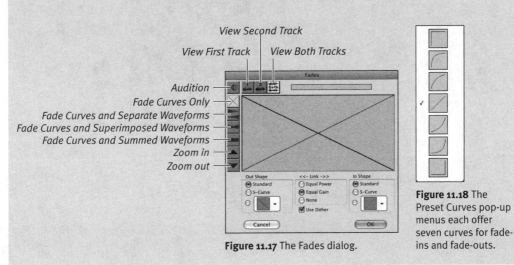

Figure 11.18 The Preset Curves pop-up menus each offer seven curves for fade-ins and fade-outs.

Figure 11.17 The Fades dialog.

Creating fade-ins and fade-outs

You create fades to shape the attacks and releases of regions. Fades of any length can be within a single region.

To create a fade-in:

1. Select the beginning of the region to fade in. The selection must extend to the start of the region or to an empty area before the region (**Figure 11.19**).

2. Choose Edit > Fades > Create.

   or

   Press Command-F (Mac) or Ctrl-F (Windows).

   The Fades dialog appears (Figure 11.17).

3. Choose an In Shape.

4. Click the Audition button to play the fade.

5. Adjust the fade curve by dragging it in the Fades dialog (**Figure 11.20**).

6. Click OK.

   The fade is applied and its curve appears in the region (**Figure 11.21**).

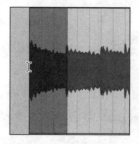

Figure 11.19 To create a fade-in, select to the start of a region or into an empty area before the region.

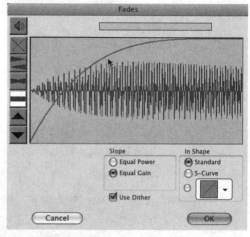

Figure 11.20 After selecting a fade curve, you can adjust it by dragging it in the Fades dialog.

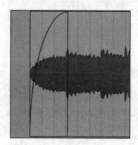

Figure 11.21 A fade-in applied to a region.

CREATING FADES AND CROSSFADES

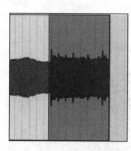

Figure 11.22 To create a fade-out, select to the end of a region or into an empty area after the region.

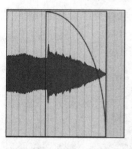

Figure 11.23 A fade-out applied to a region.

To create a fade-out:

1. Select the end of the region to fade out. The selection must extend to the end of the region or to an empty area after the region (**Figure 11.22**).

2. Choose Edit > Fades > Create.
   or
   Press Command-F (Mac) or Ctrl-F (Windows).
   The Fades dialog appears (Figure 11.17).

3. Choose an Out Shape.

4. Click the Audition button to play the fade.

5. Adjust the fade curve by dragging it in the Fades dialog.

6. Click OK.
   The fade is applied and its curve appears in the region (**Figure 11.23**).

CREATING FADES AND CROSSFADES

Creating crossfades

You create crossfades to smooth the transition between regions. Crossfades between regions can be created wherever there is the possibility of overlap. Additional material must be available beyond region boundaries, depending on the type of crossfade. The three types of crossfade include:

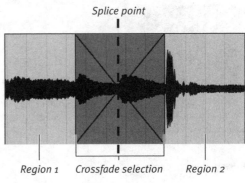

Splice point

Region 1   Crossfade selection   Region 2

Figure 11.24 A centered crossfade.

◆ **Centered crossfades** extend across both sides of the *splice point*, or the boundary between two regions (**Figure 11.24**). In a centered crossfade, the first region must have audio material beyond its end point, and the second region must have audio material before its start point.

◆ **Pre-splice crossfades** are created before the splice point (**Figure 11.25**), which maintains the volume at the very beginning of the second region. In a pre-splice crossfade, the second region must have material before its start point.

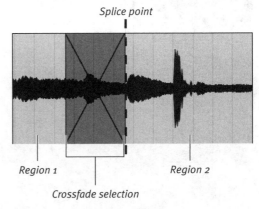

Splice point

Region 1   Region 2

Crossfade selection

Figure 11.25 A pre-splice crossfade.

◆ **Post-splice crossfades** are created after the splice point (**Figure 11.26**), which maintains the volume of the first region until its end. In a post-splice crossfade, the first region must have material after its end point.

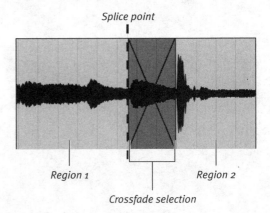

Splice point

Region 1   Region 2

Crossfade selection

Figure 11.26 A post-splice crossfade.

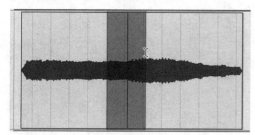

Figure 11.27 To create a crossfade, select an area across the boundary of two regions.

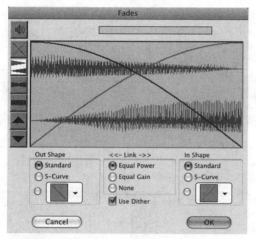

Figure 11.28 The Fades dialog showing controls for creating a crossfade.

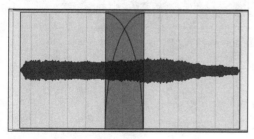

Figure 11.29 A crossfade applied across two regions.

To create a crossfade centered between two regions:

1. Select the area across the region boundary where you want to create the crossfade (**Figure 11.27**).

2. Choose Edit > Fades > Create.

   or

   Press Command-F (Mac) or Ctrl-F (Windows).

   The Fades dialog appears, showing the area where you want to create the crossfade (**Figure 11.28**).

3. Choose an Out Shape and an In Shape.

4. Select a Link option.

5. Click the Audition button to play the crossfade.

6. Adjust the fade curves by dragging them in the Fades dialog.

7. Click OK.

   A crossfade appears between the two selected regions (**Figure 11.29**).

To create a pre-splice or post-splice crossfade:

1. Click with the Selector tool before or after the region boundary where you want to create the crossfade.

2. Press Shift-Tab to extend the selection forward to the next region boundary (**Figure 11.30**).

   or

   Press Option-Shift-Tab (Mac) or Ctrl-Shift-Tab (Windows) to extend the selection back to the previous region boundary (**Figure 11.31**).

3. Choose Edit > Fades > Create.

   or

   Press Command-F (Mac) or Ctrl-F (Windows).

   The Fades dialog appears.

4. Choose an In Shape and Out Shape.

5. Select a Link option.

6. Click the Audition button to play the crossfade.

7. Adjust the fade curves by dragging them in the Fades dialog.

8. Click OK.

   A pre-splice or post-splice crossfade appears between the selected regions (**Figure 11.32**).

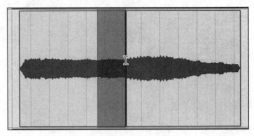

Figure 11.30 To create a pre-splice crossfade, select in the first region forward to the region boundary.

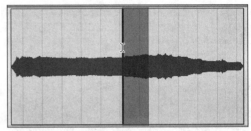

Figure 11.31 To create a post-splice crossfade, select in the second region back to the region boundary.

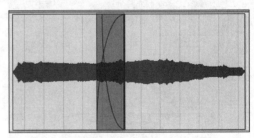

Figure 11.32 A pre-splice crossfade applied to a region.

Figure 11.33 Set defaults for the different fade types in the Edit Preferences.

Creating fades and crossfades with the Smart Tool

You can use the Smart Tool to quickly create fades and crossfades. The Default Fade settings used by the Smart Tool are set in the Editing preferences.

To set fade and crossfade preferences:

1. Choose Setup > Preferences and click Editing.

   The Fades area includes buttons for Default Fade Settings (**Figure 11.33**).

2. Click Fade In, set the Slope and In Shape, then click OK.

3. Click Fade Out, set the Slope and Out Shape, then click OK.

4. Click Crossfade, set the Linking, In Shape, and Out Shape, then click OK.

5. Click OK to close the Preferences dialog.

Linking Fade-in and Fade-out Curves

With crossfades, you can link the fade-in and fade-out curves so that when you adjust one fade curve, the other adjusts automatically. Linking curves can help smooth the transition between fade-ins and fade-outs of a crossfade. The options for linking fade-in and fade-out curves are as follows.

Equal Power is useful when crossfading between audio regions that are out of phase or differ in sound character. It can also help prevent volume dropouts that can occur with an Equal Gain crossfade.

Equal Gain is useful when crossfading between audio regions that are in phase or have similar or identical sound character (such as a drum loop). It can also help prevent the clipping that can occur when using an Equal Power crossfade.

None disables linking between the fade-in and fade-out curves so you can adjust them separately. When linking is disabled you can do the following:

◆ Option-drag (Mac) or Alt-drag (Windows) the fade-in curve to change its shape.

◆ Command-drag (Mac) or Ctrl-drag (Windows) the fade-out curve to change its shape.

◆ Drag the end points of the fade-in and fade-out curves to change their duration.

CREATING FADES AND CROSSFADES

To create a fade-in with the Smart Tool:

1. Click the Smart Tool to select it.

2. Move the cursor over the upper-left corner of the region to fade in.

   The cursor changes to a Fade tool (**Figure 11.34**).

3. Drag right from the left side of the region to set the length of the fade (**Figure 11.35**).

   A fade-in appears at the beginning of the region with the shape set according to the Fade In preference.

To create a fade-out with the Smart Tool:

1. Click the Smart Tool to select it.

2. Move the cursor over the upper-right corner of the region to fade out.

   The cursor changes to a Fade tool (**Figure 11.36**).

3. Drag left from the right side of the region to set the length of the fade (**Figure 11.37**).

   A fade-out appears at the end of the region with the shape set according to the Fade Out preference.

To create a crossfade with the Smart Tool:

1. Click the Smart Tool to select it.

2. Move the cursor over the bottom half of the boundary with another region.

   The cursor changes to a Crossfade tool (**Figure 11.38**).

3. Drag left or right from the region boundary to set the length of the crossfade (**Figure 11.39**).

   A crossfade appears over the region boundary with In and Out shapes set according to the Crossfade preference.

Figure 11.34 The Smart Tool changes to a Fade tool in the top-left corner of audio regions.

Figure 11.35 Creating a fade-in with the Smart Tool.

Figure 11.36 The Smart Tool changes to a Fade tool in the top-right corner of audio regions.

Figure 11.37 Creating a fade-out with the Smart Tool.

Figure 11.38 The Smart Tool changes to a Crossfade tool over the bottom half of region boundaries.

Figure 11.39 Creating a crossfade with the Smart Tool.

CREATING FADES AND CROSSFADES

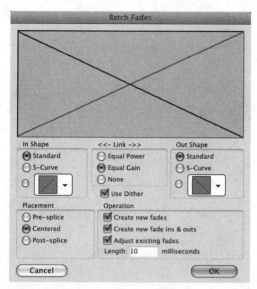

Figure 11.40 The Batch Fades dialog.

Creating Multiple Fades and Crossfades

Pro Tools lets you quickly create multiple fades and crossfades simultaneously. This makes it easy to smooth transitions between multiple audio regions in tracks with a lot of edits.

In the process of creating multiple fades or *batch fades,* you can set the properties that are applied to all fade-ins, fade-outs, and crossfades, and determine whether to create new fades, to adjust existing fades, or both.

To create multiple fades and crossfades:

1. Make a selection that includes all of the regions that require fades or crossfades.

2. Choose Edit > Fades > Create.

   or

   Press Command-F (Mac) or Ctrl-F (Windows).

   The Batch Fades dialog appears (**Figure 11.40**).

3. Under Placement, select the type of cross-fades to be created: Pre-splice, Centered, or Post-splice.

4. Under Operation, do one or more of the following:

   ▲ To create new crossfades at region boundaries that touch other regions, select "Create new fades."

   ▲ To create new fade-ins and fade-outs at region boundaries that do not touch other regions, select "Create new fade ins & outs."

   ▲ To adjust any existing fades to match the properties in the Batch Fades dialog, select "Adjust existing fades."

continues on next page

5. Type the length (in milliseconds) of the fades to be created.

6. Set the In Shape, Out Shape, and Link options to be used in creating the fades.

7. Adjust the fade curves by dragging them in the Fades dialog.

8. Click OK.

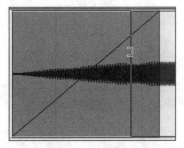

Figure 11.41 Trimming a fade with the Trimmer tool.

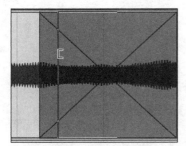

Figure 11.42 Trimming a crossfade with the Trimmer tool.

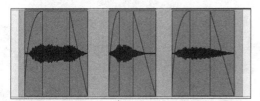

Figure 11.43 To remove fades, make a selection that includes the fades and choose Edit > Fades > Delete.

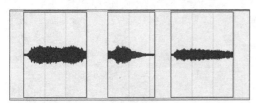

Figure 11.44 When you delete a fade, the underlying regions return to their previous state.

Editing Fades and Crossfades

After you have created a fade or crossfade, you can trim its length, modify its properties, or remove it to leave the underlying regions intact.

To trim a fade-in or fade-out:

1. Select the fade with the Grabber or Selector tool.

2. With the Trimmer tool, drag the inside edge of the fade to change its length in the region (**Figure 11.41**).

To trim a crossfade:

1. Select the crossfade with the Grabber or Selector tool.

2. With the Trimmer tool, drag the start or the end of the crossfade to change its length (**Figure 11.42**).

To modify a fade or crossfade:

1. With the Grabber tool, double-click the fade or crossfade you want to modify.

   The Fades dialog appears.

2. Modify the properties of the fade, such as Shape, Slope, or Link options.

3. Adjust the fade curves by dragging them in the Fades dialog.

4. Click OK.

To remove fades or crossfades:

1. Select the area of the track containing the fades or crossfades you want to delete (**Figure 11.43**).

2. Choose Edit > Fades > Delete.

   The fades or crossfades are removed and the underlying regions return to their previous state (**Figure 11.44**).

Compositing Tracks

Compositing or *comping* is the process of selecting the best portions from multiple takes and assembling them into a single performance. Using Playlist view to display, audition, and select material from each take, you can quickly comp together a track.

Displaying alternate takes

When loop recording, you can set Pro Tools to automatically display each take in a new playlist. Alternatively, you can expand looped takes to playlists after you are finished recording.

To automatically create new playlists while loop recording:

1. Choose Setup > Preferences and click Operation.

2. Under Recording, select Automatically Create New Playlists When Loop Recording.

3. Click OK.

To expand looped takes onto multiple playlists after recording:

1. Select the region that represents the final looped take.

2. With the Selector tool, Command-click (Mac) or Ctrl-click (Windows) the region and choose Expand Alternates To New Playlists from the pop-up menu (**Figure 11.45**).

✔ Tip

■ While track compositing is commonly done with loop recorded takes, you can use the same techniques with individually recorded takes by spotting them into playlists.

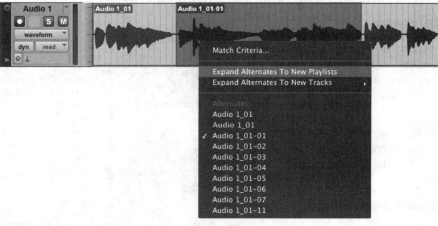

Figure 11.45 Expand alternate takes to new playlists after recording.

Viewing and auditioning takes

With the track set to Playlist view, you can organize alternate takes and resize playlist lanes.

Each playlist lane has a Solo button for auditioning a take. These buttons solo playlists in the track and have no effect on other tracks in the session.

To view multiple takes:

◆ Click the Track View selector and choose Playlist view to display the alternate playlists below the main playlist (**Figure 11.46**).

To reorder playlist lanes:

◆ Click the name of the alternate playlist and drag it up or down (**Figure 11.47**).

To resize playlist lanes:

◆ To resize all lanes along with the track, click on the amplitude scale of any lane and choose a Track Height setting (**Figure 11.48**).

or

To resize a single lane, Control-click (Mac) or Start-click (Windows) on the amplitude scale of the lane and choose a Track Height setting.

To audition multiple takes:

1. Start playback.

2. Click the Solo buttons on the track playlists to audition each take (**Figure 11.49**).

Assembling takes

As you audition selections of material in alternate playlists, you can copy and paste them to the main playlist to assemble the takes into a track.

Figure 11.46 Click the Track View selector and choose Playlist view to show alternate takes in playlists.

Figure 11.47 To reorder playlist lanes, drag them up or down in the playlist area.

Figure 11.48 To resize playlist lanes, drag their borders up or down.

Figure 11.49 To audition an alternate take, click its Solo button in Playlist view.

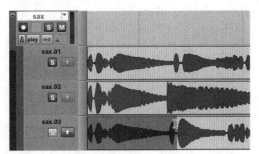

Figure 11.50 Select the portion of a take you want to use in the track.

Figure 11.51 Click the Copy Selection to Main Playlist button to move the selected portion of the take to main playlist of the track.

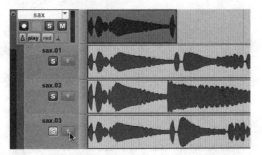

Figure 11.52 The selected portion of the take in the main playlist.

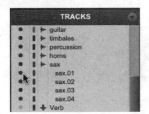

Figure 11.53 Show or hide individual playlists by clicking their Show/Hide icons in the Tracks list.

Pro Tools provides the following commands for copying and pasting selections from alternate playlists:

◆ **Copy Selection to Main Playlist** pastes the playlist selection over any material currently on the track's main playlist.

◆ **Copy Selection to New Playlist** creates an empty main playlist and pastes the playlist selection into it.

◆ **Copy Selection to Duplicate Playlist** duplicates the main playlist and pastes the playlist selection over any material in the duplicate. The duplicated playlist becomes the main playlist.

To copy a playlist selection to the main playlist:

1. In a playlist, select the portion of a take you want to use for the track (**Figure 11.50**).

2. Do one of the following:
   ▲ In the Playlist lane controls, click the Copy Selection to Main Playlist button (**Figure 11.51**).
   ▲ Choose Edit > Copy Selection to New Playlist.

   or

   ▲ Choose Edit > Copy Selection to Duplicate Playlist.

   The selected material is copied to the same time location in the destination playlist (**Figure 11.52**).

✔ Tips

■ When auditioning multiple playlists, set Pro Tools to loop playback while you solo them.

■ You can show or hide individual playlists for a track by clicking their Show/Hide icons in the Tracks list (**Figure 11.53**).

COMPOSITING TRACKS

Consolidating Audio

After you have edited an audio track, it can contain many regions, such as those created automatically when separating regions, or when looping or compositing. When you have finished editing, you can consolidate an entire track, or an Edit selection within a track, into a single audio file.

The Consolidate command is nondestructive in that it creates a new file and does not erase the original regions or files. If you want to keep the original arrangement of regions in the track for later reference, duplicate the track playlist and consolidate the duplicate.

To consolidate audio:

1. With the Selector or Grabber tool, select the area in an audio track that you want to consolidate (**Figure 11.54**).

   or

   Triple-click in the track with the Selector tool to select the entire audio track.

2. Choose Edit > Consolidate Region.

   or

   Press Shift-Option-3 (Mac) or Shift-Alt-3 (Windows).

   A new audio file is created and appears in the track as a single region (**Figure 11.55**).

✔ Tip

- Before consolidating audio, you may want to audition the boundaries between any adjacent regions and apply crossfades to prevent pops.

Figure 11.54 Select a range of material in a track to consolidate.

Figure 11.55 A consolidated audio region.

EDITING MIDI

Pro Tools offers many different methods for viewing and editing MIDI. MIDI data can be displayed in regions, allowing you to select, move, loop, and assemble material with familiar region-based editing techniques. You can also work on the level of individual MIDI notes, with powerful tools for selecting, moving, copying, transposing, quantizing, and inserting notes.

Pro Tools gives you the ability to audition changes to MIDI data in real time with the MIDI Real-Time Properties feature. It also lets you edit multiple tracks simultaneously in the MIDI Editor and allows notation-based editing in the Score Editor.

This chapter covers a range of methods for editing MIDI, from manual editing to Event Operations that transform large sections of material.

Viewing MIDI in the Edit Window

MIDI tracks and Instrument tracks show MIDI data arranged in playlists. From the Edit window, you can carry out MIDI editing operations on entire regions, selections of notes, or individual notes.

You can display MIDI data in the following track views:

Regions view (Figure 12.1) shows MIDI notes contained by regions. A MIDI region can be edited in the same way as an audio region, such as separating, moving, trimming, and looping. You can also apply MIDI operations such as Transpose or Change Duration to a region. When you apply a MIDI operation to a region, it affects all notes within the region.

Blocks view (Figure 12.2) is similar to Regions view, but shows region information only.

Notes view (Figure 12.3) shows individual MIDI notes and allows note-by-note editing operations such as changing the pitch, duration, or time location of notes. You can also make selections and apply MIDI operations to multiple notes.

Velocity view (Figure 12.4) shows individual MIDI notes along with their velocity information in the form of *velocity stalks*, vertical lines that can be adjusted to change the notes' attack velocity.

MIDI tracks and Instrument tracks can also show controller views such as MIDI volume, MIDI mute, MIDI pan, pitch bend, and many others. See "Editing MIDI Continuous Controller Data," later in this chapter.

To set the track view:

◆ Click the Track View selector and choose a view from the pop-up menu (**Figure 12.5**).

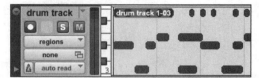
Figure 12.1 MIDI data shown in Regions view.

Figure 12.2 MIDI data shown in Blocks view.

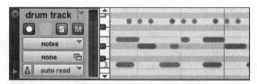
Figure 12.3 MIDI data shown in Notes view.

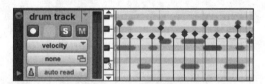
Figure 12.4 MIDI data shown in Velocity view.

Figure 12.5 Click the Track View selector to set the track view.

256

Figure 12.6 Click the Main Counter selector to select a Time Scale.

Figure 12.7 Click the Grid Value selector to select a grid size.

Settings for MIDI Editing

Before you begin editing MIDI, review the following settings and options for aligning, creating, and auditioning notes.

Setting the Main Time Scale and Grid value

When working with MIDI, you will most often use Grid mode with the Main Time Scale set to Bars|Beats. For more information, see Chapter 9, "Working with Selections."

To set the Main Time Scale:

◆ In the Edit window, click the Main Counter selector and select a Time Scale (**Figure 12.6**).

To set the Grid value:

◆ In the Edit Toolbar, click the Grid Value selector and select a grid size (**Figure 12.7**).

Setting the Edit mode

When separating, moving, or trimming MIDI regions or notes, you will usually want to constrain these edits to the grid, so that material maintains its relationship to beats in the session. You can choose between two variants of Grid mode:

◆ **Absolute Grid** snaps the moved regions or notes to grid boundaries, regardless of their original relationship to the grid. Use this mode if you want to conform material to the grid.

◆ **Relative Grid** preserves the original relationship of the moved regions or notes to the grid. Use this mode if you want to move material by grid increments while maintain its original rhythmic feel.

Enabling Mirrored MIDI Editing

As with audio regions, you can use multiple copies of MIDI regions in a session—for example, in loops or in songs that have verses and choruses. One important difference with MIDI is that you can choose to *mirror* edits to MIDI regions. With Mirrored MIDI Editing enabled, when you edit a region, the edit is automatically applied to all copies of that region in the session.

To mirror edits to MIDI regions:

◆ In the Edit window, click the Mirrored MIDI Editing icon so that it is highlighted (**Figure 12.8**).

✔ Tip

■ If you are editing looped regions or region groups, enable Mirrored MIDI Editing in order to maintain the loops or region groups. If you do not, the region loops will be flattened (creating individual regions) or the region groups will be ungrouped.

Setting the Default Note Duration and Note Velocity

When you manually insert MIDI notes, they are created with a duration and velocity that you can choose.

To set the default duration for inserted MIDI notes:

◆ In the MIDI Selection Indicators area of the Edit Toolbar, click the Default Note Duration selector and choose a note value from the pop-up menu (**Figure 12.9**).

or

Choose Follow Grid from the pop-up menu to have the Default Note Duration automatically update to match the current Grid value setting.

Figure 12.8 Click the Mirrored MIDI Editing icon to highlight it.

Figure 12.9 Select a Default Note Duration for manually inserted notes.

SETTINGS FOR MIDI EDITING

Figure 12.10 Drag up or down to set the default velocity for manually inserted notes.

Figure 12.11 Highlight the small speaker icon to play MIDI notes while editing.

To set the default velocity for inserted MIDI notes:

◆ In the MIDI Selection Indicators area of the Edit Toolbar, click the Default Note Velocity value and drag up or down to change the value (**Figure 12.10**).

Auditioning MIDI notes while editing

When working in Notes view, you can set Pro Tools to play MIDI notes when you insert, select, or move notes in tracks.

To enable MIDI notes to play while editing:

◆ In the MIDI Selection Indicators area of the Edit Toolbar, click the Play MIDI Notes When Editing icon (the small speaker) so that it is highlighted (**Figure 12.11**).

Create a Backup Playlist Before Editing MIDI

While some types edits to MIDI regions can be nondestructive, any MIDI editing that changes individual MIDI notes is destructive, changing the region permanently.

Even though Pro Tools has powerful multiple Undo capabilities, it's still a good idea to duplicate the track playlist before you begin editing MIDI. That way, even if you perform destructive edits, you can always revert back to the original.

Editing MIDI Regions

MIDI regions can be captured, placed, moved, looped, cut, copied, and pasted in the same manner as audio regions. However, because MIDI regions contain discrete notes instead of continuous waveforms, there are some differences in how they behave.

In MIDI Regions view, the Edit tools work the same way as in audio regions. The Smart Tool also changes function in the same way, depending on its location in a MIDI region, as follows (**Figure 12.12**):

◆ Selector at the top center

◆ Grabber at the bottom center

◆ Trimmer at the left and right

Separating MIDI regions

Because MIDI regions contain discrete notes, separating regions can affect the notes in several ways.

◆ When you separate MIDI regions in Regions view, any notes that cross the region boundary are not separated (**Figure 12.13**).

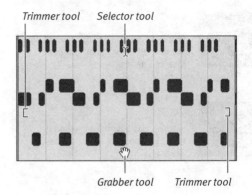

Trimmer tool   *Selector tool*

Grabber tool   *Trimmer tool*

Figure 12.12 The Smart Tool can change to the Selector, Grabber, or Trimmer in different parts of a MIDI region.

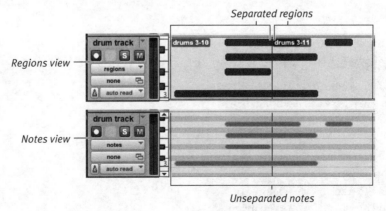

Separated regions

Regions view

Notes view

Unseparated notes

Figure 12.13 Notes that cross region boundaries are not separated.

◆ When you create a MIDI region from a selection, all notes that start in the selection are included in the region, even if they extend beyond the region end point (**Figure 12.14**).

◆ Any notes extending beyond a region end can overlap other material when the region is moved (**Figure 12.15**).

◆ For more information on separating regions, see Chapter 10, "Working with Regions."

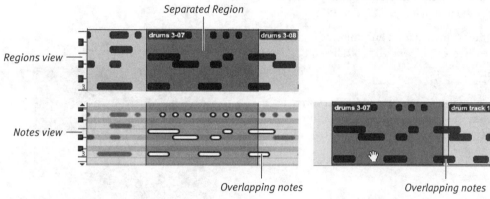

Separated Region

Regions view

Notes view

Overlapping notes

Overlapping notes

Figure 12.14 Notes that start in an Edit selection are included in newly created regions, even if they overlap the end of the region.

Figure 12.15 Notes that overlap the end of a region can also overlap other regions.

Trimming MIDI regions

You can trim the length of MIDI regions in two ways: by hiding or revealing notes, or by time-scaling notes.

◆ When you trim a MIDI region with the Standard Trimmer, notes in the region are hidden or revealed, but notes do not change in length (**Figure 12.16**).

◆ When you trim a MIDI region with the Time Compression/Expansion (TCE) Trimmer, the lengths of all notes in the region are adjusted proportionally to fit the new region length (**Figure 12.17**).

◆ For more information on trimming regions, see Chapter 10, "Working with Regions."

✔ Tip

■ To conform an imported MIDI region to the session tempo, use the TCE Trimmer in Grid mode to scale the region to grid boundaries.

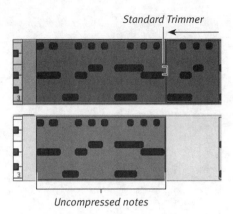

Standard Trimmer

Uncompressed notes

Figure 12.16 Trimming a MIDI region with the Standard Trimmer.

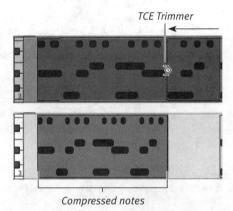

TCE Trimmer

Compressed notes

Figure 12.17 Trimming a MIDI region with the TCE Trimmer.

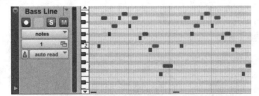

Figure 12.18 A MIDI track set to Notes view.

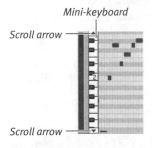

Figure 12.19
The mini-keyboard in Notes view.

Mini-keyboard

Scroll arrow

Scroll arrow

Figure 12.20
Click the Track View selector and choose Notes view.

Viewing MIDI Notes

When you display MIDI or Instrument tracks in Notes view, individual notes are shown in piano roll format, with pitch represented by the vertical position of each note and duration represented by the horizontal length of each note in the track (**Figure 12.18**).

In Notes view, a mini-keyboard on the left of the track lets you scroll notes into view (**Figure 12.19**). You can click in the mini-keyboard to audition the pitch associated with a vertical location in the track.

There are several ways to set a track to Notes view; here we discuss two of them.

To set the track view to Notes view:

◆ Click the Track View selector and choose Notes from the pop-up menu (**Figure 12.20**).

To change from Regions view to Notes view:

◆ Click a region in the track with the Pencil tool.

Selecting MIDI Notes

There are many ways to select MIDI notes, depending on the editing task. For example, it can be useful to select all notes of a given pitch in a percussion part and transpose them to change an instrument sound.

In Notes view, the Smart Tool changes its function depending on its location relative to a note (**Figure 12.21**), as follows:

◆ Selector anywhere outside the note

◆ Grabber on the center of the note

◆ Trimmer at the left and right edges of the note

To select a single MIDI note:

◆ With the Grabber tool, click the note so that it is highlighted (**Figure 12.22**).

The attributes of the selected note appear in the MIDI Selection indicators in the Edit Toolbar (**Figure 12.23**).

To select additional MIDI notes:

◆ With the Grabber tool, Shift-click the additional notes to highlight them.

To deselect a MIDI note:

◆ With the Grabber tool, Shift-click the selected note.

To select multiple MIDI notes:

◆ With the Selector tool, drag to select the notes so they are highlighted (**Figure 12.24**).

To select all MIDI notes in a region:

◆ In Notes view, double-click with the Selector tool inside the region boundaries (**Figure 12.25**).

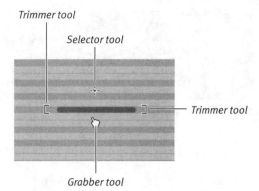

Trimmer tool

Selector tool

Trimmer tool

Grabber tool

Figure 12.21 The Smart Tool can change to the Selector, Grabber, or Trimmer depending on its location relative to a MIDI note.

Figure 12.22 Selecting a note with the Grabber tool.

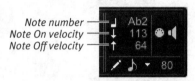

Note number

Note On velocity

Note Off velocity

Figure 12.23 The attributes of a selected MIDI note are displayed in the MIDI Selection indicators.

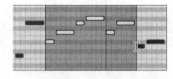

Figure 12.24 Drag with the Selector tool to select multiple notes.

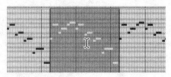

Figure 12.25 Double-click with the Selector to select all notes in a region.

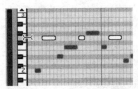

Figure 12.26 Click a key in the mini-keyboard to select all notes of that pitch throughout an entire track.

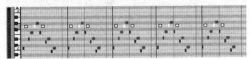

Figure 12.27 Notes of a single pitch selected across a track.

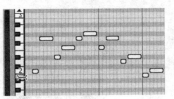

Figure 12.28 Drag in the mini-keyboard to select a range of notes across an entire track.

To select all MIDI notes of a given pitch throughout an entire track:

◆ Click a key in the track's mini-keyboard (**Figure 12.26**).

All notes corresponding to the pitch are selected (**Figure 12.27**).

To select a range of MIDI notes throughout an entire track:

◆ Drag up or down across a range of keys in the mini-keyboard (**Figure 12.28**).

Inserting and Deleting MIDI Notes

After you record MIDI into a track, you can easily edit your performance by manually adding or removing individual notes.

In Notes view, the Pencil tool lets you insert, delete, and edit notes. The Pencil tool works much like the Smart Tool, changing its function depending on its location relative to a note (**Figure 12.29**), as follows:

◆ Pencil anywhere outside the note

◆ Grabber on the center of the note

◆ Trimmer at the left and right edges of the note

To insert a MIDI note:

1. Click the Pencil tool and select Free Hand from the pop-up menu (**Figure 12.30**).

2. Click at the location where you want to insert a note (**Figure 12.31**).

   or

   Click to insert a note and drag to determine its length (**Figure 12.32**).

   A note with the specified duration is inserted at the location.

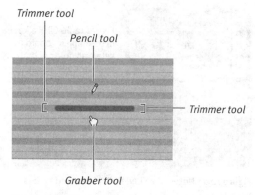

Trimmer tool
Pencil tool
Trimmer tool
Grabber tool

Figure 12.29 The Pencil tool can change to the Pencil, Grabber, or Trimmer depending on its location relative to a MIDI note.

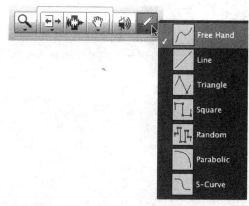

Figure 12.30 Select the Free Hand Pencil tool.

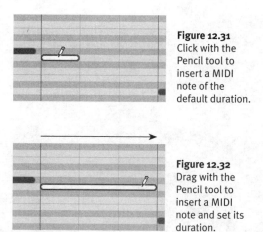

Figure 12.31 Click with the Pencil tool to insert a MIDI note of the default duration.

Figure 12.32 Drag with the Pencil tool to insert a MIDI note and set its duration.

Figure 12.33 To delete notes, Option-click (Mac) or Alt-click (Windows) with the Pencil tool.

To delete a MIDI note:

1. Position the Pencil tool in a track and hold the Option key (Mac) or the Alt key (Windows).

   The Pencil turns upside down to indicate that it will erase notes (**Figure 12.33**).

2. With the upside-down Pencil, click the note you want to delete.

To delete multiple MIDI notes:

1. With the Grabber tool, drag to select the notes to delete.

2. Press Delete (Mac) or Backspace (Windows).

INSERTING AND DELETING MIDI NOTES

267

Separating and Consolidating MIDI Notes

Individual MIDI notes can be separated in much the same way as regions, with the Separate Notes At Selection and Separate Notes On Grid commands in the Edit menu. Consecutive MIDI notes of the same pitch can be consolidated with the Consolidate command.

Special Separate and Consolidate tools are also available to use when editing MIDI notes. The behavior of separated notes depends on the Edit mode.

To separate a MIDI note:

◆ With the Grabber tool or Pencil tool, Control-Shift-Click (Mac) or Start-Shift-Click (Windows) at the point where you want to separate the note.

The cursor turns into a knife icon to indicate its function as a Separation tool (**Figure 12.34**).

To consolidate MIDI notes:

◆ With the Grabber tool or Pencil tool, Control-Shift-Click (Mac) or Start-Shift-Click (Windows) at the intersection of the notes.

The cursor turns into a bandage icon to indicate its function as a Consolidation tool (**Figure 12.35**).

Knife icon

Figure 12.34 Control-Shift-Click (Mac) or Start-Shift-Click (Windows) a note to separate it.

Bandage icon

Figure 12.35 Control-Shift-Click (Mac) or Start-Shift-Click (Windows) a separation between notes to consolidate them.

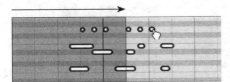

Figure 12.36 Drag MIDI notes to the right or left to move them in time.

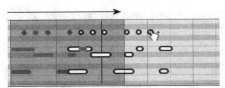

Figure 12.37 Option-drag (Mac) or Alt-drag (Windows) MIDI notes to make copies of them.

Moving and Copying MIDI Notes

You can move MIDI notes horizontally to change their placement in time or copy them to another location in the session. (If you move notes vertically, this transposes them to another pitch; see "Transposing MIDI Notes" later in this chapter.)

In Grid mode, the horizontal motion of notes is constrained by the current Grid value.

To move MIDI notes:

1. Select one or more MIDI notes to move.

2. With the Pencil tool or Grabber tool, drag the notes to the left or right to move them earlier or later in time (**Figure 12.36**).

To copy MIDI notes:

1. Select one or more MIDI notes to copy.

2. With the Pencil tool or Grabber tool, Option-drag (Mac) or Alt-drag (Windows) the notes to the left or right to copy them earlier or later in time (**Figure 12.37**).

✔ Tip

- To prevent vertical motion while moving or copying notes, hold Shift while dragging.

Transposing MIDI Notes

You can transpose, or change the pitch of, MIDI notes by moving them vertically.

To transpose a MIDI note:

1. Select one or more MIDI notes to transpose.

2. With the Pencil tool or Grabber tool, drag the notes up or down (**Figure 12.38**).

To copy and transpose a MIDI note:

1. Select one or more MIDI notes to copy and transpose.

2. With the Pencil tool or Grabber tool, Option-drag (Mac) or Alt-drag (Windows) the notes up or down to copy them higher or lower (**Figure 12.39**).

✔ Tip

■ To prevent horizontal motion while transposing notes, hold Shift while dragging.

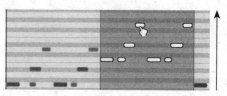

Figure 12.38 Drag notes up or down to transpose them higher or lower.

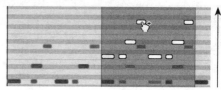

Figure 12.39 Option-drag (Mac) or Alt-drag (Windows) MIDI notes up or down to copy and transpose them.

TRANSPOSING MIDI NOTES

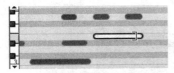

Figure 12.40
Changing the
duration of a
note with the
Trimmer.

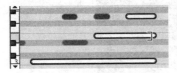

Figure 12.41
Trimming the
duration of
multiple notes.

Changing the Duration of MIDI Notes

You can change the duration of an individual note by adjusting the start or end time of the note with the Trimmer tool.

In Grid mode, the boundaries of notes are constrained by the current Grid value.

To change the duration of a note:

1. With the Pencil tool or Smart Tool, position the cursor over the left or right edge of a note.

   The cursor turns into the Standard Trimmer (**Figure 12.40**).

2. Drag with the Trimmer tool to adjust the start or end of the note.

To change the duration of multiple notes:

1. With the Grabber tool, drag to select the notes to change.

2. With the Pencil tool or Smart Tool, position the cursor over the left or right edge of a selected note.

   The cursor turns into the Standard Trimmer.

3. Drag with the Trimmer to move the start or end of any selected note.

   All selected notes are trimmed by the same amount (**Figure 12.41**).

CHANGING THE DURATION OF MIDI NOTES

Editing MIDI Velocity

Velocity, a measure of the strength of a MIDI note's attack, is displayed in a separate Velocity view in the Edit window. In this view, the velocity of each note is shown by a *velocity stalk* or vertical line that indicates the velocity value.

In Velocity view, you can edit the velocity of individual notes by dragging their velocity stalks up or down. To edit velocity values for multiple notes, you use the Pencil tool to draw a velocity contour.

To edit velocity for a MIDI note:

1. Click the Track View selector and choose Velocity from the pop-up menu (**Figure 12.42**).

2. With the Grabber tool, drag the diamond at the top of a velocity stalk up or down.

   The velocity value is temporarily displayed in the track (**Figure 12.43**).

To edit velocity for multiple MIDI notes:

1. With the Grabber tool, drag to select the notes to change.

   The notes and their velocity stalks highlight to indicate that they are selected (**Figure 12.44**).

2. Drag a selected velocity stalk.

   All selected velocity stalks change by a proportionate amount (**Figure 12.45**).

Figure 12.42 Click the Track View selector and choose Velocity view.

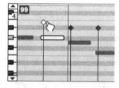

Figure 12.43 Editing velocity by dragging a velocity stalk.

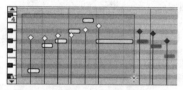

Figure 12.44 Select multiple notes to select their velocity stalks.

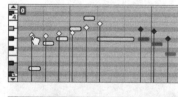

Figure 12.45 Editing the velocity of multiple notes with the Grabber tool.

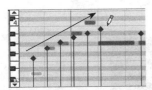

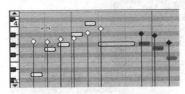

Figure 12.46
Drawing a velocity contour with the Pencil tool.

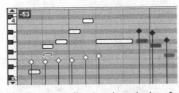

Figure 12.47 Adjusting the velocity of multiple notes with the Trimmer tool.

To draw a velocity contour for multiple MIDI notes:

1. Click the Pencil tool and select a curve from the pop-up menu (Figure 12.30).

2. With the Pencil tool, drag across the tops of the velocity stalks to adjust their values (**Figure 12.46**).

To trim velocity values for multiple MIDI notes:

1. With the Selector or Grabber tool, drag to select the notes to change.

   The notes and their velocity stalks highlight to indicate that they are selected.

2. With the Trimmer tool, drag up or down to adjust all selected velocity stalks (**Figure 12.47**).

✔ Tip

■ You can move, transpose, change duration, and delete MIDI notes while in Velocity view.

EDITING MIDI VELOCITY

Editing MIDI Continuous Controller Data

In addition to the standard MIDI parameters of pitch, duration, and velocity, there is a wide variety of performance parameters that fall into the category of *continuous controller events*. Pro Tools displays continuous controller (CC) data in separate track views in the Edit window.

Pro Tools can record, edit, and play back events for any continuous controller (numbers 0-127). However, continuous controllers for MIDI volume (CC 3) and MIDI pan (CC 10) are handled differently from other controllers. Pro Tools classifies these, along with MIDI mute, as automation parameters that can be written, read, and suspended like their counterparts on audio tracks. For more information on automation, see Chapter 15, "Automating Mix Controls."

To edit continuous controller data:

1. Click the Track View selector and choose a controller from the pop-up menu (**Figure 12.48**).

2. With the Grabber tool, drag a breakpoint on the graph to adjust its value (**Figure 12.49**).

   or

   With the Pencil tool, draw a curve in the playlist to modify the controller data (**Figure 12.50**).

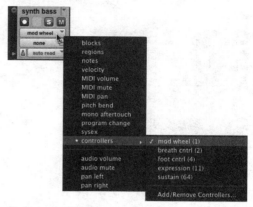

Figure 12.48 Click the Track View selector and choose a continuous controller view.

Figure 12.49 Editing a continuous controller value with the Grabber tool.

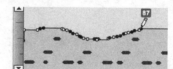

Figure 12.50 Drawing a controller value curve with the Pencil tool.

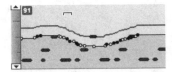

Figure 12.51 Adjusting multiple continuous controller values with the Trimmer tool.

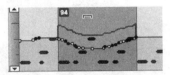

Figure 12.52 Adjusting selected continuous controller values with the Trimmer.

To trim continuous controller data:

◆ With the Trimmer tool, drag up or down to adjust the values of all breakpoints (**Figure 12.51**).

or

1. With the Selector tool, drag to select the range of data to trim.

2. With the Trimmer tool, drag up or down in the selection to adjust the values of selected breakpoints (**Figure 12.52**).

Using MIDI Event Operations

In addition to commands for manually editing individual MIDI regions and notes, Pro Tools offers a set of powerful functions for performing more complex edits on MIDI data across selections and tracks.

The MIDI Event Operations window lets you perform the following types of edits:

◆ **Quantize** aligns MIDI notes with the grid or with a groove template extracted from another performance.

◆ **Change Velocity** adjusts Note On and Note Off velocity values for MIDI notes.

◆ **Change Duration** adjusts the length and overlap of MIDI notes.

◆ **Transpose** changes the pitch of MIDI notes by interval or according to a key.

◆ **Select/Split Notes** lets you set criteria for selecting notes in a track and moving or copying them to new tracks.

◆ **Input Quantize** automatically aligns MIDI data to a grid during recording.

◆ **Step Input** lets you enter individual MIDI notes in a track using an external MIDI controller.

◆ **Restore Performance** reverts MIDI note attributes to their original state (or to their previously flattened state), prior to any subsequent edits.

◆ **Flatten Performance** commits the current state of any edited MIDI note attributes, making them permanent.

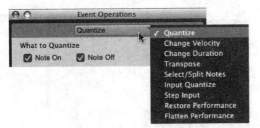

Figure 12.53 Select a MIDI Event Operation from the pop-up menu.

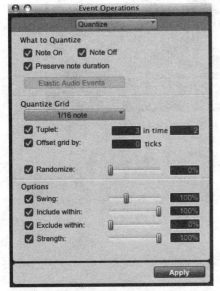

Figure 12.54 The Quantize page of the Event Operations window.

To open the Event Operations window:

1. Choose Event > Event Operations > Event Operations Window.

2. In the Event Operations window, select the operation you want to perform from the pop-up menu (**Figure 12.53**).

Quantizing MIDI notes

The Quantize operation can be used to clean up a performance by conforming it to a grid, or to impart a particular rhythmic feel to a performance from a predetermined rhythmic map, or *groove*.

The editing options in the Event Operations window are different for grid and groove quantization.

To quantize MIDI notes to a grid:

1. Select the notes to quantize.

2. Choose Event > Event Operations > Quantize.

   The Quantize page of the Event Operations window opens (**Figure 12.54**).

3. Under Quantize Grid, select a grid value from the pop-up menu, then select any of the following options, including:

   ▲ **Tuplet** lets you set the grid to irregular note values; for example, for quintuplet sixteenth notes, choose 1/16 note, then select Tuplet and type 5 in time of 4.

   ▲ **Offset grid by** advances or delays the grid to achieve a rushed or dragged feel.

4. Under What to Quantize, select whether to quantize the beginning of the note (Note On), end of the note (Note Off), or both.

continues on next page

5. Select whether to preserve the duration of quantized notes.

   If both Note On and Note Off are quantized, this option is not available.

6. Under Options, select any of the following:

   ▲ **Swing** adjusts alternating grid boundaries to achieve a swing feel. The maximum triplet setting is 100 percent.

   ▲ **Include within** and **Exclude within** determine how far (in percentage) a note must deviate from the grid before it is quantized.

   ▲ **Strength** determines the extent to which quantized notes are conformed to the grid. A setting of 100 percent aligns notes precisely with the grid.

7. Click Apply.

✔ Tip

■ To introduce slight variations in the quantize operation and thus avoid a "mechanical" feel, select Randomize and set a percentage.

To quantize MIDI notes to a groove:

1. Select the notes to quantize. The selection should start and end directly on beats, and it should match the number of bars in the groove template that you intend to use (see Step 3).

2. Choose Event > Event Operations > Quantize.

3. Under Quantize Grid, select a groove template from the pop-up menu.

   A brief description of the template appears below the pop-up menu (**Figure 12.55**).

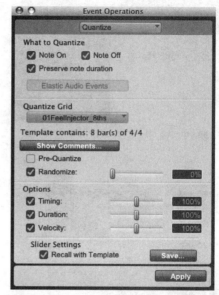

Figure 12.55 Select a groove template for quantizing MIDI notes.

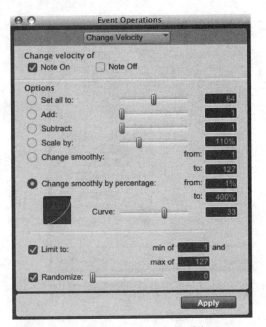

Figure 12.56 The Change Velocity page of the Event Operations window.

4. Under Options, select any of the following:

▲ **Timing** determines the extent to which the quantized notes are conformed to the template. A setting of 100 percent aligns notes precisely with the template.

▲ **Duration** determines the extent to which note durations are conformed to the template. A setting of 100 percent changes note durations to precisely match the template.

▲ **Velocity** determines the extent to which note velocities are conformed to the template. A setting of 100 percent changes velocities to precisely match the template.

5. Click Apply.

✔ Tip

■ If the original material deviates greatly from the groove template, it may be useful to select Pre-Quantize, which conforms the material to a basic sixteenth-note grid before applying the groove template.

Changing MIDI note velocity

The Change Velocity operation can be used to affect the attacks of notes by changing note velocities in a variety of ways, including adding or subtracting set amounts, scaling, or applying curves across a selection.

To change the velocity of notes:

1. Select the notes whose velocity you want to change.

2. Choose Event > Event Operations > Change Velocity.

The Change Velocity page of the Event Operations window opens (**Figure 12.56**).

continues on next page

3. Under "Change Velocity of," select whether to change the velocity of the attack (Note On), the release (Note Off), or both.

4. Under Options, select one of the following:

   ▲ **Set all to** changes the velocity of notes to the specified value.

   ▲ **Add** and **Subtract** change the velocity of notes by the specified amount.

   ▲ **Scale by** adjusts the velocity values of notes by the specified percentage.

   ▲ **Change smoothly** applies a linear change of velocity from the specified start and end values.

   ▲ **Change smoothly by percentage** applies a percentage change of velocity across the selected range of notes. You can specify a curve for this change.

5. To impose absolute limits to all velocity changes, select "Limit to" and enter minimum and maximum values.

6. Click Apply.

✔ Tip

- To introduce slight variations in the Change Velocity operation, select Randomize and set a percentage.

Changing MIDI note duration

The Change Duration operation can be used to adjust the length of notes in order to make them more detached from or more connected to other notes.

To change the duration of notes:

1. Select the notes whose duration you want to change.

2. Choose Event > Event Operations > Change Duration.

   The Change Duration page of the Event Operations window opens (**Figure 12.57**).

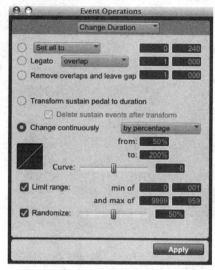

Figure 12.57 The Change Duration page of the Event Operations window.

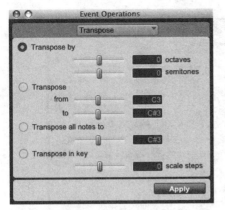

Figure 12.58 The Transpose page of the Event Operations window.

3. Select one of the following:
   - ▲ **Set all to** changes the duration of notes to the specified value.
   - ▲ **Legato** lets you specify the amount of overlap or gap between adjacent notes.
   - ▲ **Remove overlaps and leave gap** eliminates overlap for adjacent notes of the same pitch.
   - ▲ **Transform sustain pedal to duration** converts sustain pedal information to note duration.
   - ▲ **Change continuously** applies a gradual change of duration across the selected range of notes. You can specify a curve for this change.

4. To impose absolute limits on all duration changes, select "Limit range" and enter minimum and maximum values.

5. Click Apply.

Transposing MIDI notes

In addition to chromatic transposition of individual notes, the Transpose operation can be used across regions to modulate material within a key, or across entire tracks to change the key of a song.

To transpose notes:

1. Select the notes that you want to transpose.

2. Choose Event > Event Operations > Transpose.

   The Transpose page of the Event Operations window opens (**Figure 12.58**).

continues on next page

3. Select one of the following:

▲ **Transpose by** moves all selected notes up or down by octaves or chromatically by half-steps.

▲ **Transpose from/to** moves all selected notes up or down chromatically by the specified interval.

▲ **Transpose all notes to** changes all selected notes to the single specified pitch.

▲ **Transpose in key** moves notes in scale steps according to the current key signature as specified in the Key Change dialog.

4. Click Apply.

Selecting and splitting MIDI notes

When you are working with tracks that have multiple musical lines or chords, you can use the Select/Split Notes operation to select individual voices or notes in chords, cut or copy them, and send them to a new track.

To select or split notes:

1. Make a selection that includes the notes you want to select or split.

or

To select or split notes across an entire track, click in the track with the Selector tool.

2. Choose Event > Event Operations > Select/Split Notes.

The Select/Split Notes page of the Event Operations window opens (**Figure 12.59**).

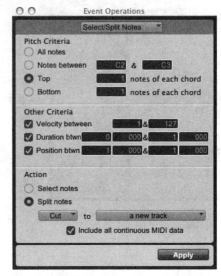

Figure 12.59 The Select/Split Notes page of the Event Operations window.

USING MIDI EVENT OPERATIONS

3. Under Pitch Criteria, select one of the following:

   ▲ **All notes** selects all notes in the selection range or track.

   ▲ **Notes between** specifies a pitch range for notes to be selected.

   ▲ **Top notes of each chord** and **Bottom notes of each chord** specify the positions of notes in chords to be selected.

4. Under Other Criteria, select any of the following:

   ▲ **Velocity between** specifies a range of velocities for notes to be selected.

   ▲ **Duration btwn** specifies a range of note lengths to be selected.

   ▲ **Position btwn** specifies a range of beats within each bar to be selected.

5. Under Action, select one of the following:

   ▲ **Select notes** causes notes that meet the specified criteria to be selected.

   ▲ **Split notes** causes notes that meet the specified criteria to be cut or copied to the clipboard or to a new track in the session.

6. To include all continuous controller MIDI data along with the specified selection, select "Include all continuous MIDI data."

7. Click Apply.

USING MIDI EVENT OPERATIONS

Using MIDI Real-Time Properties

The Real-Time Properties feature lets you make changes to MIDI data properties and audition their effects in real time during playback. This lets you make changes while playing through or looping a passage, then decide whether to apply those changes.

The MIDI Real-Time Properties feature lets you perform the following real-time changes to regions or entire tracks:

◆ **Quantize** aligns MIDI notes with the grid or with a groove template.

◆ **Duration** adjusts the length and overlap of MIDI notes.

◆ **Delay** causes playback of MIDI notes to be delayed or advanced by the specified amount.

◆ **Velocity** adjusts Note On velocity values for MIDI notes.

◆ **Transpose** changes the pitch of MIDI notes by interval, to a pitch, or in a key.

Controls for Real-Time Properties are accessible from the Real-Time Properties window (for regions and tracks) or from the Real-Time Properties view in the Edit window (for tracks). The Real-Time Properties window offers expanded views with additional settings for Quantize, Duration, and Velocity.

To open the Real-Time Properties window:

◆ Choose Event > MIDI Real-Time Properties.

◆ The Real-Time Properties window opens (**Figure 12.60**).

Figure 12.60 The Real-Time Properties window.

Figure 12.61 Click the Edit window View selector and choose Real-Time Properties view.

Figure 12.62 Click the name of a MIDI Real-Time Property to enable it.

Figure 12.63 A MIDI region with Real-Time Properties applied displays an "R."

Figure 12.64 In tracks with Real-Time Properties applied, regions display a "T."

Figure 12.65 Click Write to Region to write MIDI Real-Time Properties settings.

✔ Tip

■ When auditioning Real-Time Properties, toggle the property on and off by clicking the property name.

To enable Real-Time Properties view in the Edit window:

◆ Choose View > Edit Window Views > Real-Time Properties.

or

At the top left of the Tracks area, click the Edit Window View selector and select Real-Time Properties (**Figure 12.61**).

To audition MIDI Real-Time Properties:

1. Select a MIDI or Instrument track with material you want to adjust in real time.

   or

   In a MIDI or Instrument track, select a region you want to adjust in real time.

2. In the Real-Time Properties window or view, click the property name you want to modify.

   The property name highlights and its settings are displayed (**Figure 12.62**).

   When Real-Time Properties are applied to a region, the region shows an "R" icon in the top-right corner (**Figure 12.63**).

   When Real-Time properties are applied to an entire track, each region in the track displays a "T" icon in the top-right corner (**Figure 12.64**).

3. Adjust the property settings and play the session to audition the results.

To write MIDI Real-Time Properties:

◆ In the Real-Time Properties window, click Write to Region (**Figure 12.65**) or Write to Track.

   or

   Choose Track > Write MIDI Real-Time Properties.

USING MIDI REAL-TIME PROPERTIES

285

Real-Time Quantize settings

The Quantize Real-Time Properties include the following settings:

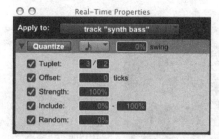

Figure 12.66 The expanded Quantize settings in the Real-Time Properties window.

- ◆ **Grid Value pop-up menu** lets you select the Quantize grid value or groove template.

- ◆ **Swing** adjusts alternating grid boundaries to achieve a swing feel.

- ◆ **Tuplet** lets you set the grid to irregular note values.

- ◆ **Offset** advances or delays the grid to achieve a rushed or dragged feel.

- ◆ **Strength** determines the extent to which quantized notes are conformed to the grid.

- ◆ **Include** determines how far a note must deviate from the grid before it is quantized.

- ◆ **Random** introduces slight variations in the Quantize operation.

To adjust Real-Time Quantize settings:

1. Choose Event > MIDI Real-Time Properties.

2. Click the Quantize button.

3. Click the Quantize disclosure triangle to show the Quantize settings (**Figure 12.66**).

4. Select a value for the Quantize grid or choose a groove template from the pop-up menu (**Figure 12.67**).

5. Click the check box for the setting you want to adjust, and enter a value for the setting.

6. Audition the material to hear the effect of the settings.

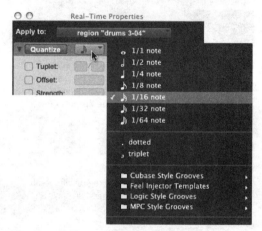

Figure 12.67 Choose a Grid value or select a groove template from the pop-up menu.

Figure 12.68 The expanded Duration settings in the Real-Time Properties window.

Figure 12.69 Choose a Duration setting from the pop-up menu.

Real-Time Duration settings

The Duration Real-Time Properties include the following settings, available from the Duration pop-up menu:

◆ **Set** changes note durations to the specified value.

◆ **Add** and **Subtract** change note durations by the specified value.

◆ **Scale** changes note durations by the specified percentage.

◆ **Legato/gap** extends the end of each note to the beginning of the subsequent note, leaving a gap of the specified amount.

◆ **Legato/overlap** extends the end of each note to the beginning of the subsequent note, overlapping by the specified amount.

The **Min/Max** check boxes let you specify absolute limits to note duration.

To adjust Real-Time Duration settings:

1. Choose Event > MIDI Real-Time Properties.

2. Click the Duration button.

3. Click the Duration disclosure triangle to show the Duration settings (**Figure 12.68**).

4. Choose the setting you want to adjust from the pop-up menu (**Figure 12.69**), and enter a value for that setting.

5. Audition the material to hear the effect of the settings.

Real-Time Delay settings

The Delay Real-Time Properties let you delay or advance MIDI playback.

To adjust Real-Time Delay settings:

1. Choose Event > MIDI Real-Time Properties.

2. Click the Delay button.

3. Choose "+ delay" or "– advance" from the pop-up menu (**Figure 12.70**).

4. Enter a value for the advance or delay.

5. Audition the material to hear the effect.

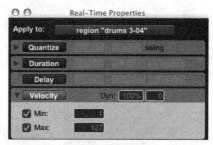

Figure 12.70 Choose a setting from the Delay pop-up menu.

Real-Time Velocity settings

The Velocity Real-Time Properties include the following settings:

◆ **Dyn** (Dynamics) scales velocity values by a percentage based on the average velocity value of 64.

◆ **Offset value** changes the velocity of notes by the specified amount (a negative value decreases and a positive value increases the offset).

◆ The **Min/Max** check boxes let you specify absolute limits to velocity values.

Figure 12.71 The expanded Velocity settings in the Real-Time Properties window.

To adjust Real-Time Velocity settings:

1. Choose Event > MIDI Real-Time Properties.

2. Click the Velocity button.

3. Click the Velocity disclosure triangle to show the Velocity settings (**Figure 12.71**).

4. Enter values for the scaling and offset of Velocity values.

5. Audition the material to hear the effect of the settings.

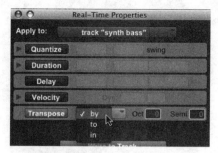

Figure 12.72 Choose a Transposition type from the pop-up menu.

Real-Time Transpose settings

The Transpose Real-Time Properties include the following settings, available from the Transpose pop-up menu:

◆ **Transpose by** moves notes by octaves or chromatically.

◆ **Transpose to** changes notes to the specified pitch.

◆ **Transpose in** moves notes in scale steps based on the current key signature.

To adjust Real-Time Transpose settings:

1. Choose Event > MIDI Real-Time Properties.

2. Click the Transpose button.

3. Choose the type of transposition from the pop-up menu (**Figure 12.72**), and enter a value for the setting.

4. Audition the material to hear the effect of the setting.

Viewing and Editing MIDI in the MIDI Editor

One limitation of the Edit window for editing MIDI is that you can edit only one track at a time. The MIDI Editor provides a way to view and edit MIDI data on one or more MIDI and Instrument tracks simultaneously.

In addition, you can open multiple MIDI Editor windows, each with its own Edit mode settings, Zoom levels, Grid and Nudge values, and Edit Tool selections. This lets you focus on details of a session while keeping the big picture in the Edit window.

MIDI notes are edited in exactly the same way in the MIDI Editor as in the Edit window.

Opening MIDI Editor windows

You can open a MIDI Editor view at the bottom of the Edit window, or open separate MIDI Editor windows to focus on different parts of a session.

To open a MIDI Editor window:

◆ To open the MIDI Editor view in the Edit window, choose View > Other Displays > MIDI Editor.

The MIDI Editor appears, docked to the bottom of the Edit window (**Figure 12.73**).

or

To open a separate MIDI Editor window, choose Window > MIDI Editor.

A separate MIDI Editor window appears.

VIEWING AND EDITING MIDI IN THE MIDI EDITOR

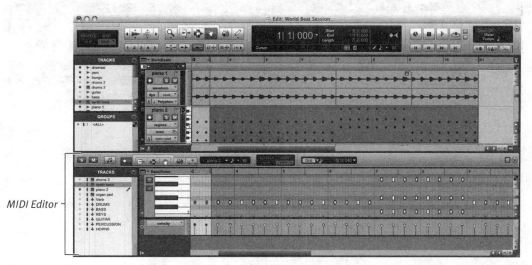

MIDI Editor

Figure 12.73 The MIDI Editor, docked to the bottom of the Edit window.

To display a selection in a new MIDI Editor window:

1. Select the material to view in the Edit window. The selection can span multiple tracks.

2. Choose Window > MIDI Editor.

   A MIDI Editor window opens with the selection zoomed in, showing the MIDI notes from all tracks superimposed (**Figure 12.74**).

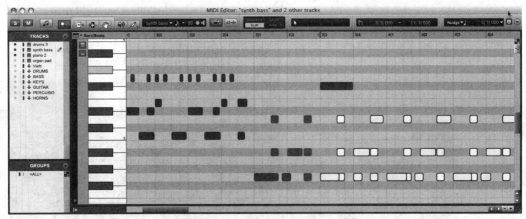

Figure 12.74 Displaying an Edit selection in a new MIDI Editor window.

Figure 12.75 To show or hide a track in the MIDI Editor, click its Show/Hide icon in the Tracks list.

Color Code Notes by Track

Color Code Notes by Velocity

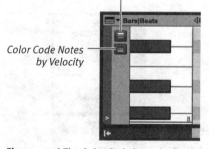

Figure 12.76 The Color Code icons in the top left of the MIDI Editor window.

To display a region in a new MIDI Editor window:

◆ With the Grabber tool, double-click a MIDI region.

A MIDI Editor window opens with the region zoomed in.

Showing and hiding tracks

The Tracks list in the MIDI Editor window lets you show or hide any of the MIDI, Instrument and Auxiliary Input tracks in session. The Tracks list menu and commands work the same as in the Edit and Mix windows. See "Showing and Hiding Tracks" in Chapter 4, "Working with Tracks."

To show and hide tracks:

◆ In the Tracks list, click the Show/Hide icon for the tracks you want to show or hide (**Figure 12.75**).

The MIDI data in the shown MIDI and Instrument tracks is superimposed in the Tracks area of the window.

Color coding MIDI notes

You can set the color coding of notes in the MIDI Editor to indicate which track they belong to, or to indicate their velocity. If no color coding is selected, MIDI notes show their normal Edit window region color in the MIDI Editor.

To set the color coding of MIDI notes:

◆ At the top left of the MIDI Editor, click the Color Code Notes by Track icon or the Color Code Notes by Velocity icon (**Figure 12.76**).

VIEWING AND EDITING MIDI IN THE MIDI EDITOR

Showing velocity, controller, and automation data

MIDI Editor windows can show MIDI velocity, MIDI continuous controller data, and mix automation. Each type of data can be shown in a separate lane at the bottom of the window, with the data from all shown tracks superimposed in the lane.

To show and hide velocity, controller, and automation lanes:

◆ At the bottom left of the MIDI Editor window, click the Show/Hide Lanes icon (**Figure 12.77**).

To show and hide additional lanes:

◆ Click the Add Lanes (Plus sign) or Remove Lanes (Minus sign) icon at the left side of a lane (**Figure 12.78**).

To change the view in a lane:

◆ Click the Lane View selector and choose a view from the pop-up menu (**Figure 12.79**).

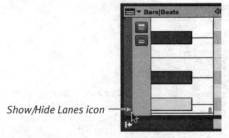

Show/Hide Lanes icon

Figure 12.77 The Show/Hide Lanes icon at the bottom left of the MIDI Editor window.

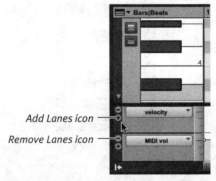

Add Lanes icon

Remove Lanes icon

Figure 12.78 The Add Lanes icon at the left side of a lane.

Figure 12.79 Click the Lane View selector and choose a new view for the lane.

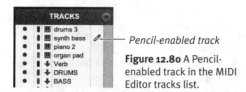

Pencil-enabled track

Figure 12.80 A Pencil-enabled track in the MIDI Editor tracks list.

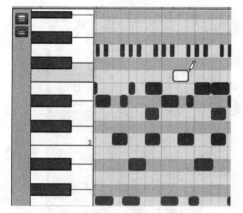

Figure 12.81 Click in the MIDI Editor window to add a MIDI note to the Pencil-enabled track.

Figure 12.82 Enabling Notation View in the MIDI Editor window.

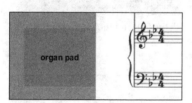

Figure 12.83 In Notation view, tracks are displayed in a Grand Staff by default.

Inserting MIDI notes

You can manually insert notes in the MIDI Editor in the same way as in the Edit window. However, because the MIDI Editor shows multiple tracks, you first need to Pencil enable the track on which you want to insert notes.

To insert MIDI notes on a track:

1. In the Tracks list of the MIDI Editor, click in the column to the right of the track name.

   A pencil icon appears to indicate that the track is Pencil enabled (**Figure 12.80**).

2. With the Pencil tool, click at the location where you want to add a note (**Figure 12.81**).

Editing MIDI with Notation view

The MIDI Editor lets you display and edit MIDI notes in the form of musical notation in the session timeline. Each MIDI or Instrument track appears in its own musical staff.

When you enter Notation view, Pro Tools automatically enters Grid mode. The musical notes in Notation view align with bars and beats and with data in velocity and controller lanes in the MIDI Editor window.

To enable Notation view:

◆ In the MIDI Editor Toolbar, click the Notation view icon so that it is highlighted (**Figure 12.82**).

   Each track is displayed in a Grand Staff (Treble clef plus Bass clef) by default (**Figure 12.83**).

To adjust the display of notes in the MIDI Editor:

1. Double-click any clef symbol at the beginning of a music staff (**Figure 12.84**).

   The Notation Display Track Settings window opens (**Figure 12.85**).

2. Select a track to adjust from the Track pop-up menu.

3. Choose a clef for the track from the Clef pop-up menu.

4. Adjust the transposition and quantization values used for display of notes.

5. For Grand Clef displays, set the split point between the Treble and Bass clef.

6. Close the Notation Display Settings window.

To select notes in Notation view:

1. Click the Selector tool in the MIDI Editor window (**Figure 12.86**).

2. Drag to select notes on one or more staves.

   The noteheads highlight to indicate that they are selected (**Figure 12.87**).

To transpose notes in Notation view:

1. With the Selector tool or the Grabber tool, select the notes you want to transpose.

2. Drag the notes up or down in the staff (**Figure 12.88**).

Figure 12.84 Double-click a track's clef symbol to open the Notation Display Track Settings.

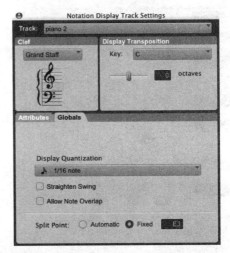

Figure 12.85 The Notation Display Track Settings window.

Figure 12.86 Click the Selector tool in the MIDI Editor window.

Figure 12.87 Drag to select notes in Notation view.

Figure 12.88 Drag notes up or down in the staff to transpose them higher or lower.

Figure 12.89 Drag MIDI notes to the right or left to move them in time.

Figure 12.90 Click with the Pencil tool to insert a note of default duration.

Figure 12.91 Drag with the Pencil tool to insert a MIDI note and set its duration.

Figure 12.92 To delete notes, Option-click (Mac) or Alt-click (Windows) with the Pencil tool.

To move notes in Notation view:

1. With the Selector or Grabber tool, select the notes you want to move.

2. Drag the notes left or right in the staff (**Figure 12.89**).

To nudge notes in Notation view:

1. With the Selector or Grabber tool, select the notes you want to nudge.

2. To move the note ahead by the Nudge value, press the Plus key on the numeric keypad.

   or

   To move the note back by the Nudge value, press the Minus key on the numeric keypad.

To insert notes in Notation view:

1. In the MIDI Editor Toolbar, select the default note duration from the Note Duration pop-up menu.

2. Click the Pencil tool and select Free Hand from the pop-up menu.

3. Click at the location where you want to add a note (**Figure 12.90**).

   or

   Click to add a note and drag to determine its length (**Figure 12.91**).

   A note with the specified duration is inserted at the location.

To delete notes in Notation view:

1. Position the Pencil tool over a note and hold the Option key (Mac) or the Alt key (Windows).

   The Pencil turns upside down to indicate that it will erase notes (**Figure 12.92**).

2. With the upside-down Pencil, click the note you want to delete.

Viewing and Editing MIDI in the Score Editor

The Score Editor shows MIDI data as musical notation in full score format.

In the Score Editor, you can insert, edit, and delete MIDI notes in the same way as in MIDI Editor Notation view, except that the notes are shown in page layout instead of in individual staves.

To open the Score Editor window:

◆ Choose Window > Score Editor.

To display a selection in the Score Editor window:

1. Select the material to view in the Edit window or a MIDI Editor window. The selection can span multiple tracks.

2. Right-click the selection and choose Open In Score Editor.

   The Score Editor window opens with the selection zoomed in (**Figure 12.93**).

Figure 12.93 Displaying an Edit selection in the Score Editor window.

Figure 12.94 Zooming in the Score Editor window.

Figure 12.95 The Zoom In and Zoom Out buttons in the lower right of the Score Editor window.

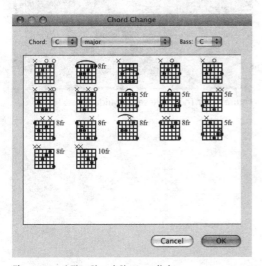

Figure 12.96 The Chord Change dialog.

To zoom the Score Editor window display:

◆ Drag with the Zoomer tool in the area you want to view (**Figure 12.94**).

or

Click the Zoom In (+) and Zoom Out (–) buttons in the lower right of the Score Editor window (**Figure 12.95**).

To add chord symbols in the Score Editor:

1. With the Selector tool, Right-click at the location where you want to add a chord symbol, and select Insert > Chord.

   The Chord Change dialog appears (**Figure 12.96**).

2. In the Chord Change dialog, use the pop-up menus to select the root of the chord, the quality of the chord, and the bass note.

3. Select a chord diagram to include at the chord change.

4. Click OK.

Printing a Score

You can print music directly from Pro Tools, or export it for additional formatting in Sibelius notation software.

To set up a score for printing:

1. Choose File > Score Setup.

   The Score Setup window appears (**Figure 12.97**).

2. Enter information about the score and choose which attributes you want to display on the page.

3. Under Spacing, enter values to set the distance between elements on the page.

4. Under Layout, choose the page size from the pop-up menu and enter values for staff size and page margins.

To print a score:

◆ Choose File > Print Score.

To export a score to Sibelius:

◆ Choose File > Send to Sibelius.

   All MIDI and Instrument tracks are exported to a Sibelius (.sib) file. If Sibelius is installed on your system, it automatically launches and opens the score.

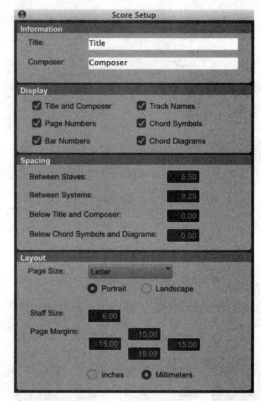

Figure 12.97 The Score setup window.

13

MIXING

With Pro Tools, the mixing process can begin from the moment you start your session as you adjust the balance between tracks, pan tracks in stereo, and apply effects. After you've selected your best takes, finished editing MIDI tracks, and arranged the material in your session, you're ready to shift your attention to building a final mix.

This chapter covers the use of groups to help organize a session and simplify mixing tasks. It also covers the fundamentals of signal routing for mixing, including configuring bus paths and outputs, using inserts to process audio, and using sends to create submixes and share effects across multiple tracks.

Adjusting Track Controls

The controls on Audio, Auxiliary Input, Instrument, and Master Fader tracks let you control volume, pan, solo, and mute functions. For an overview of track controls, see Chapter 4, "Working with Tracks."

Track volume and metering

The Volume faders on Audio, Auxiliary Input Instrument, and Master Fader tracks provide up to 12 decibels (dB) of gain during playback (**Figure 13.1**).

The meters on these track types show output levels in decibels relative to full scale (dBFS), and have peak hold and clip indication functions. Track metering can be set to indicate pre-fader or post-fader levels. When set to pre-fader, track meters show level at the track input. When set to post-fader, they show the effect of the volume fader on output.

To adjust track volume:

◆ Drag the track's Volume fader up or down.

To adjust track volume with fine control:

◆ Command-drag (Mac) or Ctrl-drag (Windows) the track's Volume fader up or down.

To set meter peak hold and clip indication:

1. Choose Setup > Preferences and click Display.

2. Under Meters, choose Peak Hold and Clip Indication settings (**Figure 13.2**).

3. Click OK.

Figure 13.1 The Volume fader and meter on an Audio track, showing fader gain scale (on the right) and the meter scale (on the left).

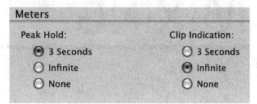

Figure 13.2 Choose meter display settings in the Display Preferences.

Figure 13.3 An Output window for a track with a mono output.

To set pre- or post-fader metering:

◆ Select or deselect Options > Pre-Fader Metering.

Adjusting track pan controls

Pan controls let you position track output in the stereo field. The pan controls available on a track depend on its channel format and its output format.

◆ A track assigned to a mono output does not have pan controls (**Figure 13.3**).

◆ A mono track assigned to a stereo output has one pan control (**Figure 13.4**).

◆ A stereo track assigned to a stereo output has two pan controls (**Figure 13.5**).

Each pan control is adjustable from full left (indicated as –100) to full right (indicated as +100), with the center point at zero.

Figure 13.4 An Output window for a mono track with a stereo output.

Figure 13.5 An Output window for a stereo track with a stereo output.

To adjust track pan:

◆ Click the Track Pan knob and drag up or down (**Figure 13.6**).

To adjust track pan with fine control:

◆ Command-drag (Mac) or Ctrl-drag (Windows) the Track Pan knob up or down.

Linking stereo pan controls

On tracks with stereo pan controls, you can link the left and right controls so that they move in tandem, either in the same direction or in opposite directions.

To link pan controls on a stereo track:

1. Click the Output Window button on the track.

   The Output window opens (**Figure 13.7**).

2. In the Output window, click the Panner Linking button so that it is highlighted (**Figure 13.8**).

3. To link pan controls in an inverse manner, click the Inverse Pan button so that it is highlighted (**Figure 13.9**).

Soloing and muting tracks

When you solo a track, other tracks in the session are implicitly muted, and you hear the soloed track in the outputs of the session. When you mute a track, the output of that track is explicitly silenced.

To solo a track:

◆ Click the track's Solo button (**Figure 13.10**). The Solo button highlights to indicate the track is soloed, and the Mute buttons on all other tracks are both highlighted and dimmed to indicate that they are implicitly muted.

Figure 13.6 Drag up or down on the Track Pan knob to adjust the setting.

Figure 13.7 Click the Output Window button to open the track Output window.

Figure 13.8 Click the Panner Linking button to link pan controls on a stereo track.

Figure 13.9 Click the Inverse Pan button to link stereo pan controls in opposite directions.

Figure 13.10 Click the Solo button to solo a track.

Figure 13.11 Click the Mute button to mute a track.

Figure 13.12 Command-click (Mac) or Ctrl-click (Windows) the Solo button to Solo Safe the track.

To mute a track:

◆ Click the track's Mute button (**Figure 13.11**).

The Mute button highlights to indicate the track is explicitly muted. Mute buttons latch, allowing multiple tracks to be muted simultaneously.

Setting Solo Latch options

You can set Solo buttons to behave in one of two ways:

◆ **X-OR (Cancel Previous Solo)** causes any other soloed tracks to become unsoloed.

◆ **Latching** allows multiple tracks to be soloed simultaneously.

To set the Solo Latch option:

◆ Choose Options > Solo Mode > and select X-OR (Cancel Previous Solo) or select Latching.

Solo Safing tracks

You can prevent tracks from being muted when other tracks are soloed. This is useful on an Auxiliary Input track to maintain its function as an effects return, or on a MIDI track to ensure it plays back while you are soloing Audio tracks.

To Solo Safe a track:

◆ Command-click (Mac) or Ctrl-click (Windows) the track's Solo button.

The Solo button grays out to indicate that the track is in Solo Safe mode (**Figure 13.12**).

ADJUSTING TRACK CONTROLS

Assigning Track Inputs and Outputs

Audio and Auxiliary Input tracks have Input and Output selectors that let you route audio to and from each track.

Instrument tracks also have Input and Output selectors for routing audio, but in most cases the input on an Instrument track is automatically assigned to an instrument plug-in on the track.

Master Fader tracks are used to control outputs in a session, so they have Output selectors only.

For more information on assigning track inputs and outputs, see Chapter 4, "Working with Tracks," and Chapter 6, "Recording Audio."

Assigning multiple outputs

Pro Tools lets you assign the outputs on Audio, Auxiliary Input, and Instrument tracks to more than one destination. This makes it possible to send the same signal to discrete outputs—for example, to multiple monitor feeds or recording devices. This also makes it possible to output different mixes simultaneously.

To assign multiple outputs on a track:

1. Assign the first output by clicking the Output selector and choosing an audio interface or bus output path (**Figure 13.13**).

2. Assign an additional output by holding Control (Mac) or Start (Windows) and choosing an additional output path.

   The Output selector shows a Plus sign next to the first path name to indicate that the track has multiple output assignments (**Figure 13.14**).

Figure 13.13 Click the track's Output selector to assign the first output.

Figure 13.14 The Output selector shows a Plus sign to indicate multiple output assignments.

Figure 13.15 Command-Control-click (Mac) or Ctrl-Start-click (Windows) an output to make it inactive.

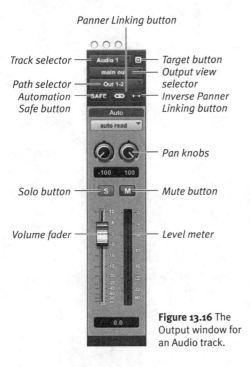

Panner Linking button

Track selector — *Target button*
Output view selector
Path selector —
Automation Safe button — *Inverse Panner Linking button*

Pan knobs

Solo button — *Mute button*

Volume fader — *Level meter*

Figure 13.16 The Output window for an Audio track.

Making outputs inactive

Making an output inactive both silences the track output and frees up the processing power used by the output.

To toggle the active/inactive state of an output:

◆ Command-Control-click (Mac) or Ctrl-Start-click (Windows) the Output selector.

When inactive, an output is grayed out and the output name is italicized (**Figure 13.15**).

Using track Output windows

Pro Tools lets you open separate Output windows for tracks (**Figure 13.16**). These floating windows provide convenient access to mixing controls when the Mix window is obscured or showing other tracks.

Output windows for Audio, Auxiliary Input, Instrument, or Master Fader tracks all have the same controls as their corresponding track type in the Mix window, including Volume fader, Level meter, Solo and Mute buttons, Pan controls, Automation Mode selector, and Output selector.

In addition, track Output windows have the following controls:

◆ **Track selector** lets you choose any Audio, Auxiliary Input, Instrument, or Master Fader track for display in the window.

◆ **Output view selector** lets you display any of the outputs on the selected track (the track's Main Output or Sends A–J).

continues on next page

◆ **Path selector** lets you assign the Output path for the currently displayed output view.

◆ **Automation Safe button** prevents existing automation on the track from being overwritten.

◆ **Panner Linking button** links the left and right pan knobs of stereo tracks.

◆ **Inverse Panner Linking button** sets left and right pan knobs to move in opposite directions.

◆ **Target button** determines the focus when you open a new Output window. If you deselect the Target, the window is anchored to its current location and output display.

To open a track Output window:

◆ Click the Output Window button located next to the output selector for the track (Figure 13.7).

Figure 13.17 Inserts view in the Mix window, showing selectors for Inserts A–J.

Figure 13.18 Click an Insert selector to select a plug-in or hardware I/O insert.

Using Inserts

Pro Tools lets you add up to ten inserts on each Audio, Auxiliary Input, Instrument, or Master Fader track. Inserts can be software plug-ins that process audio internally, or hardware inserts that route audio to external processors and back.

For more information on using plug-ins, see Chapter 14, "Using Plug-Ins."

Inserts on Audio, Auxiliary Input, and Instrument tracks are pre-fader, processing the audio signal before it reaches the track's Volume fader. Inserts on Master Fader tracks are post-fader, processing the audio signal after it is modified by the track's Volume fader.

When more than one insert is placed on the same track, they process the audio signal in series, from top to bottom as they are displayed in the Inserts view.

Adding inserts to tracks

In Inserts view, you can display inserts on tracks in two groups of five (labeled Inserts A–E and Inserts F–J) (**Figure 13.17**).

To display Inserts view in the Mix window:

◆ Choose View > Mix Window Views > Inserts A–E or Inserts F–J.

To add an insert to a track:

◆ Click the Insert selector on the track and select a plug-in or a hardware I/O pair (**Figure 13.18**).

To remove an insert from a track:

◆ Click the Insert selector and choose "no insert."

✔ Tips

■ To add the same insert to all tracks with the same channel format, hold Option (Mac) or Alt (Windows) while adding it to a track.

■ To add the same insert to all currently selected tracks with the same channel format, hold Option-Shift (Mac) or Alt-Shift (Windows) while adding it to a track.

Bypassing plug-ins

You can bypass software plug-ins, but not hardware inserts. When you bypass a plug-in, it disables the effect but does not free up the processing power that the plug-in uses.

To toggle the bypass state of a plug-in:

◆ In Inserts view, Command-click (Mac) or Ctrl-click (Windows) the insert.

The insert turns blue to indicate that is it bypassed (**Figure 13.19**).

or

In the Plug-In window, click the Bypass button (**Figure 13.20**).

The Bypass button highlights to indicate that the plug-in is bypassed.

Figure 13.19 Command-click (Mac) or Ctrl-click (Windows) an insert to bypass it.

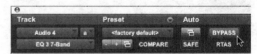

Figure 13.20 Click the Bypass button in the Plug-In window to bypass it.

Figure 13.21 Command-Control-click (Mac) or Ctrl-Start-click (Windows) an insert to make it inactive.

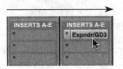

Figure 13.22 Drag an insert to move it to a new position.

Making inserts inactive

Making an insert inactive both disables the effect and frees up the processing power used by the insert.

To toggle the active/inactive state of an insert:

◆ In Inserts view, Command-Control-click (Mac) or Ctrl-Start-click (Windows) the insert.

When inactive, an insert is grayed out and the insert name is italicized (**Figure 13.21**).

Moving and copying inserts

After you have added an insert to a track, you can move or copy that insert to other tracks with the same channel format, or to another insert position on the same track.

When you move or copy a plug-in, any adjustments to the plug-in settings are preserved or copied. If you move or copy an insert onto an existing insert, the original insert is replaced.

To move an insert:

◆ Drag the insert to a new position (**Figure 13.22**).

To copy an insert:

◆ Option-drag (Mac) or Alt-drag (Windows) the insert to a new position.

Using Sends

Pro Tools lets you assign up to ten sends on each Audio, Auxiliary Input, or Instrument track. Sends can be used for a variety of purposes, such as creating an effects loop, a cue mix, or a submix.

A send can be routed to an internal bus or to an external device through an audio interface output.

Assigning sends to tracks

In Sends view, you can display sends on tracks in two groups of five (labeled Sends A–E and Sends F–J), or you can display the controls for individual sends.

To display Sends view in the Mix window:

◆ Choose View > Mix Window Views > Sends A–E or Sends F–J.

The corresponding Sends view is displayed in the Mix window (**Figure 13.23**).

To display individual send controls in Sends view:

◆ Choose View > Sends A–E or Sends F–J and select a send position.

or

Command-click (Mac) or Ctrl-click (Windows) the Send selector at the send position you want to display.

The controls for the selected send are displayed in the Mix window (**Figure 13.24**).

Figure 13.23 Sends view in the Mix window, showing Send selectors for Sends A–J.

Figure 13.24 The controls for an individual send shown in the Mix window.

To assign a send to a track:

1. Click the Send selector on the track and select an audio interface output or bus path.

   The Send window for the track appears (**Figure 13.25**).

2. In the Send window, drag the fader to set the level for the send.

To remove a send from a track:

◆ Click the Send selector and choose "no send."

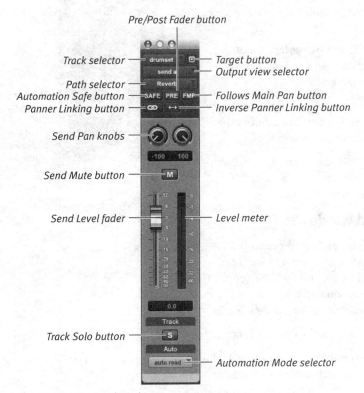

Pre/Post Fader button

Track selector

Target button
Output view selector

Path selector
Automation Safe button
Panner Linking button

Follows Main Pan button
Inverse Panner Linking button

Send Pan knobs

Send Mute button

Send Level fader

Level meter

Track Solo button

Automation Mode selector

Figure 13.25 The Send window.

Creating a return for a send

After you've routed a send to an internal bus or an external output, you need to return the signal to the mix with an Auxiliary Input track.

To create a return for a send:

1. Create a new Auxiliary Input track with the appropriate channel format (mono or stereo).

2. Click the Input selector on the Auxiliary Input track (**Figure 13.26**) and do one of the following:

   ▲ Assign the bus you chose for the send.

   or

   Assign the audio interface input to which the output of the external device is connected.

3. Click the Output selector of the Auxiliary Input track and assign its output to the main output for the session.

4. Adjust the Volume fader of the Auxiliary Input track to control the amount of returned signal in the mix.

Figure 13.26 To create a return for a send, assign the input of an Auxiliary Input track to the bus or audio interface input you chose for the send.

Using Send windows

Send windows show all of the controls for sends, which include the Send Level fader, the Send Mute button, and Send Pan controls. The Send window also shows the track Solo button and Automation Mode selector.

Send windows also have the following controls:

◆ **Track selector** lets you choose any Audio, Auxiliary Input, Instrument, or Master Fader track for display in the window.

◆ **Output view selector** lets you display any of the outputs on the selected track (the track's Main Output or Sends A–J).

◆ **Path selector** lets you assign the Output path for the currently displayed output view.

USING SENDS

Figure 13.27 Click the send to open the Send window.

◆ **Automation Safe button** prevents existing automation for the send from being overwritten.

◆ **Pre/Post Fader** sets the send for pre- or post-fader operation.

◆ **Follows Main Pan** links the Send pan controls to the main pan controls for the track.

◆ **Panner Linking button** links the left and right pan knobs of stereo sends.

◆ **Inverse Panner Linking button** sets left and right pan knobs to move in opposite directions.

◆ **Target button** determines the focus when you open a new Output window. If you deselect the Target button, the window is anchored to its current location and output display.

To open a Send window:

◆ In Sends view, click the send (**Figure 13.27**).

Setting send pre-fader or post-fader operation

You can set sends to operate in two ways:

◆ **Pre-fader** sends are located before the track's Volume fader in the signal path, so the send level is not influenced by the track volume setting. Pre-fader sends are useful for monitor and cue mixes, when you want the sends to remain audible regardless of the track volume setting.

◆ **Post-fader** sends are located after the track's Volume fader in the signal path, so the send level is dependent on the track volume setting. Post-fader sends are often used for effects processing, when you want the effect to be proportional to the overall level. Sends are post-fader by default.

continues on next page

USING SENDS

To toggle send pre- and post-fader operation:

◆ In the Send window, click the Pre/Post Fader button. The button highlights to indicate that the send is pre-fader (**Figure 13.28**).

or

In Sends view with the individual send controls displayed, click the Pre/Post Fader button. The button highlights to indicate that the send is pre-fader (**Figure 13.29**).

Adjusting send pan controls

Send pan controls let you balance send output across a stereo output path. As with track panning, the available controls depend on the channel formats involved.

◆ A send assigned to a mono path does not have pan controls (**Figure 13.30**).

◆ A send on a mono track assigned to a stereo path has one pan control (**Figure 13.31**).

Figure 13.28 The Pre/Post Fader button in the Send window.

Figure 13.29 The Pre/Post Fader button in the individual send controls.

Figure 13.30 A Send window for a send assigned to a mono path.

Figure 13.31 A Send window for a mono send assigned to a stereo path.

Figure 13.32 A Send window for a stereo send assigned to a stereo path.

Figure 13.33 Drag up or down on the Send pan knob to adjust the Send pan setting.

Figure 13.34 Click the Panner Linking button to link pan controls on a Stereo send.

Figure 13.35 Click the Inverse Pan button to link stereo send pan controls in opposite directions.

◆ A send on a stereo track assigned to a stereo output has two pan controls (**Figure 13.32**).

As with track pan controls, each send pan control is adjustable from full left to full right.

To adjust send pan:

◆ Click a Send Pan knob and drag up or down (**Figure 13.33**).

To adjust send pan with fine control:

◆ Command-drag (Mac) or Ctrl-drag (Windows) the Send Pan knob up or down.

Linking send pan controls

As with track pan controls, on stereo sends you can link the left and right pan controls so that they move in tandem.

To link pan controls on a stereo send:

1. In the Send window, click the Panner linking button so that it is highlighted (**Figure 13.34**).

2. To link send pan controls in an inverse manner, click the Inverse Pan button (**Figure 13.35**).

USING SENDS

Linking send pan and track pan controls

If you don't want to adjust a send's pan controls independently, you can set them to follow the track's main pan controls.

Figure 13.36 Click the Follows Main Pan button to link a send's pan controls to the track pan controls.

To link send pan controls to track pan controls:

◆ In the Send window, click the Follows Main Pan button so that it is highlighted (**Figure 13.36**).

The send pan controls are grayed out; they now follow the pan settings for the track.

Figure 13.37 Command-click (Mac) or Ctrl-click (Windows) a send to mute it.

Muting sends

Muting a send silences its output, without freeing up any of the processing power that the send uses.

Figure 13.38 Click the Mute button in the individual Send controls to mute the send.

To mute a send:

◆ In Sends view, Command-click (Mac) or Ctrl-click (Windows) the send.

The send turns blue to indicate that it is muted (**Figure 13.37**).

◆ In Sends view with individual Send controls displayed, click the Mute button. The button highlights to indicate that the send is muted (**Figure 13.38**).

or

In the Send window, click the Mute button.

The Mute button highlights to indicate that the send is muted (**Figure 13.39**).

Figure 13.39 Click the Mute button in the Send window to mute the send.

Figure 13.40 Command-Control-click (Mac) or Ctrl-Start-click (Windows) a send to make it inactive.

Figure 13.41 Drag a send to move it to new position.

Making sends inactive

Making a send inactive both silences its output and frees up the processing power it uses.

To toggle the active/inactive state of a send:

◆ In Sends view, Command-Control-click (Mac) or Ctrl-Start-click (Windows) the send.

When inactive, a send is grayed out and the send name is italicized (**Figure 13.40**).

Moving and copying sends

You can move or copy sends to other tracks or to another send position on the same track. If you move the send to a track with a different channel format, the send pan controls change accordingly.

When you move or copy a send, all of its settings are preserved or copied. If you move or copy a send onto an existing send, the original send is replaced.

To move a send:

◆ Drag the send to a new position (**Figure 13.41**).

To copy a send:

◆ Option-drag (Mac) or Alt-drag (Windows) the send to a new position.

Working with Groups

Pro Tools lets you group tracks so that you can edit them and adjust their controls simultaneously. Grouping is useful for multi-miked instruments, or for related sections of an ensemble, or for categories of tracks that you might include in a submix.

You can create up to 104 groups in four banks of 26 (labeled a–z) within a session. In addition, every session automatically includes the All group, which affects all tracks in the session. When the All group is active, all tracks are affected by operations performed on a single track.

The names of groups in a session appear in the Groups list, which is on the bottom left of the Edit and Mix windows. From the Groups list, you can activate and modify groups, select and display tracks in groups, and delete groups.

Types of groups

There are three types of groups: Edit groups, Mix groups, and combined Mix/Edit groups. When editing, you can use groups to change views across multiple tracks, and make sure the same edits are applied to grouped tracks. When mixing, you can group tracks to maintain their relative levels.

Edit groups affect the following:

◆ Track View, Track Height, and Track Timebase settings

◆ Audio and MIDI editing operations

◆ Automation editing operations

Mix groups affect the following:

◆ Track volume

◆ Automation mode

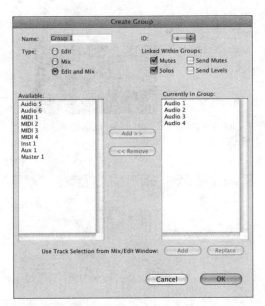

Figure 13.42 The Create Group dialog.

Figure 13.43 A new, activated group in the Groups list.

Mix groups can also be set to affect the following:

◆ Track mute and Track solo

◆ Send level and Send mute

Creating groups

You can group tracks at any time during a session.

To create a new group:

1. Select the tracks you want to include in the group.

2. Choose Track > Group.

   or

   Press Command-G (Mac) or Ctrl-G (Windows).

   The Create Group dialog appears (**Figure 13.42**).

3. Type a name for the group.

4. Select the type of group to create. In most cases, choosing the combined "Edit and Mix" group is suitable.

5. The next available group ID is automatically displayed. If you want to assign a different group ID, select it from the ID pop-up menu.

6. Under Linked Within Groups, select any attributes you want the group to affect.

7. To change track membership in the group, select track names and click the Add or Remove buttons.

8. Click OK.

   The new group appears in the Groups list and is selected to indicate that it is active (**Figure 13.43**).

WORKING WITH GROUPS

To modify an existing group:

1. Click the Groups list menu button and choose Modify Groups from the pop-up menu (**Figure 13.44**).

   The Modify Groups dialog appears (**Figure 13.45**).

2. Choose the group you want to modify from the ID pop-up menu.

3. Make any changes to the name, type, or track membership in the group.

4. Click OK.

To delete a group:

◆ In the Groups list, right-click the group name and choose Delete from the pop-up menu (**Figure 13.46**).

Activating and deactivating groups

When a group is active, the controls on member tracks are linked; for example, if you move a Volume fader on one track, the faders on all other tracks in the group move by the same amount. When the group is not active, track controls operate independently. When you create a new group, it is automatically activated.

Figure 13.44 Click the Groups list menu button and choose Modify Groups.

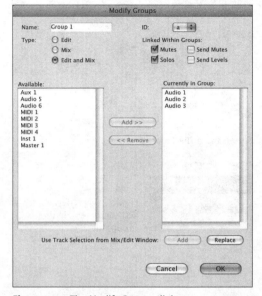

Figure 13.45 The Modify Groups dialog.

Figure 13.46 Right-click the Group name and choose Delete.

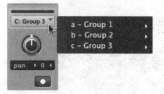

Figure 13.47 Click the Group name to activate the group.

Figure 13.48 To view a track's group membership, click its Group ID indicator.

To toggle the active state of a group:

◆ In the Groups list, click the group name (**Figure 13.47**).

The group name is highlighted to indicate that it is activated.

Viewing group membership

In the Mix window, a track's group membership is shown in its Group ID indicator as a lowercase letter (a–z) and the group name. If a track belongs to more than one active group, an uppercase letter is displayed, along with the name of the larger or parent group.

To view the group membership of a track:

◆ In the Mix window, click the track's Group ID indicator.

A pop-up menu appears, showing a list of currently active groups (**Figure 13.48**).

Selecting tracks in a group

You can select tracks in a group from the Groups list. The list shows different symbols depending on how many tracks in a group are selected (**Figure 13.49**):

◆ A **dot** indicates that all of the group's tracks are selected.

◆ A **circle** indicates that only some of the group's tracks are selected.

continues on next page

WORKING WITH GROUPS

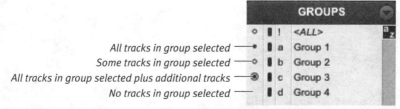

All tracks in group selected ——
Some tracks in group selected ——
All tracks in group selected plus additional tracks ——
No tracks in group selected ——

Figure 13.49 Symbols in the Groups list indicate which tracks in the group are selected.

- A **dot inside a circle** indicates that all of the group's tracks are selected, plus additional tracks.

- **No symbol** means that no tracks in the group are selected.

To select the members of a group:

- In the Groups list, click in the column to the left of the Group ID.

   A dot appears, indicating that all tracks in the group are selected (**Figure 13.50**).

Figure 13.50 Click in the column to the left of a Group name to select all tracks in the group.

Showing and hiding tracks in a group

From the Groups list, you can show or hide tracks that are members of a group. Tracks are shown or hidden in both the Edit and the Mix windows, regardless of the Group type.

Figure 13.51 Right-click a Group name and choose Show Only Tracks in Group.

To show only the members of a group:

- In the Groups list, right-click a group name and choose Show Only Tracks in Group from the pop-up menu (**Figure 13.51**).

To hide the members of a group:

- In the Groups list, right-click a group name and choose Hide Tracks in Group from the pop-up menu.

To show all tracks:

- In the Groups list, right-click a group name and choose Show All Tracks from the pop-up menu.

Creating a Submix

In sessions where you have a group of related tracks such as drums and percussion or a horn section, you can create a submix to control their overall volume with a single fader. You can also apply effects to the submix instead of to each individual track.

In a submix, you route the outputs from related tracks to the same internal bus path and control that path with an Auxiliary Input track (**Figure 13.52**).

Outputs of Audio tracks —

Input of Auxiliary Input track

Volume fader of Auxiliary Input track controls the overall submix level

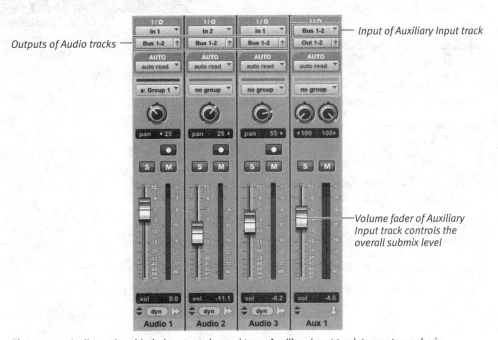

Figure 13.52 Audio tracks with their outputs bussed to an Auxiliary Input track to create a submix.

To create a submix:

1. On each track you want to include in the submix, set the track output to the same stereo bus path (**Figure 13.53**).

2. Create a new stereo Auxiliary Input track.

3. Click the Input selector on the Auxiliary Input track and assign the same bus path you chose for the track outputs (**Figure 13.54**).

4. Click the Output selector of the Auxiliary Input track and assign its output to the main output for the session.

5. Adjust the Volume faders of the individual tracks to set relative levels within the submix.

6. Adjust the pan controls of the individual tracks to place them in the stereo field.

7. Adjust the Volume fader of the Auxiliary Input track to control the overall level of the submix.

8. To apply an effect to the submix, add an insert to the Auxiliary Input track.

9. Adjust the mix or wet/dry controls on the plug-in or external effects processor to determine the amount of processing applied to the submix.

Figure 13.53 Set the output of each source track to the same stereo bus path.

Figure 13.54 Set the input of the Auxiliary Input track to the bus that the source track outputs were routed to.

Creating a Shared Effects Loop

In sessions where you want to apply the same effect to several tracks and also control the overall amount of the effect applied, you can create a send-return arrangement called an *effects loop* (**Figure 13.55**). This is especially useful for time-based effects such as reverbs, delays, or echoes.

Sends from Audio tracks →

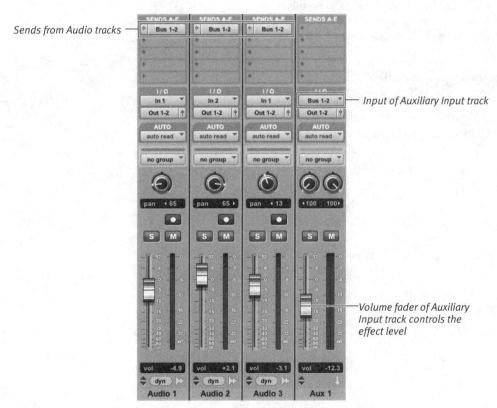

Input of Auxiliary Input track

Volume fader of Auxiliary Input track controls the effect level

Figure 13.55 Audio tracks with sends bussed to an Auxiliary Input track to create an effects loop.

To create a shared effects loop:

1. On each track you want to send to the effect, assign a send to the track and then send the signal to a stereo bus path (**Figure 13.56**).

2. Create a new stereo Auxiliary Input track.

3. Click the Input selector on the Auxiliary Input track and assign the same bus path you chose for the track sends (Figure 13.53).

4. Click the Output selector of the Auxiliary Input track and assign its output to the main output for the session.

5. Add an insert for the effect to the Auxiliary Input track.

6. Adjust the Volume fader of the Auxiliary Input track to determine the amount of processed signal in the mix.

Figure 13.56 Create sends and route them to a stereo bus path.

USING PLUG-INS

Much of the power and versatility of Pro Tools comes from its use of software add-ons, or plug-ins. There are a variety of plug-ins available for Pro Tools, ranging from the essential (equalizers, compressors, reverbs) to the esoteric (amp emulators, vocoders, virtual instruments, and more).

This chapter shows how to use plug-ins and introduces four essential types of plug-in effects: equalization, compression, reverb, and delay.

Plug-In Types

Pro Tools LE uses two types of plug-ins:

RTAS (Real-Time AudioSuite) plug-ins operate during playback and are nondestructive. Audio is routed through an RTAS plug-in as it is played back, but the original audio material remains unmodified. Equalization (EQ), compression, reverb, and delay are types of commonly used RTAS plug-ins (**Figure 14.1**).

AudioSuite plug-ins are applied when playback is stopped, creating a new audio file. Use them to add a permanent effect to selected audio. Gain, Normalize, and Invert are commonly used AudioSuite plug-ins (**Figure 14.2**).

Plug-ins are available in four channel formats:

◆ **Mono** plug-ins are used on single-channel tracks.

◆ **Multi-channel** plug-ins are used on stereo tracks.

◆ **Mono/stereo** plug-ins are used on mono tracks and change their output to two-channel (stereo) output. This makes it possible to apply a stereo effect directly to a mono track. Any other plug-ins inserted after a mono/stereo plug-in automatically convert to stereo format.

◆ **Multi-mono** plug-ins can be used on stereo tracks if a multi-channel version of the plug-in is not available. The Click plug-in, for example, is available only in mono and multi-mono formats.

Figure 14.1 DigiRack 1-band EQ III is a nondestructive, real-time plug-in.

Figure 14.2 DigiRack AudioSuite Normalize is a destructive plug-in that is applied after playback.

Inserting Plug-Ins on Tracks

To use a plug-in, insert it on any of the ten inserts available on Audio, Auxiliary Input, or Instrument tracks (**Figure 14.3**). When more than one effects plug-in is inserted on the same track, each effect is added after the previous one (**Figure 14.4**).

EQ plug-in insert

Figure 14.3 The DigiRack RTAS 1-band EQ III plug-in inserted on an audio track.

EQ plug-in insert
Compressor plug-in insert

Figure 14.4 An EQ and a compressor plug-in are inserted on the same track. The compressor's effect is added after the EQ.

Certain plug-ins are best suited to specific track types.

◆ Insert a virtual instrument plug-in such as a synthesizer or drum machine on an Instrument track. You can then play it with a MIDI controller connected to your system.

◆ Insert a reverb on an Auxiliary Input track so that it can be shared by several other tracks.

See "Sharing Reverb with Other Tracks in an Effects Loop" later in this chapter.

To add a plug-in to a track:

1. Show track inserts by choosing View > Mix Window Views > Inserts A–E or Inserts F–J.

2. Click the Insert selector on the track and select a plug-in (**Figure 14.5**).

To remove a plug-in:

◆ Click the Insert selector and choose "no insert" (**Figure 14.6**).

✔ Tip

■ You can insert or remove a plug-in during playback, but not during recording.

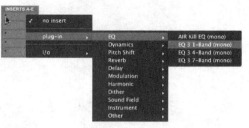

Figure 14.5 To insert a plug-in, click the Insert selector and choose from the plug-ins menu.

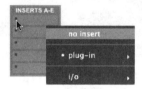

Figure 14.6 To remove a plug-in, click the Insert selector and choose "no insert."

Plug-In Favorites

If you regularly use a certain plug-in, make it easier to access by designating it as a "favorite" by pressing Command (Mac) or Ctrl (Windows) and selecting it from the Insert selector. It will then always appear at the top of the plug-in menu for quick selection.

The RTAS Plug-In Window

When an RTAS plug-in is inserted, it appears in a floating window. There you can adjust its controls, manage its library of presets, and enable its parameters for mix automation.

While parameters vary, all RTAS plug-ins share a common set of controls that appear in the header area of the window (**Figure 14.7**).

Track controls

Track controls let you choose which plug-in to display in the window (Figure 14.7).

◆ **Track selector** lets you select any track in the session, with the exception of MIDI tracks.

◆ **Insert Position selector** lets you choose any insert on the current track.

◆ **Plug-in selector** lets you select any RTAS plug-in installed in your system.

◆ **Key Input** lets you route audio from an input or bus and use it to trigger a plug-in such as a compressor. This menu appears only on plug-ins that feature side-chain processing.

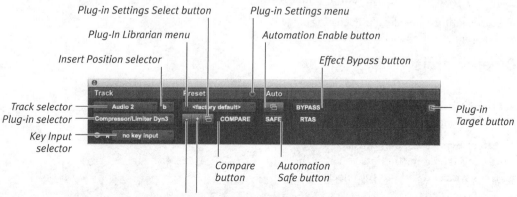

Figure 14.7 The plug-in header has controls for managing presets, enabling automation, and other essential functions.

Preset controls

Preset controls let you select from a library of presets or create new presets (Figure 14.7).

◆ **Plug-in Settings menu** lets you copy, paste, save, and import plug-in settings.

◆ **Plug-in Librarian menu** lets you recall plug-in presets.

◆ **Next Setting and Previous Setting** let you select the next or previous preset from the Librarian menu.

◆ **Plug-in Settings Select** lets you access the Plug-in Settings dialog, which lists all presets for the selected plug-in. From this list, you can select and audition presets by clicking on their name, or by tabbing through the list with your keyboard's up, down, left, and right arrows.

◆ **Compare** toggles between the original state of a preset and any changes you have made.

Automation controls

Automation controls let you enable specific plug-in controls for mix automation (Figure 14.7).

◆ **Automation Enable** opens the Plug-in Automation dialog, where you can select plug-in parameters for mix automation.

◆ **Automation Safe** safeguards existing plug-in automation from being overwritten.

Other controls

Other controls include Effect Bypass, a Target button, a clip indicator, and linking controls for multi-mono plug-ins (Figure 14.7).

◆ **Effect Bypass** disables the currently displayed plug-in. This lets you hear the track with and without the effect.

◆ **Target** selects that plug-in as the target for any keyboard commands.

Figure 14.8 To open a plug-in window, click the Insert button.

Figure 14.9 Click the Target button to make a plug-in window remain on screen with other plug-ins.

Opening and Managing Plug-In Windows

Normally, Pro Tools displays a single plug-in window at a time. However, you can open multiple plug-in windows for quick access to their controls.

To open a plug-in window:

◆ Click an Insert button (**Figure 14.8**).

The Plug-in window appears.

To open multiple plug-in windows:

1. Click the Insert selector and select a Plug-in.

2. Click the Plug-in Target button (**Figure 14.9**).

The Target button grays out, indicating that the plug-in is active, but that the window is not the target of keyboard commands.

3. Click the Insert selector and select another plug-in.

The plug-in opens. The previously opened Plug-in window remains open.

4. Repeat steps 2–3 to open additional plug-in windows.

    or

    Shift-click the Insert button for another plug-in.

    The selected plug-in window opens. Any previously open plug-in windows remain open as well.

To select a different plug-in on the same track:

◆ Click the Plug-in selector and choose a plug-in from the pop-up menu (**Figure 14.10**).

The new plug-in appears.

To select a plug-in on a different track:

◆ Click the Track selector and choose a track from the pop-up menu (**Figure 14.11**).

The first plug-in inserted on that track appears.

OPENING AND MANAGING PLUG-IN WINDOWS

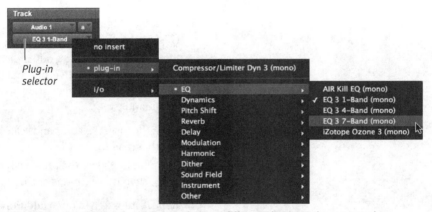

Plug-in selector

Figure 14.10 Use the Plug-in selector to choose a different plug-in on the same track.

Track selector

Figure 14.11 Use the Track selector to choose a plug-in on another track.

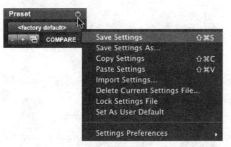

Figure 14.12 The Plug-In Librarian lets you load presets for a plug-in.

Figure 14.13 Use the Save Settings command to store your own presets.

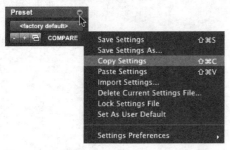

Figure 14.14 You can copy and paste settings between plug-ins.

Previous Setting button

Next Setting button

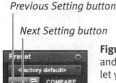

Figure 14.15 The Next Setting and Previous Setting buttons let you quickly tab through a plug-in's presets.

Auditioning, Storing, and Recalling Presets

Most plug-ins provide a library of useful presets. Pro Tools provides an easy way to not only recall and audition these presets, but also create and store your own.

To load a preset:

◆ Click the Plug-in Librarian menu and choose a preset (**Figure 14.12**).

To save a preset:

1. Set the controls of the plug-in to create the effect you want.

2. Choose Save Settings from the Plug-In Settings menu (**Figure 14.13**).

3. Enter a name and click OK.

   The new preset appears in the Plug-in Librarian menu.

To copy settings from one instance of a plug-in to another:

1. Choose Copy Settings from the Plug-in Settings menu (**Figure 14.14**).

2. Open the destination plug-in.

3. Choose Paste Settings from the Plug-in Settings menu.

Selecting presets with Next Setting and Previous Setting

You can manually scroll through the presets for a plug-in using the Next Setting and the Previous Setting buttons (**Figure 14.15**).

To scroll through presets:

1. Begin audio playback.

2. Click the Next Setting button to select the next preset; click the Previous Setting button to select the previous preset.

Auto-auditioning presets

Pro Tools provides an auto-audition feature that scrolls through presets during audio playback.

To auto-audition presets:

1. Click the Settings Select button on the plug-in.

   The Plug-in Settings dialog appears (**Figure 14.16**).

2. Click the check box to enable Increment Setting Every, then enter a value for the number of seconds between each preset change.

3. Select a preset.

4. Begin audio playback.

5. When you find a preset you like, deselect the Increment Setting Every option.

6. Click Done.

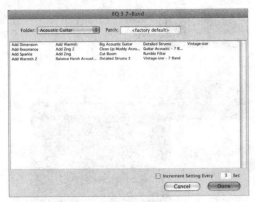

Figure 14.16 The Plug-in Settings dialog displays a list of all available presets.

Figure 14.17 The DigiRack 1-Band EQ III plug-in.

Figure 14.18 The DigiRack 4-Band EQ III plug-in.

Using EQ Plug-Ins

The purpose of EQ is to change the tonal quality of an audio signal by boosting or cutting the gain of specific frequencies within the signal. EQ has both creative and corrective uses.

Pro Tools provides 1-band, 4-band, and 7-band parametric RTAS EQ plug-ins. A parametric EQ lets you choose the specific range of frequencies that you want to boost or cut. To use a parametric EQ, select a specific frequency, set the bandwidth around that frequency, then select how much you will boost or cut the gain of those frequencies.

The DigiRack 1-Band EQ III (**Figure 14.17**) lets you apply a single EQ filter to an audio signal. The DigiRack 4-Band EQ III (**Figure 14.18**) lets you apply up to four different EQ filters simultaneously. The DigiRack 7-Band EQ III (**Figure 14.19**) lets you apply up to seven different EQ filters to a signal.

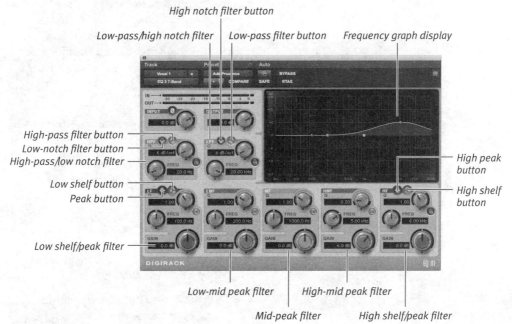

High notch filter button

Low-pass/high notch filter   *Low-pass filter button*   *Frequency graph display*

High-pass filter button
Low-notch filter button
High-pass/low notch filter

High peak button

Low shelf button
Peak button

High shelf button

Low shelf/peak filter

Low-mid peak filter   *High-mid peak filter*

Mid-peak filter   *High shelf/peak filter*

Figure 14.19 The DigiRack 7-Band EQ III plug-in.

USING EQ PLUG-INS

339

DigiRack EQ plug-ins offer the following types of filters:

◆ **High Pass/Low Pass.** Pass filters eliminate unwanted frequency ranges. A high-pass filter lets high frequencies pass while cutting low frequencies. A low-pass filter lets low frequencies pass while cutting high frequencies.

◆ **High Shelf/Low Shelf.** Shelf filters cut or boost both high- and low-frequency ranges. A high-shelf filter cuts or boost frequencies above a selected frequency. A low-shelf filter cuts or boosts frequencies below a selected frequency.

◆ **High Notch/Low Notch.** Notch filters cut or boost a narrow band of frequencies. The Q button sets the notch width of the filter's frequency range.

◆ **Peak.** Peak filters cut or boost frequencies around a selected frequency in a bell shape. The Peak filter's Q button sets the targeted frequency range.

Using EQ Effectively

There are many ways to use EQ to improve a mix. Your ultimate goal is to make the various instruments blend well together while adding clarity to each. Carefully divide the frequency spectrum among the various instruments in your mix and give each its own space.

◆ If a mix lacks definition, try boosting the key frequency range of each of the main instruments.

◆ If the instruments in your mix don't blend well, try cutting the key frequency range of each one.

◆ To add presence to vocals, try boosting the 3 kHz range.

◆ Avoid boosting the same frequencies on multiple instruments.

◆ Use the Bypass button frequently to audition tracks with and without EQ.

Knee   Attack

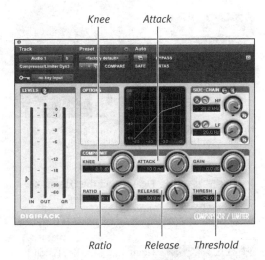

Ratio   Release   Threshold

Figure 14.20 The DigiRack Compressor/Limiter plug-in.

Using Compression Plug-Ins

A compressor is like an automatic volume control: it reduces the level of loud sounds when their volume exceeds a specific threshold.

In this way, a compressor controls the dynamic range of audio material so that the difference between its quietest and loudest parts is decreased. The more a signal is compressed, the higher its average energy level. Hence, compression has the added effect of increasing the average volume of a recording.

Compression can be used to bring out subtle details, give a track more consistent levels, and in some cases, add more presence and punch to a mix. Typically, a recording engineer will use compression on individual instruments (vocals, bass guitar, drums) as well as on the overall mix.

Pro Tools provides the DigiRack Compressor/ Limiter plug-in. It has the following settings (**Figure 14.20**):

◆ **Threshold** is the level above which compression is applied.

◆ **Ratio** is the amount that a signal's volume is decreased relative to the signal's original volume. With the ratio set to 2:1, an increase in input of 2 dB above the threshold will result in an increased output level of only 1 dB. Higher ratios yield more compression, but only to signals that pass above the threshold.

◆ **Attack** controls the length of time in milliseconds that the compressor takes to reduce the gain once the audio signal has passed the threshold.

continues on next page

◆ **Release** controls the length of time in milliseconds that the gain takes to return to normal after the audio signal has fallen back below the threshold.

◆ **Knee** sets the rate at which the compressor reaches full compression once the threshold has been exceeded.

Side-chain processing

The DigiRack Compressor/Limiter features side-chain processing, which allows the compressor to be triggered by audio from a different track. The audio source used to trigger the compressor is called the *key input*. You can use any Pro Tools bus or input as the key input.

A common use for a side chain is to use a voiceover track as a key input to strongly reduce or *duck* the volume of a music bed. In this case, whenever the voiceover occurs, it triggers the compressor, which reduces the volume of the music bed. This improves the clarity and intelligibility of the voiceover in the mix.

To use a key input for side-chain processing:

1. From the Key Input menu, choose the input or bus carrying the audio that you want to trigger the compressor (**Figure 14.21**).

2. Click the External Key button to activate side-chain processing (**Figure 14.22**).

3. Click the Key Listen button to audition the key input audio source (**Figure 14.23**).

4. Begin playback.
   The compressor uses the key input to trigger its effect. If necessary, adjust the controls to achieve the desired effect.

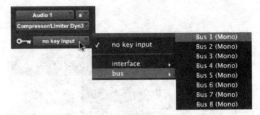

Figure 14.21 The Key Input lets you trigger the compressor from a separate audio source.

Figure 14.22 The External Key button enables side-chain processing.

Figure 14.23 The Key Listen button lets you audition the key input audio source.

✔ Tip

■ The DigiRack Compressor/Limiter features high- and low-pass key input filters. Use these to define specific frequency ranges to trigger compression. For example, set the high-pass filter so that only specific high frequencies, such as a hi hat, trigger the effect. Alternatively, set the low-pass filter so that only specific low frequencies, such as a kick drum, trigger the effect.

Using Reverb Plug-Ins

Reverb is used to impart a sense of acoustic space to a recording by simulating the complex pattern of echoes and reflections that occur in that space, whether large or small.

Because individual instruments in a mix are typically recorded *dry*, without room ambience, reverb can help acoustically connect them by placing them within a common sonic environment: the vastness of a cathedral, or the intimacy of a small room.

The D-Verb reverb plug-in (**Figure 14.24**) provided with Pro Tools features a library of presets that simulate various halls, churches, plates, and rooms. You can also create your own settings with these parameters:

◆ **Algorithm** lets you choose the type of acoustic space simulated.

◆ **Size** lets you choose from three room sizes: small, medium, and large. You can create a variety of reverbs with very different characteristics by choosing a reverb Algorithm, then varying its Size setting.

continues on next page

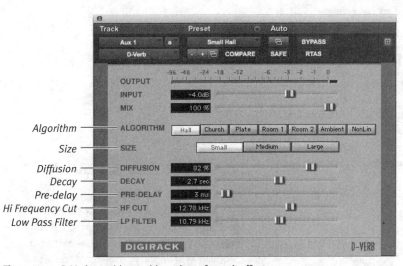

Figure 14.24 D-Verb provides a wide variety of reverb effects.

- **Diffusion** determines the overall density of the reverb effect. Use diffusion to adjust the perceived reflectivity of a space. Lower diffusion simulates a more reflective space; higher diffusion simulates a less reflective space.

- **Decay** controls the length of the reverb effect. It interacts with the Size and Algorithm controls. Longer decay times simulate larger acoustic spaces.

- **Pre-delay** determines the amount of time between the beginning of an audio signal and the beginning of its reverberations. Longer settings add definition to the source audio by separating it from its reverb.

- **High Frequency Cut** filter controls the decay of high-frequency components in the reverb. Use it with the Low Pass filter to shape the overall high-frequency contour of the reverb. Lower settings increase high-frequency damping.

- **Low Pass** filter controls the volume of high frequencies in the reverb. The Low Pass filter applies a 6 dB cut to audio above the frequency you've selected.

Sharing Reverb with other tracks in an effects loop

In most cases, you will want to share a reverb plug-in among several tracks. There are two reasons for this. First, it helps unify a mix by placing the tracks in the same acoustic space. Second, it helps minimize the number of plug-ins used in a session, thereby conserving valuable processing power.

Use Reverb Judiciously

When it comes to reverb, less is more. A good rule of thumb is this: You shouldn't actually hear the reverb as an effect in its own right—but if you remove it, you should get the sense that something is missing.

Send to bus named "Reverb"

Figure 14.25 Use Sends to bus audio to an Auxiliary Input where a reverb plug-in is inserted.

To share a reverb among several tracks, you create an effects loop, in which you will bus audio from multiple tracks to an Auxiliary Input track. The reverb plug-in is then inserted on the Auxiliary Input. You can control the wet/dry balance—the signal with/without effects—between the track and the reverb effect using the track faders (dry level) and Auxiliary Input fader (wet level).

To create an effects loop:

1. Assign a Send on each source track to the same mono or stereo bus (**Figure 14.25**).

2. Assign each track's main output to the main mix outputs (typically channels 1–2).

3. Choose Track > New.
   The New Track dialog box appears.

4. Choose Auxiliary Input (stereo or mono), and click Create.

5. Insert a reverb plug-in on the Auxiliary Input track.

6. Set the reverb's Mix or Balance parameter to 100% Wet, and set any other parameters as desired.

7. Set the Input selector of the Auxiliary Input to the same bus path as the Sends on the source tracks (**Figure 14.26**).

continues on next page

Input from bus named "Reverb"

Figure 14.26 Set the Input selector of the auxiliary input to the same bus as the Sends on the source tracks.

USING REVERB PLUG-INS

8. Click the Output selector of the Auxiliary Input and choose the main mix outputs.

9. Adjust the volume faders of the individual tracks to set their dry (unprocessed) levels.

10. Adjust the level of the Auxiliary Input to set the overall level of the reverb in the mix.

11. Adjust the Send Level faders on each track to set the amount of reverb applied (**Figure 14.27**).

— *Send Level fader*

Figure 14.27 The Send Level fader on the source tracks controls the amount of reverb applied to the track.

Using Delay Plug-Ins

Like reverb, delay effects can add space, depth, and dimension to tracks in a mix. In simple terms, a delay repeats an audio signal for a certain number of repetitions.

By varying the rate of delay and the number of repetitions, and by introducing pitch or time modulation, you can create a wide variety of different effects.

◆ **Doubling** makes a track sound thicker. The effect is typically created with a single delay of between 30 and 80 milliseconds (ms).

◆ **Slapback** is a punchy, short-delay effect often applied to vocals. The effect is typically created with a single delay of between 75 and 120 ms.

◆ **Echo** is a long-delay effect. It is typically created with one or more repeats at delay times of 120–1,000 ms or more.

◆ **Phase shifting** produces an out-of-phase "swirling" effect. It is created by mixing the original audio signal with a slightly delayed (1–3 ms) version of itself that is pitch or time modulated.

◆ **Flanging** produces an even more dramatic swirling effect than phase-shifting. It is created with a slightly longer delay time (1–20 ms) and modulation.

◆ **Chorus** uses short delay times (20–40 ms) and modulation to create the effect of multiple instruments or voices.

The DigiRack RTAS Mod Delay II plug-ins (**Figure 14.28**) provide the following settings:

◆ **Delay** controls the delay time of the effect.

◆ **Depth** controls the amplitude of modulation applied to the delayed signal.

◆ **Rate** controls the speed of the pitch modulation applied to the delayed signal.

◆ **Feedback** controls the number of repeats. The higher the feedback level, the greater the number of repeats.

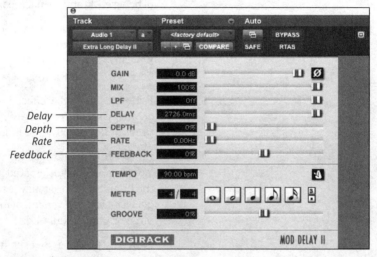

Figure 14.28 The Mod Delay Plug-In window.

Figure 14.29 Enabling Tempo Sync synchronizes the delay to the session tempo.

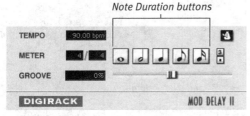

Figure 14.30 Selecting a note duration.

Synchronizing Delay Effects to Session Tempo

Synchronizing delay effects to the session tempo is a common music production technique with many creative applications. The DigiRack Mod Delay II plug-ins provide a Tempo Sync feature that makes this easy to do.

To synchronize a delay effect to session tempo:

1. Click the Insert selector on a track and select Extra Long Delay II.

   The Mod Delay Plug-In appears (Figure 14.28).

2. Begin playback.

3. Adjust the delay parameters for the approximate effect that you want.

4. Click the Tempo Sync button (**Figure 14.29**). The delay tempo changes to match the current session tempo.

5. Select a note duration (**Figure 14.30**).

   The Note Duration buttons select a delay from a musical perspective: whole note, half note, quarter note, eighth note, or sixteenth note. Select the Dot or Triplet modifier buttons to dot the selected note value or make it a triplet.

✔ Tip

■ When using a stereo delay, set each channel to a different note duration for complex rhythmic effects.

Using AudioSuite Plug-Ins

In contrast to RTAS plug-ins, AudioSuite plug-ins cannot be applied during playback. They process audio to disk, creating a new audio file with the chosen effect permanently applied.

To use an AudioSuite plug-in, you must first select the audio material you want to process either in the track where it occurs or in the Region list. When using reverb or delay effects, make the selection longer than the source audio or the reverb tail or delay repeat will be truncated.

To process audio with an AudioSuite plug-in:

1. Select the audio that you want to process, either from within a track or from the Region list.

2. Choose a plug-in from the AudioSuite menu (**Figure 14.31**).

   The AudioSuite plug-in window appears (**Figure 14.32**).

3. In the plug-in window, adjust the controls for the effect.

4. Click the Preview button to audition the effect. Use the Preview Volume control to adjust the volume level if necessary.

5. Click the Process button.

   To process a selected region only in the track in which it appears, choose Playlist from the Selection Reference pop-up menu.

   To process all occurrences of a selected region in the session, click the Use In Playlist button, then choose Region List from the Selection Reference pop-up menu.

   The selected audio is processed. An acronym indicating the AudioSuite process is appended to the region name, and the new audio file appears in the session.

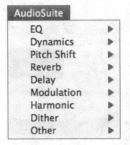

Figure 14.31 Choose AudioSuite plug-ins from the AudioSuite menu.

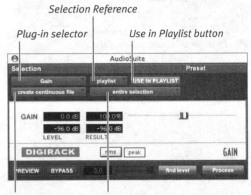

Figure 14.32 AudioSuite plug-ins permanently apply their effect to a selected region of audio.

✔ Tip

■ To ensure that the original audio is preserved with AudioSuite processing, choose Create Individual Files from the File Mode pop-up menu. This creates a new audio file for each region processed. The source file remains intact.

USING AUDIOSUITE PLUG-INS

Automating Mix Controls

All but the simplest mixes involve adjustments to mix controls during the course of the session. Pro Tools automation gives you the ability to record these adjustments in real time, reproducing them exactly when you play back the session. It also lets you view and edit automation data in graphic form alongside audio or MIDI, using the same tools.

This chapter provides an overview of the different types of automation and the various ways to display them. It also describes the automation modes that determine how your moves are captured, the special editing commands for working with automation data across tracks, and how to automate send controls and plug-in parameters.

Viewing Automation

Pro Tools LE lets you automate the following controls, depending on the track type:

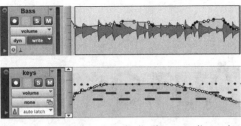

◆ Track volume (Audio, Auxiliary Input, Instrument, and Master Fader tracks)

◆ Track pan (Audio, Auxiliary Input, and Instrument tracks)

Figure 15.1 An automation playlist for an audio track (top) and a MIDI track (bottom).

◆ Track mute (Audio, Auxiliary Input, Instrument, and Master Fader tracks)

◆ Send level, pan, and mute (Audio, Auxiliary Input, and Instrument tracks)

◆ Plug-in controls (for plug-ins only)

◆ MIDI volume, pan, and mute (MIDI and Instrument tracks)

Each track has an automation playlist for each of its automatable controls. These playlists can be displayed for each track in the Edit window, either in the Track view or in an automation lane.

Viewing automation playlists

You can view one automation playlist at a time in a track.

To display an automation playlist:

◆ Click the Track View selector and choose the name of the automation playlist from the pop-up menu.

The automation playlist shows a breakpoint graph for the control, superimposed over the audio or MIDI data for the track (**Figure 15.1**).

✔ Tip

■ When no automation has been written for a control, a single breakpoint appears at the very beginning of the track. This breakpoint updates to reflect the current setting of the control.

Show/Hide Lanes icon

Figure 15.2 Click the Show/Hide Lanes icon at the bottom left of the track to show an automation lane.

Add Lanes icon

Figure 15.3 Click the Add Lanes icon at the left side of a lane to show additional automation lanes.

Figure 15.4 Click the Lane View selector and choose a new view for the lane.

Viewing automation lanes

Pro Tools lets you view multiple automation playlists for a track in automation lanes beneath the track. You can edit data in automation lanes in the same way as in playlists.

To display automation lanes for a track:

◆ At the bottom left of the track, click the Show/Hide lanes icon (**Figure 15.2**).

To show and hide additional lanes:

◆ Click the Add Lanes (Plus sign) icon or Remove Lanes (Minus sign) icon at the left side of a lane (**Figure 15.3**).

To change the view in a lane:

◆ Click the Lane View selector and choose a view from the pop-up menu (**Figure 15.4**).

Types of Automation Displays

The appearance of automation data depends on the type of control you are viewing. The graph for continuously variable controls such as track volume (**Figure 15.5**) or send level can have many possible shapes, while the graphs for on/off controls such as mute (**Figure 15.6**), or stepped controls such as a plug-in effect type (**Figure 15.7**), are much more restricted in shape.

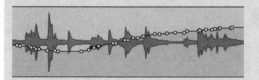

Figure 15.5 An automation graph for track volume showing a continuous series of breakpoints.

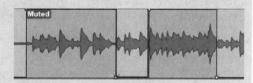

Figure 15.6 An automation graph for track mute showing on/off states.

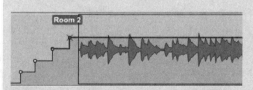

Figure 15.7 An automation graph for a plug-in effect selector with discrete, stepped settings.

VIEWING AUTOMATION

Setting the Automation Mode

Automation modes determine how automation data is read or written during playback. You can set the automation mode for each track independently. The default setting for tracks is Read mode.

Pro Tools LE provides the following automation modes:

◆ **Off** turns off automation for all automation parameters on a track.

◆ **Read** plays back any automation that was previously written for a track.

◆ **Write** writes automation data during playback, overwriting any previous automation data on the track. After you stop playback in Write mode, Pro Tools automatically switches to Touch mode, preventing you from accidentally overwriting automation data during subsequent playback.

◆ **Touch** writes automation data only when you click or move a control that can be automated. When you release the control, or stop moving it, automation writing stops and the control returns to its previous position.

◆ **Latch** starts writing automation data only when you click or move a control that can be automated, as in Touch mode. However, in Latch mode, automation writing continues until playback stops. This mode can be useful for automating pan or plug-in controls, because they don't return to their previous position when automation writing stops.

To set the automation mode:

◆ Click the Automation Mode selector on a track and choose the mode from the pop-up menu (**Figure 15.8**).

Figure 15.8 Click the Automation Mode selector and choose the mode for the track.

SETTING THE AUTOMATION MODE

Figure 15.9 The Automation window lets you suspend writing and playback of automation in the session.

Figure 15.10 Click to suspend writing of automation for a control type.

Enabling and Suspending Automation

The Automation window lets you enable or suspend writing and playback of all automation across all tracks. You can also enable or suspend writing of automation for each type of automation (track volume, pan, and mute; send level, pan, and mute; and plug-ins) across all tracks.

To suspend writing and playback of all automation:

1. Choose Window > Automation.

   The Automation window appears (**Figure 15.9**).

2. Click the Suspend button.

   The Suspend button highlights to indicate the all automation is suspended. Automation Mode selectors on all tracks are grayed out and the mode is displayed in italics.

To suspend writing of automation for a control on all tracks:

1. Choose Window > Automation.

2. Under Write Enable, click the button for the control that you want to suspend, so that the button is not highlighted (**Figure 15.10**).

   Writing of automation is suspended for the control. Existing automation for the suspended control will continue to play back.

To suspend writing and playback of automation on individual tracks:

1. In the Edit window, click the Track View selector and choose the automation parameter that you want to suspend.

2. Command-click (Mac) or Ctrl-click (Windows) the name of the displayed parameter in the Track View selector. The name of the parameter is italicized to indicate that it is suspended (**Figure 15.11**).

Figure 15.11 Command-click (Mac) or Ctrl-click (Windows) the Track view selector to suspend automation for the parameter on that track.

Figure 15.12 Set the automation mode for each track to be automated.

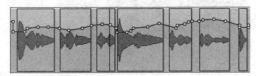

Figure 15.13 Automation moves appear in the automation playlist.

Writing Automation

You can write automation in real time by moving controls during playback. As you move the controls, Pro Tools writes the moves to the corresponding automation playlists. By using Touch or Latch modes, you can perform multiple automation passes on a section of a track, and later resume writing automation on the next section.

To write automation:

1. Make sure the controls you want to automate are enabled in the Automation window.

2. On each track that you want to automate, set the automation mode (**Figure 15.12**). For a first automation pass, Write mode works well.

3. Start playback to begin writing automation.

4. Move the controls that you want to automate.

5. Stop playback when you are finished. An automation graph appears in the automation playlist for each control (**Figure 15.13**). Tracks in Write mode automatically switch to Touch mode after an automation pass.

WRITING AUTOMATION

To resume writing automation after an automation pass:

1. Make sure Link Edit and Timeline Selection is enabled (**Figure 15.14**).

2. In the Edit window, place the cursor or make a selection where you want to write automation (**Figure 15.15**).

3. On each track that you want to automate, make sure the automation mode is set to Touch or Latch (**Figure 15.16**).

4. Start playback. When you reach the location where you want to change existing automation data, click or move the controls that you want to automate.

5. Stop playback when you are finished.

Figure 15.14 Click the Link Timeline and Edit Selection icon so that it is highlighted.

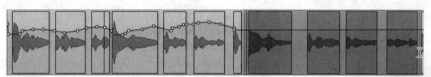

Figure 15.15 Select the area to resume writing of automation.

Figure 15.16 Make sure the automation mode is set to Touch or Latch before resuming an automation pass.

Figure 15.17 Enable the Send controls you want to automate in the Automation window.

Figure 15.18 Display controls for the send you want to automate.

Automating Send Controls

Pro Tools lets you write automation for Send Level, Send Pan, and Send Mute controls. This can be useful for controlling the levels of effects or stereo placement of effects during a mixdown.

To write send level, mute, or pan automation:

1. Make sure the controls you want to automate are write-enabled in the Automation window. The Send Volume, Send Level, or Send Mute buttons should be highlighted (**Figure 15.17**).

2. On each track that you want to automate, set the automation mode.

3. Choose View > Sends A–E, or Sends F–J, and select a send position to display controls for an individual send.

   or

   Click a send to display its Send Output window (**Figure 15.18**).

4. Start playback to begin writing automation.

5. Move the controls that you want to automate.

6. Stop playback when you are finished.

Automating Plug-In Controls

Pro Tools lets you automate nearly every plug-in control, but each control must first be enabled for automation.

To enable plug-in controls for automation:

1. Open the plug-in that you want to automate.

2. In the plug-in window, click the Automation Enable button (**Figure 15.19**).

   The Plug-in Automation dialog appears (**Figure 15.20**).

3. To choose which controls to automate, select the names of the controls and click the Add button.

4. Click OK.

   The selected controls are enabled for automation in the plug-in window (**Figure 15.21**).

To enable a single plug-in control for automation:

1. Open the plug-in that you want to automate.

2. In the plug-in window, Command-Option-Control-click (Mac) or Ctrl-Alt-Start-click (Windows) on the control you want to automate (**Figure 15.22**).

Figure 15.19 Click the Automation Enable button in the plug-in window.

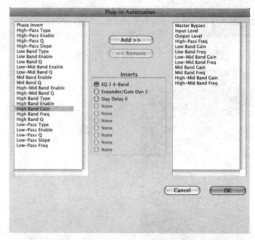

Figure 15.20 The Plug-In Automation dialog lets you enable individual plug-in controls for automation.

Automation Enable indicators

Figure 15.21 Plug-In controls indicate they are enabled for automation.

Figure 15.22 Command-Option-Control-click (Mac) or Ctrl-Alt-Start-click (Windows) on a control to enable it for automation.

Figure 15.23 Click the Plug In button in the Automation window.

Figure 15.24 Click the Automation Safe button to prevent overwriting of plug-in automation.

To enable all plug-in controls for automation:

1. Open the plug-in that you want to automate.

2. In the plug-in window, Command-Option-Control-click (Mac) or Ctrl-Alt-Start-click (Windows) the Automation Enable button (Figure 15.19).

   The controls that can be automated indicate that they are enabled for automation in the Plug-In window.

To write plug-in automation:

1. Make sure that plug-ins are write enabled in the Automation window. The Plug In button should be highlighted (**Figure 15.23**).

2. Open the plug-in that you want to automate.

3. Make sure the plug-in controls you want to automate are enabled for automation.

4. On the track containing the plug-in you want to automate, set the automation mode.

5. Start playback to begin writing automation.

6. Move the plug-in controls that you want to automate.

7. Stop playback when you are finished.

Plug-In Automation Safe mode

You can prevent overwriting of a specific plug-in's automation by putting the plug-in into Automation Safe mode.

To enable Automation Safe mode for a plug-in:

1. Open the window for the plug-in.

2. Click the Automation Safe button so that it is highlighted (**Figure 15.24**).

Editing Automation

Pro Tools lets you edit automation data in track automation playlists or automation lanes. You can edit the automation line graph directly by moving breakpoints, or by using standard Cut, Copy, and Paste commands.

In addition, Pro Tools provides edit commands specifically for editing automation data (Cut Special, Copy Special, Paste Special, and Clear Special).

Graphical editing of automation

You can create and move breakpoints in the automation graph. Moving breakpoints up or down increases or decreases their value, and moving them to the left or right moves the automation event earlier or later on the timeline.

To create a breakpoint:

◆ With the Grabber tool or Pencil tool, click on the automation playlist's line graph (**Figure 15.25**).

A new breakpoint appears on the line graph.

To move a breakpoint:

◆ With the Grabber tool, drag a point on the line graph to a new position (**Figure 15.26**).

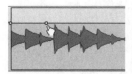

Figure 15.25 Click on the automation graph to create an editable breakpoint.

Figure 15.26 Drag breakpoints on the automation graph to change their value or their location on the timeline.

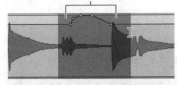

Breakpoints before nudging

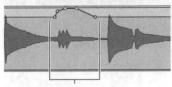

Breakpoints after nudging

Figure 15.27 Breakpoints before (top) and after nudging (bottom).

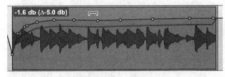

Figure 15.28 Adjust multiple breakpoints up or down with the Trimmer tool.

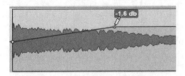

Figure 15.29 Use the Line Pencil tool to draw a volume automation ramp.

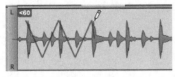

Figure 15.30 Use the Triangle Pencil tool to draw a pan effect.

To nudge breakpoints:

1. Select a range of breakpoints to move in the automation playlist.

2. To nudge the breakpoints ahead, press the Plus key on the numeric keypad.

or

To nudge breakpoints back, press the Minus key on the numeric keypad (**Figure 15.27**).

The breakpoints move by the current nudge value.

To change all breakpoint values in a region:

◆ Click in the region with the Trimmer tool and drag the breakpoints up or down (**Figure 15.28**).

Drawing automation

You can use the Pencil tool to draw an automation graph in an automation playlist or MIDI controller playlist.

The different Pencil tool shapes can create a range of automation effects: For example, the Line Pencil can be used to draw a volume automation ramp (**Figure 15.29**), or the Triangle Pencil can be used to draw a periodic pan effect (**Figure 15.30**).

Cutting, copying, and pasting automation

You can cut, copy, and paste automation data to different locations within a track or to the same automation playlist on another track. You cannot paste automation data into a different automation playlist with the standard edit commands.

When you cut or paste a range of automation data, Pro Tools adds anchor breakpoints to preserve the value and slope of data inside and outside the edit (**Figure 15.31**).

To cut or copy automation data:

1. Select the range of data you want to cut or copy.

2. Choose Edit > Cut or Edit > Copy.

To paste automation data:

1. Click with the Selector tool to place the cursor in the same track or in another track displaying the same automation playlist.

2. Choose Edit > Paste.

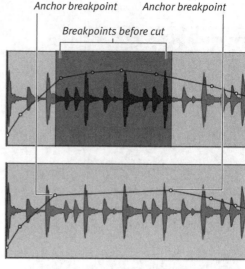

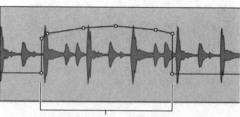

Figure 15.31 When you cut or paste automation data, anchor breakpoints are created around the edit.

Special automation editing commands

Pro Tools provides special Edit commands for working with automation data on Audio, Auxiliary Input, Instrument, and Master Fader tracks. You can also use these special Edit commands to edit MIDI controller data. (You cannot, however, copy automation data or controller data between tracks that contain audio tracks and tracks that contain MIDI.)

These commands let you edit automation data exclusively, regardless of the current track view. For example, you can cut and paste volume, pan, or mute automation data on Audio tracks without leaving Waveform view; or you can cut and paste MIDI controller data on MIDI tracks without leaving Notes view.

You can also use special Edit commands to copy data between different automation playlists, for example, from Right Pan to Left Pan.

Cut Special, Copy Special, and Clear Special commands

The Cut Special, Copy Special, and Clear Special commands include the following:

◆ **All Automation** cuts, copies, or clears all automation data or MIDI controller data, whether it is shown or not.

◆ **Pan Automation** cuts, copies, or clears only pan automation data or MIDI pan data, whether it is shown or not.

◆ **Plug-in Automation** cuts, copies, or clears only plug-in automation data that is shown.

Paste Special commands

The Paste Special commands include the following:

◆ **Merge** combines copied MIDI note data with preexisting MIDI note data.

◆ **Repeat to Fill Selection** pastes successive copies of audio and MIDI regions, automation data, or MIDI controller data to fill the current Edit selection.

◆ **To Current Automation Type** pastes automation or MIDI controller data to automation playlists. This lets you use automation data interchangeably between all types of automation, and MIDI data interchangeably between all MIDI functions.

To copy and paste automation data only:

1. With the Selector tool, drag in an Audio track or Auxiliary Input track to make an Edit selection (**Figure 15.32**).

The source track does not need to be in an automation playlist view.

2. Choose Edit > Copy Special > All Automation.

3. Click with the Selector tool to place the cursor in the same track or in another Audio or Auxiliary Input track where you want to paste the automation data.

The destination track does not need to be in an automation playlist view.

4. Choose Edit > Paste.

The automation data is pasted at the new location without changing the audio in the track (**Figure 15.33**).

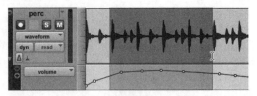

Figure 15.32 Drag in an Audio or Auxiliary Input track to make a selection. The selection does not need to be in an automation playlist view when you use Copy Special to copy automation data.

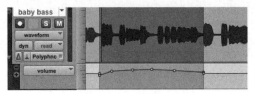

Figure 15.33 Copied automation data is pasted and the audio in the main playlist is unchanged.

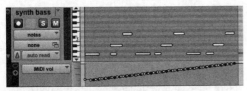

Figure 15.34 Drag in a MIDI or Instrument track to make a selection. The selection does not need to be in a MIDI controller playlist when you use Copy Special to copy controller data.

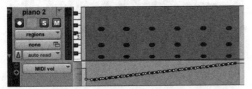

Figure 15.35 Copied MIDI Controller data is merged with existing controller data and the MIDI notes remain unchanged.

To copy and paste MIDI controller data only:

1. With the Selector tool, drag in a MIDI or Instrument track to make an Edit selection (**Figure 15.34**).

   The source track does not need to be in a MIDI controller playlist view.

2. Choose Edit > Copy Special > All Automation.

3. Click with the Selector tool to place the cursor in the same track or in another MIDI or Instrument track where you want to paste the controller data.

   The destination track does not need to be in MIDI controller playlist view.

4. Choose Edit > Paste Special > Merge.

   The MIDI controller data is pasted at the new location without changing the MIDI in the track (**Figure 15.35**).

To copy automation data between different automation playlists:

1. On the source track, click the Track View selector and choose the automation playlist that contains the data you want to copy.

2. With the Selector tool, drag in the automation playlist to select the data (**Figure 15.36**).

3. Choose Edit > Copy.

4. In the destination track, click the Track View selector and choose the automation playlist where you want to paste the data.

5. Click with the Selector tool to place the cursor in the destination track.

6. Choose Edit > Paste Special > To Current Automation Type.

   The pasted data appears in the new playlist (**Figure 15.37**).

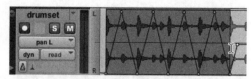

Figure 15.36 Copying automation data to a different playlist.

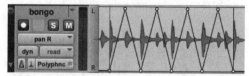

Figure 15.37 Pasted data in the new playlist.

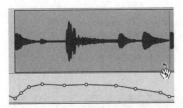

Figure 15.38 With the Grabber tool, click the Loop icon of the individual region.

Automating Looped Regions

When you loop an audio region, any automation data associated with the source region is not looped.

You can copy and paste automation from the source region to individual loop iterations by using special Edit commands to copy the original automation and repeat it for the duration of the loop.

To repeat automation for a looped region:

1. Click the Loop icon in the source region to select the region (**Figure 15.38**).

2. Choose Edit > Copy Special > All Automation.

3. Click in the center of a looped region to select the entire region loop.

4. Choose Edit > Paste Special > Repeat to Fill Selection.

   The automation data from the source region is pasted and repeated to fill the loop iterations (**Figure 15.39**).

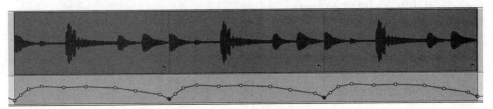

Figure 15.39 Pasting the copied automation to fill the selection.

Deleting automation

To delete automation data, display the auto-mation parameter that you want to edit by selecting it from the Track View selector. You can then delete automation breakpoints or remove data in automation playlists.

To delete an automation breakpoint:

◆ With the Grabber tool or Pencil tool, Option-click (Mac) or Alt-click (Windows) the breakpoint (**Figure 15.40**).

To delete multiple automation breakpoints:

1. With the Selector tool, drag to select the breakpoints to delete (**Figure 15.41**).

2. Press Delete (Mac) or Backspace (Windows).

   All breakpoints within the selected range are erased (**Figure 15.42**).

To delete data in all automation playlists on a track:

1. With the Selector tool, drag to select a range of data to be deleted.

2. Press Control-Delete (Mac) or Start-Backspace (Windows).

   All data within the selected range is deleted on each of the track's automation playlists.

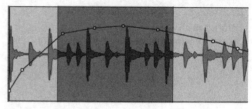

Figure 15.40 To delete breakpoints, Option-click (Mac) or Alt-click (Windows) with the Pencil tool.

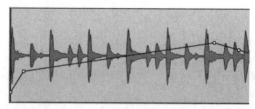

Figure 15.41 Select the breakpoints to delete.

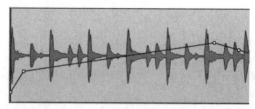

Figure 15.42 When you delete automation instead of cutting it, no anchor breakpoints are created.

Mixing Down and Mastering

Mixing down is the final stage in a recording project. In the mixdown process, you render your recording into a final stereo mix that includes all audio and MIDI tracks, plus any effects and automation you've applied to them. You can record the final mix within Pro Tools by either bouncing to disk or bus-recording it, or you can output it to an external device such as a CD recorder.

This chapter covers methods for recording a final mix within Pro Tools and creating an MP3 file of a mix. It also discusses *mastering*, the process of optimizing a final mix for reproduction.

Mixdown Options

You can record the final mix in several ways, including:

Bouncing to disk consolidates the output of all audible tracks into a new audio file on disk. Sample rate, bit depth, file format, and other attributes of the new audio file must be selected before you perform the bounce. With this method, you cannot manually adjust mixer controls during mixdown.

Bus recording to new audio tracks records the output of all audible tracks to new audio tracks within the same session. Sample rate, bit depth, file format, and other attributes of the new tracks match those in the session. With this method, you can manually adjust track faders and other controls during mixdown.

Recording directly to a digital recorder uses the S/PDIF digital outputs of your audio interface to send your main stereo mix directly to a CD, DAT, or DVD recorder.

Preparing for Mixdown

Before you bounce a mix to disk, or bus record a mix to new audio tracks, do the following:

◆ Audition your session to make sure all of the tracks you want to include in the mix are audible. If any are not, check for muted tracks, deactivated tracks, or muted regions.

◆ Ensure that overall track levels are high, but do not clip. If the red clip indicator lights up on a track meter, reduce the track's level or insert a compressor/limiter plug-in on the track. Keep signal peaks within the meter's orange zone (**Figure 16.1**).

◆ If any track includes automation, make sure that its Automation Mode selector is set to Read (**Figure 16.2**).

◆ Determine whether you want to mix down the entire session or just a portion of it. See the "Mixing a Selection" sidebar for details.

Avoid this range.
Keep signal peaks within this range.

Figure 16.1 Before mixdown, audition your session and watch your meters for clipping. Keep signal peaks within the meter's orange zone.

Automation mode selector

Figure 16.2 Make sure all automated tracks are set to Read mode.

Mixing a Selection

In most cases, you will mix down an entire session. But Pro Tools also allows you to select just a portion of a session for mixdown. You might do this to create an excerpt from a longer piece of music, for example.

If you make a selection in any track in a session, the bounced or bus-recorded mix will be exactly the length of the selection. If the material includes delay or reverb effects, make sure your selection includes any delay repeats or reverb tails that occur at the end of the material.

Without a selection, the bounced or bus-recorded mix will be the length of the longest track in the session.

Bouncing a Mix to Disk

The Bounce to Disk command allows you to render your mix to a new audio file on disk. You can then archive the file, burn it to CD, or prepare it for mastering and reproduction.

Using dither when mixing down

If you want to distribute a 24-bit master mixdown via any medium with lower resolution—such as on CD, or as an MP3 file, for example—you will need to convert your mixdown to a lower bit depth. To ensure the best possible sonic results, insert one of the Dither plug-ins included with Pro Tools (Dither or POW-r Dither) on a Master Fader track that carries the main output mix, then bounce the mix to disk.

Bounce Output Options

The Bounce dialog (**Figure 16.3**) provides several options.

Bounce Source lets you choose the main output or bus path that carries the audio for the mixdown.

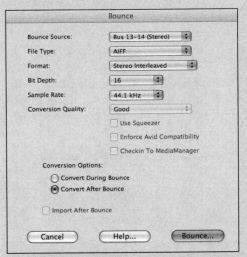

Figure 16.3 To access the Bounce dialog, select File > Bounce To > Disk.

File Type lets you choose a file type for the bounced mix. Some commonly used file types include the following:

◆ **SDII (Sound Designer II)** is compatible with older Mac OS–based Pro Tools systems and many CD burning applications.

◆ **WAV** is compatible with current Pro Tools systems and many other audio applications, including CD burning software.

◆ **AIFF (Audio Interchange File Format)** is for use in CD burning applications and other software that supports this format.

continues on next page

Bounce Output Options (*continued*)

◆ **MP3 (MPEG-1 Layer 3)** is for downloading, distribution, and streaming audio over the Internet.

◆ **QuickTime** is for use with compatible media players and software applications.

Format lets you choose a channel format for the mixdown:

◆ **Mono (summed)** creates a single mono disk file.

◆ **Multiple mono** creates as many mono disk files as there are source paths. For example, if the source is stereo, two mono files are created, with the suffixes ".L" (left) and ".R" (right) appended to their names.

◆ **Stereo interleaved** creates a stereo interleaved file containing of all of the bounced tracks.

Bit Depth lets you choose the resolution of the mixdown.

◆ **8-bit** is sometimes used by multimedia applications. Use this setting if high-quality audio is not required.

◆ **16-bit** is the standard resolution for audio CDs.

◆ **24-bit** provides the highest possible sound quality. Use it for archiving master stereo mixdowns.

Sample Rate lets you choose among several different sample rates. The higher the sample rate, the better the audio quality. Some commonly used sample rates include:

◆ **44.1 kHz**, the standard for CDs

◆ **48 kHz**, the standard for DVD video, DAT, and ADAT decks

◆ **96 kHz,** the standard for audio DVDs

◆ **192 kHz,** for highest fidelity on audio DVDs that support this sample rate

Conversion Quality determines the quality of conversion applied if you choose a sample rate other than the session's current sample rate. Generally, the higher the conversion quality, the longer it takes for Pro Tools to convert the sample rate. Choose from Low (fastest), Good, Better, Best, and TweakHead (slowest).

Conversion Options lets you specify whether Pro Tools performs the selected bounce processing options during or after the bounce.

◆ Choose **Convert After Bounce** for the highest level of automation accuracy.

◆ Chose **Convert During Bounce** for faster conversion, but lower accuracy.

Import After Bounce lets you automatically import a newly bounced file into the current session's Audio Regions list. Choose this option if you want to create submixes for use in the current session.

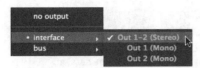

Figure 16.4 Setting an output path to Out 1-2.

Figure 16.5 On a Master Fader track, Dither should always be the last plug-in in the signal chain.

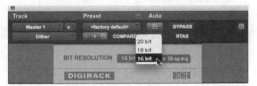

Figure 16.6 The Dither plug-in.

Figure 16.7 The POW-r Dither plug-in.

Because Pro Tools performs much of its internal processing at higher bit depths (32-bits for audio processing, for example), using dither is also recommended for creating a 16-bit mixdown from a session that is already in 16-bit format.

To use the dither plug-ins:

1. Choose Track > New and create a stereo Master Fader track (see Chapter 4, "Working with Tracks").

2. Set the outputs of all audio tracks to the same path, typically, Out 1-2 (**Figure 16.4**).

3. Set the output of the Master Fader track to same path you selected in step 2.

   The Master Fader track now controls the output levels of all tracks routed to it.

4. Insert the Dither plug-in on the Master Fader track. If there are other plug-ins on the Master Fader, insert Dither last in the signal chain (**Figure 16.5**).

5. In the Dither plug-in window, choose an output Bit Resolution (**Figure 16.6**).

   or

   If you are using POW-r Dither, choose a Noise Shaping setting (**Figure 16.7**) in addition to the Bit Resolution.

To bounce a mix to disk:

1. Arrange track levels, automation, and all other elements of your mix.

2. To bounce the entire session, click Return to Zero in the Transport window (**Figure 16.8**).

   or

   To bounce only part of the session, select Options > Link Timeline and Edit Selection (**Figure 16.9**), and then make a selection in the Edit window.

Figure 16.8 Click Return to Zero to set the session to its beginning and bounce the entire session.

Figure 16.9 Before you make a selection, link the Edit and Timeline selections.

Figure 16.10 Naming the bounced file.

3. Choose File > Bounce To > Disk.

4. Configure the output settings in the Bounce dialog (Figure 16.3).

5. Click Bounce.

6. Enter a name for the bounced file and click Save (**Figure 16.10**).

   Session playback begins and the bounce is performed in real time.

What Is Dither?

Dither is a special type of very low-level randomized noise. It is used to minimize distortion and other undesirable audio artifacts that can occur when you reduce the bit depth of an audio file. If dither is not added during this process, *quantization* noise (errors due to rounding off the bits) can occur, particularly at the low end of a signal's dynamic range. Adding dither while mixing down allows you to more effectively convert 24-bit audio into a 16-bit format.

The Dither and POW-r Dither plug-ins included with Pro Tools use noise shaping to reduce the effects of quantization by shifting the noise to less-audible audio frequencies. POW-r Dither lets you choose from three types of noise shaping:

Type 1, for material with low stereo complexity

Type 2, for material with medium stereo complexity

Type 3, for material in wide-field stereo

Bus Recording a Mix

Instead of bouncing to disk, you can bus record the final mix to a new stereo track in the same session. This technique has the added benefit of allowing you to adjust track levels, change panning and muting, and perform other mixing actions during the recording process. You can also add live input to the session.

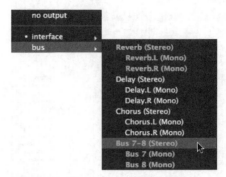

Figure 16.11 Set the output of all tracks in the submix to an available bus path.

To bus record a master stereo mix:

1. Arrange the track levels, automation, effects, and other elements of your mix.

2. Set the output of all tracks you want to include in the submix to an available bus path (**Figure 16.11**).

3. Choose Track > New and create a new stereo track.

4. Set the input of the stereo track to the bus path you selected as the output of the tracks in the submix (**Figure 16.12**).

Figure 16.12 Set the input of the new stereo track.

Play Record

Figure 16.13 In the Transport window, click Record, then Play.

5. Set the output of the new stereo track to your main output path.

6. To record the entire session, click Return to Zero in the Transport window (Figure 16.8).

   or

   To record only part of the session, select Options > Link Timeline and Edit Selection, and then make a selection in the Edit window.

7. Record enable the new stereo track.

8. In the Transport window, click Record, then click Play (**Figure 16.13**).

   Recording begins.

   If you are recording an audio selection, recording will stop automatically at the end of the selection. If no audio is selected, click Stop to end recording at the appropriate spot.

Recording Digital Output

Another alternative for mixdown is to record digitally to a S/PDIF-equipped CD, DAT, DVD, or other digital media recorder. The specific recording procedure will differ according to the device.

To record directly to a digital recorder:

1. Connect the S/PDIF inputs and outputs of your audio interface to the S/PDIF inputs and outputs of the digital recorder.

2. Configure the digital recorder to accept S/PDIF input.

3. Set the digital recorder as slave to the Pro Tools digital clock.

4. Press Record on the digital recorder.

5. In Pro Tools, click Play in the Transport window (Figure 16.13).

6. When Pro Tools playback has finished, stop the digital recorder.

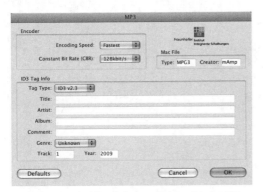

Figure 16.14 The MP3 dialog, available with the MP3 Export Option.

Creating an MP3

To create an MP3 file, you will need to purchase and install the Digidesign MP3 Export Option, which is available online. You will then bounce your recording to disk, selecting MP3 as the File Type.

To create an MP3 of your mix:

1. Arrange track levels, automation, and other elements of your mix.

2. Choose File > Bounce To > Disk.

3. Choose MP3 as the File Type, and in the MP3 dialog configure the export options (**Figure 16.14**).

4. Click OK.

5. Enter a name for the MP3 file and click Save.

   Session playback begins and the bounce is performed in real time.

MP3 Output Options

The MP3 Export Option provides the following options for output:

Encoding Speed lets you choose the audio quality of the bounced file. Choose Highest Quality for the best possible fidelity. Be aware, however, that this option can take up to five times as long to process audio than the Fastest Encoding option.

Constant Bit Rate lets you choose a bit rate for the bounced audio. The 128 kbit/s option is generally the best choice for streaming audio over the Internet.

ID3 Tag Info lets you store information about the encoded audio. MP3 players use this information to display details about a recording.

CREATING AN MP3

Mastering

The goal of mastering is to prepare a final mixdown for duplication and distribution. Skillful mastering is an art. For this reason, many people enlist the services of a professional mastering engineer.

Mastering differs from mixdown in that a mastering engineer takes a mixdown and makes further adjustments to its sound—typically using additional equalization and compression—to ensure that it is as sonically balanced as possible and ready for mass reproduction.

If a mixdown is just one of several recordings on an album, a mastering engineer must also ensure that each recording is sonically consistent with the others with respect to volume and tone.

If you choose to master your own recordings, consider the following:

◆ Volume should be should be consistent from track to track and equal to commercial standards.

◆ Compression and limiting should be used sparingly. These techniques should add fullness and presence without sacrificing dynamic range.

◆ Equalization should be used carefully. It should add warmth, depth, balance, and clarity—but not harshness.

◆ Sequencing of multi-song content should create a dynamic listening experience that has good musical and dramatic flow.

The recommendations above are general guidelines and not iron-clad rules for every project. When mastering, it's crucial to consider your source material and its ultimate destination medium, and prepare it accordingly.

MASTERING

WORKING WITH VIDEO

This chapter covers the basics of working with video in Pro Tools, including how to import and view video, how to spot audio to video, and how to bounce to a new QuickTime video file. These techniques will give you the essential tools you'll need for composing music to picture or performing basic audio post production for a video project.

Importing QuickTime or Windows Media Video Files

Figure 17.1 Setting the playback priority for QuickTime video.

Pro Tools LE works with QuickTime video, and with Windows Media video files created using the VC-1 Advanced Profile codec. You can import a single video file and view a single Video track in a session. To work with QuickTime movies, QuickTime must be installed on your computer.

Once you have imported a video file, you can compose music to picture or "spot" audio regions to specific locations in the video.

To set QuickTime movie playback priority:

1. From the Pro Tools LE menu, choose Preferences and click the Operation tab.

2. In the Video section, select a playback priority (**Figure 17.1**).

3. To view imported QuickTime movies at the highest possible resolution, select the High Quality QuickTime Image option.

Before Beginning a Project

To ensure optimal system performance and work as accurately as possible with imported video, follow these tips:

◆ Use a separate hard drive for video. Your system will perform better if audio files and video files are kept on separate hard drives.

◆ Know the frame rate of your video source material. Set your Pro Tools session to this frame rate using the Session Setup window.

◆ If possible, use source material with timecode superimposed, or *burned in,* on the video image. This will make it possible to align audio to timecode locations in the video even though Pro Tools LE doesn't display the timecode in its main counter or time ruler.

◆ If you are working with video that has timecode burned in, set the Session Start time to match the start time of the video file. See "Spotting Audio" later in this chapter.

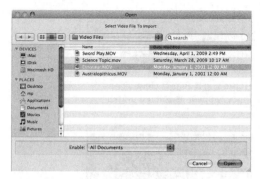

Figure 17.2 Selecting a video file to import.

Figure 17.3 Use the Location pop-up menu to select where to place the imported video in the Timeline.

To import a QuickTime or Windows Media video:

1. Choose File > Import > Video, then select the movie you want to import. Click the Open button (**Figure 17.2**).

    or

    Drag a QuickTime or Windows Media video file into the Timeline.

2. In the Video Import Options dialog, use the Location menu to select where in the Timeline to place the imported video (**Figure 17.3**). The options are:

    ▲ **Session Start** places the imported video at the start of the session.

    ▲ **Selection** places the imported video at the cursor's current location.

    ▲ **Spot** allows you to use the Spot dialog to place the imported video at a precise numeric location on the Timeline.

3. Select the Import Audio from File option if you also want to import the audio associated with the video.

4. Click OK.

The movie appears in a new Video track (**Figure 17.4**). Any associated audio appears in a new Audio track.

Figure 17.4 An imported video appears in a Video track.

IMPORTING QUICKTIME OR WINDOWS MEDIA

Working with the Video Track

Imported video appears in a Video track, where it can be viewed, played, scrubbed, and referenced for aligning audio events.

Figure 17.5 In Blocks view, video frames appear as colored blocks.

Choosing a Video track view

You can display a Video track in either Frames or Blocks view. In Frames view, data appears as individual video frames. In Blocks view, video frames appear as colored blocks (**Figure 17.5**). If video playback is inconsistent or intermittent, switching to Blocks view will improve system performance.

Figure 17.6 Choosing a view for the Video track.

To choose a view for the Video track:

◆ Click the Track View selector and choose Frames or Blocks from the pop-up menu (**Figure 17.6**).

QuickTime Playback Options

Pro Tools LE uses your computer's processing power for all audio and video playback. If video playback quality is paramount, use the Operation tab in the Preferences dialog to set QuickTime Playback Priority. This option allows you to give extra priority to video playback at the expense of other Pro Tools screen update tasks. Playback options include the following.

Normal gives no priority to movie playback. This setting should be used in most cases, unless movie playback is sluggish or sporadic.

Medium gives movie playback higher priority at the expense of Pro Tools screen update tasks such as metering and on-screen fader movement.

Highest disables Pro Tools screen activity to give movie playback first priority.

High Quality QuickTime Image displays an imported movie at its highest resolution by decompressing the two fields of interlaced video frames. Disable this option if system performance is sluggish in a session with QuickTime video.

Taking the Video track offline

To further improve system performance, you may choose to disable video display by taking the Video track offline. When offline, the video window is black during audio playback.

To toggle video playback:

◆ Click the Video Online button. The button is gray when the Video track is offline (**Figure 17.7**).

◆ To put the Video track online again, click the Video Online button a second time. The button is blue when the Video track is online. The video window displays the video image again.

Click here to take the Video track offline

Figure 17.7 Click the Video Online button to toggle the Video track offline. The Video window is black when offline.

Resizing the Video Window

The Video window can be resized for easier viewing.

To resize the video window:

◆ Drag the bottom-left or -right corner of the video window (**Figure 17.8**).

   or

   Control-click (Mac) or right-click (Windows) anywhere on the Video window and choose a view size (**Figure 17.9**).

Scrubbing video

You can use the Scrubber tool to quickly find a video frame location for spotting audio events. Scrubbing on the Video track scrubs video playback only. Scrubbing on an Audio track scrubs video and audio playback.

To scrub video playback:

1. Select the Scrubber tool (**Figure 17.10**).

2. Drag the Scrubber tool in the Video track or Audio track.

Figure 17.8 Drag a bottom corner of the video window to resize it.

Figure 17.9 Control-click (Mac) or right-click (Windows) the video window to select a view size.

Figure 17.10 Use the Scrubber tool to scrub video playback and find a frame location.

Figure 17.11
Selecting a
Nudge value.

Figure 17.12
Use the Selector
to place the edit
cursor at the
approximate
location you want.

Nudging video

Another way to navigate to a specific video
frame location is to move or *nudge* the edit
cursor in precise increments using the Plus
and Minus keys on your numeric keypad.

To nudge video playback:

1. Select a Nudge value from the Nudge
   value selector (**Figure 17.11**).

2. Select the Selector tool (**Figure 17.12**).

3. Click the Selector tool in the Video track
   at the approximate location of the video
   data you want to nudge.

4. Press the Plus key on your numeric
   keypad to move the cursor forward or the
   Minus key to move the cursor backward
   by the selected Nudge value.

WORKING WITH THE VIDEO TRACK

Spotting Audio

You can use Spot mode to align music cues or sound effects to specific time locations. To locate a specific frame location, or *hit point*, in the video, scrub or nudge video playback to that frame, then align or *spot* a music or sound effect cue to that location. In Spot mode, you specify the placement of a region by entering a start time—or if it has a predefined sync point, a sync point time.

If you are working with video that has a burned-in timecode and want to spot audio to specific timecode frames, set the Session Start time to match the start time of the video file. Although Pro Tools LE doesn't display the timecode in its main counter or time ruler, this makes it possible to spot audio to burned-in timecode frame locations.

To set the Session Start time:

1. Choose Setup > Session.

2. In the Session Start field, enter a time that matches the first frame of the burned-in timecode in the imported video (**Figure 17.13**).

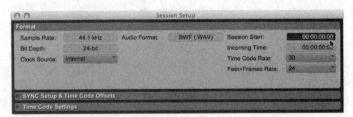

Figure 17.13 Setting the Session Start time.

Figure 17.14 Enabling Spot mode.

Figure 17.15 In Spot mode, you specify the placement of a region by entering a start or end time, or a sync point time if it has a predefined sync point.

To spot audio to a hit point:

1. Using the Scrubber tool, locate the general frame location you're looking for in the Video track.

2. Switch to the Selector tool and click near where you stopped scrubbing.

3. Use the Plus and Minus keys on your numeric keypad to nudge the insertion point to the exact frame you want.

4. Click the Spot button (**Figure 17.14**).

5. Drag a music cue or sound effect from the Regions list into an available Audio track. The Spot dialog appears (**Figure 17.15**).

6. Enter a value for the Start, Sync Point, or End of the region you are spotting.

7. Click OK.

   The region is placed at the specified location.

SPOTTING AUDIO

Bouncing to a QuickTime Movie

When you have finished spotting audio to video, you can export and save the video with a mixdown of your Audio tracks using the Bounce to QuickTime Movie command.

To bounce session audio and video to a new QuickTime movie:

1. To bounce the entire session, click Return to Zero in the Transport window (**Figure 17.16**).

   or

   To bounce only part of the session, select Options > Link Timeline and Edit Selection, then make a selection in the Edit window (**Figure 17.17**).

2. Choose File > Bounce To > QuickTime Movie (**Figure 17.18**).

Figure 17.16 Click Return to Zero to set the session to its beginning and bounce the entire session.

Figure 17.17 When bouncing only part of a session, be sure to enable the Link Timeline and Edit Selection option when selecting material for the bounce.

Figure 17.18 Choose File > Bounce To > QuickTime Movie to export and save the video and a mixdown of your Audio tracks.

Figure 17.19 Configuring bounce settings.

Figure 17.20 Naming the new QuickTime movie.

3. Configure the output settings in the Bounce dialog (**Figure 17.19**). The File Type is automatically set to QuickTime.

4. Click Bounce.

5. Enter a name for the bounced file and click Save (**Figure 17.20**).

Session playback begins and the bounce is performed in real time. A new QuickTime movie is saved to disk.

BOUNCING TO A QUICKTIME MOVIE

INDEX

INDEX

INDEX